Women's Voices on American Stages in the Early Twenty-First Century

Women's Voices on American Stages in the Early Twenty-First Century
Sarah Ruhl and Her Contemporaries

Leslie Atkins Durham

WOMEN'S VOICES ON AMERICAN STAGES IN THE EARLY TWENTY-FIRST CENTURY
Copyright © Leslie Atkins Durham, 2013.
Softcover reprint of the hardcover 1st edition 2013 978-1-137-28710-6

All rights reserved.

First published in 2013 by PALGRAVE MACMILLAN® in the United States—a division of St. Martin's Press LLC, 175 Fifth Avenue, New York, NY 10010.

Where this book is distributed in the UK, Europe and the rest of the world, this is by Palgrave Macmillan, a division of Macmillan Publishers Limited, registered in England, company number 785998, of Houndmills, Basingstoke, Hampshire RG21 6XS.

Palgrave Macmillan is the global academic imprint of the above companies and has companies and representatives throughout the world.

Palgrave® and Macmillan® are registered trademarks in the United States, the United Kingdom, Europe and other countries.

ISBN 978-1-349-44951-4   ISBN 978-1-137-28711-3 eBook
DOI 10.1057/9781137287113

Library of Congress Cataloging-in-Publication Data is available from the Library of Congress.

A catalogue record of the book is available from the British Library.

Design by Scribe Inc.

First edition: February 2013

10 9 8 7 6 5 4 3 2 1

Transferred to Digital Printing in 2013

For Craig and Kate

Contents

Acknowledgments		ix
Introduction: The Context for Ruhl and Her Contemporaries, or Women's Playwriting: Strictly Prohibited in the New Century?		1
1	Educating Sarah Ruhl	13
2	Emotional Journeys	31
3	Caring Labor	53
4	Theatrical Devotion	75
5	Mobile Lines	99
6	Natural Forces	131
Epilogue: "The Curtain Goes Up"		159
Notes		165
Bibliography		193
Index		207

Acknowledgments

This book would not exist without my students at Boise State University. The questions they ask, the opinions they share, and the art they make challenges and inspires me. I am also truly privileged to have an extraordinary friend and colleague at Boise State—Jacqueline O'Connor. She has supported and encouraged me in more ways than I can count during every phase of this project. I would also like to thank the Department of Theatre Arts, the College of Arts and Sciences, and the Office of Research and Economic Development at Boise State University for giving me time to write and money to travel. For that I am truly grateful.

I would also like to offer my sincere thanks to the Idaho Humanities Council for supporting the book with a Research Grant. This funding came at a crucial point in my writing: it allowed me to travel during a pivotal theater season, and it provided much-needed encouragement. I am very appreciative of the IHC's generosity.

Sarah Ruhl and Quiara Alegría Hudes allowed me to read their work before it was published. This assistance was absolutely invaluable.

Robyn Curtis and Desiree Browne at Palgrave and the readers of the draft manuscript have also earned my lasting gratitude. I was also truly fortunate to have Suzanne Sherman Aboulfadl's expert assistance with the index.

Most of all I'm thankful for the support and love of my family, immediate and extended. They've helped me in more ways than I can list here.

Introduction

The Context for Ruhl and Her Contemporaries, or Women's Playwriting: Strictly Prohibited in the New Century?

For more than a decade, activists, writers, and critics have been calling for a change to unfair working conditions faced by contemporary female playwrights. During the 1998–99 theater season, the Guerilla Girls put stickers in the stalls of women's restrooms in New York City theaters that had not produced a play by a woman that season—this included some of the city's most well-regarded companies. The stickers proclaimed, "In this theater the taking of photographs, the use of recording devices, and the production of plays by women are strictly prohibited." The Susan Jonas and Suzanne Bennett study "Report on the Status of Women: A Limited Engagement?" was released three years later, in January 2002. In their study, funded by the New York State Council on the Arts, Jonas and Bennett reported on the number of female playwrights at work in the American regional theater and in Off-Broadway theaters at several moments: from 1969 to 1975, the number was 7 percent; in the 1994–94 season, 17 percent of plays were written by women; in the 2000–2001 season, 20 percent "had a woman on the writing team"; and in the then current season of 2001–2, 17 percent of plays were written by women.[1] They observed that in 1998 in Off-Off Broadway theaters the percentage of plays written by women neared 30 percent, but if one looked uptown to Broadway houses that same year, only 8 percent of dramas and 1 percent of musicals had female authors. While women's voices might not have been literally prohibited in the years covered by the study, the statistics Jonas and Bennett gathered demonstrated that on American stages, these voices were rare. It was at roughly this time that Sarah Ruhl began her professional playwriting career.

In *The New York Times* the next year, Jason Zinoman trumpeted "The Season of the Female Playwright." Noting the perception among playwrights that Jonas and Bennett's study was a "turning point," he compared the 2002 and 2003 seasons: "Last year's fall season did include New York premieres by Caryl

Churchill, Dael Orlandersmith and Elaine May, but the majority of new plays were written by men and there were hardly any debuts by female playwrights." By contrast in 2003, he argued, "Downtown, the highest profile commercial play was *Omnium Gatherum* by Ms. [Theresa] Rebeck and Alexandra Gersten-Vassilaros. Arguably the best-reviewed plays so far this season have been Lisa Loomer's *Living Out*, Amy Freed's *Beard of Avon* and Paula Vogel's *Long Christmas Ride Home*." But before Zinoman concluded his thoughts, he did note that even in this golden season for women, "the only play written by a woman on Broadway this fall closed before it opened—*Bobbi Boland* by Nancy Hasty."[2]

The public furor over gender equity in American playwriting quieted for a time, Sarah Ruhl's list of plays and productions expanded, and tension continued to simmer just beneath the surface of critical discourse. Writing a little more than four years after Zinoman, Alexis Greene decried the lack of a new and comprehensive study mapping male and female writers' work opportunities in *American Theatre*.[3] In October 2008, female playwrights took matters into their own hands in order to restart large-scale, public conversations. Playwrights Sarah Schulman and Julia Jordan organized a town hall–style meeting at the nation's oldest organization supporting playwrights, New Dramatists, to discuss the struggles female writers continue to face if they aim to have their work produced Off-Broadway, a segment of New York theater generally hospitable to new, nonmusical plays. The then current 2008–9 season at the Public Theater would feature six new plays by men and one by a woman;[4] at the Manhattan Theatre Club five news plays were written by men and one was by a woman (Lynn Nottage, whose Pulitzer Prize–winning *Ruined* will be discussed in this study). At the time of the meeting there were no nonmusical plays on Broadway written by women.

Meanwhile, at the instigation of Jordan, Emily Glassberg Sands began studying the situation. When she shared her findings at the 59E59 Theatre in New York in June 2009, she confirmed some assumptions while upending others. Sands found that in 2008, 82 percent of plays in nonprofit theaters with more than 99 seats were written by men while only 18 percent were written by women, thus indicating no profound change from the seasons studied by Jonas and Bennett.[5] In addition, she found that there are more scripts being written by men, so the percentage of male-authored scripts that find their way to production is actually almost equal to the number authored by women; she found that women are more likely to write plays about women and that plays about women are less likely to be produced; she found that women artistic directors (those who schedule plays for production) tend to anticipate bias and thus worry more about female-authored texts' economic value than male artistic directors; and she found that while women's scripts, when they make it to

Broadway, are actually more profitable than men's by an average of 18 percent, they play for shorter runs.⁶

As summer turned to fall and the 2009–10 season began, the Sands study was fresh in people's minds, and stories about her findings turned up in a variety of mainstream and specialist publications. Marsha Norman's article in the November issue of *American Theatre*, "Not There Yet: What Will it Take to Achieve Equality for Women in Theatre?" ranks among the most influential of these pieces. Norman demanded change, calling on the major arts-funding organizations to legislate against discrimination of women writers—in the same way they protect every other kind of writer. She simply found the 80/20 divide unacceptable and argued persuasively, "We have to commit to telling all the stories of this country. We need to make some new rules for ourselves, and do our jobs fairly. We need to stop expecting plays by women to be soft. We need to see what they actually are when we read them. We should've done this a long time ago. But we can do it now. We can even up these numbers."⁷

By season's end, however, the numbers were not even. The *New York Times* ran a story in mid-May as part of its Tony Award coverage called "Disappointing Season for Broadway Women." As *The New York Times* discussed the female writers up for Tony consideration, they observed that 4 of the 22 nominees were women. Two of the four women were in musical categories—Lucy Prebble and Sherie Rene Scott.⁸ This is worth noting, because the musical theater has been hospitable to female writers in recent years.⁹ The other two women were Edna Ferber—whose *Royal Family*, coauthored with George S. Kaufman, was up for a Best Revival Tony 73 years after its 1927 debut—and the sole living author of a straight play to receive recognition, Sarah Ruhl. She was nominated for *In the Next Room*, her Broadway debut.

The other award for which *In the Next Room* was a contender, the Pulitzer Prize, also inspired controversy in the spring of 2010. Reaction to the award was nearly instantaneous. Three plays were designated nominees: *The Elaborate Entrance of Chad Diety* by Kristoffer Diaz, *Bengal Tiger at the Baghdad Zoo* by Rajiv Joseph, and *In the Next Room* by Sarah Ruhl. The Pulitzer winner was a title not originally on the list of finalists (created by a five-member jury of critics, artists, and academics) but one that several Pulitzer Prize board members went to see the night before the final vote on the year's winner.¹⁰ The Broadway musical *Next to Normal*, the only title among the four contenders running in New York at the time of the deliberations, took home what is arguably the highest prize in American playwriting.

In the 2010–11 and 2011–12 awards cycles, the Pulitzer Prize did honor work by women again. Lisa D'Amour's *Detroit* was a Pulitzer finalist; Quiara Alegría Hudes's *Water by the Spoonful*, also considered in this study, won the Pulitzer in 2012, making Hudes the first Latina author to win the award. But the Tony Awards did not honor women writers either year in the best play category. In 2011 Cheri Steinkellner was nominated for her book of *Sister Act*; in 2012 Margaret Edson's *Wit* was a nominee for best revival of a play. Neither writer won in her respective category. No women writers of straight plays were nominated in 2010–11 because there were no new straight plays on Broadway written by women that opened that season.[11] In the 2011–12 season, however, Lydia R. Diamond, Katori Hall, and Theresa Rebeck all had new work on Broadway stages.[12]

Sarah Ruhl's Serious Success

Despite these conditions, Sarah Ruhl dominated the American stage at the beginning of the twenty-first century. She had 12 premiere productions in as many years. One more script had major remountings at the Yale Repertory Theatre in January 2010 followed by the Classic Stage Company in September 2010. And four of her plays were among the ten most-produced plays in the American theaters that are members of the Theatre Communications Group's organization: in 2010–11, *In the Next Room, or the Vibrator Play* was the seventh-most-produced play and in 2011–12, the third most produced; in 2009–10, *Dead Man's Cell Phone* was tied for the second-most-produced play; in 2008–9, *Eurydice* was the fifth-most-produced play; and in 2007–8 *The Clean House* was tied for the second-most-produced play.[13] Across the country, if theatergoers were attending the premiere of a new play, there was a good chance that play was written by Sarah Ruhl.[14]

Academic scholarship has not yet succeeded in catching up with the prolific and widely produced Ruhl. The first book on her work appeared in 2011. In *Sarah Ruhl: A Critical Study of the Plays*, James Al-Shamma did an exceptional job of analyzing each of her major plays. He also amplified the primary trope running through the voluminous popular commentary on her work in newspapers and magazines. In these reviews, critics applied a limited number of adjectives to Ruhl's work over and over again, regardless of whether reviewers were praising her plays or dismissing them: they called the plays fantastical, fanciful, hallucinatory, offbeat, quirky, and, most frequently, whimsical. Al-Shamma also describes Ruhl's style, particularly in her early plays, as whimsical.[15] I am intrigued by the subtext of these words. The words critics, popular and now academic, use to describe Ruhl's plays all suggest an otherness, a strangeness, and a disconnection from some facets of reality. My goal in this study is to reveal another and equally important dimension of Ruhl's dramaturgy. I will contend that Ruhl is not simply quirky and whimsical. Instead, I intend to prove that she also has a passionate interest in the social concerns and ethical questions that characterized her (first) great decade of success. While her work generally, and sometimes emphatically, eschews psychological realism—in terms of character, subtext, and action—that does not mean she fails to engage the troubles of the world around her in profound ways. In fact, quite the opposite is true. As she has explained when discussing her admiration for Italo Calvino and her own tendency toward existential comedy, "Lightness isn't stupidity . . . It's actually a philosophical and aesthetic viewpoint, deeply serious, and has a kind of wisdom—stepping back to laugh at horrible things even as you're experiencing them."[16] Furthermore, these deeply serious matters connect her to the work of other women writing plays in the decade. Ruhl's work should not be read in isolation, because her work is part of a larger conversation by female playwrights about the values present in and missing from contemporary American culture. This conversation was taking place on Broadway and off, as well as in regional theaters around the country; well-established authors and emerging writers lent their voices to this multilogue. I will, therefore read five of Ruhl's most popular plays—those listed on Theatre Communications Group's (TCG) most-produced list, and one of the last of her plays to receive a New York premiere in the first decade of the twenty-first century, and the last published before the end of 2010, *Passion Play*, in relation to single plays by Lisa Loomer, Diana Son, Jenny Schwartz, Joan Didion, Kate Fodor, Young Jean Lee, Bathsheba Doran, Quiara Alegría Hudes, Lynn Nottage, and Kia Corthron.

My focus on the popular is quite purposeful. In "Feminist Performance Criticism and the Popular: Reviewing Wendy Wasserstein," Jill Dolan wrote, "Conducting feminist practice, as third wavers advocate, from a place admittedly within capitalism (and within dominant ideology) could be advantageous, instead of holding on to what might finally be an idealist belief that feminist practice can remain outside capitalism's reach. Many American feminist performance theorists and critics have historically looked to the outside or the margins for effective, socially critical theatre. Perhaps it is now time to acknowledge the potential of looking inside as well, and to address feminism as a critique or value circulating within our most commercial theatres."[17] While I wish to qualify what being "third wave"[18] might entail—I will discuss the relationship of third-wave feminism to this study below—I do advocate the approach Dolan describes here and find it timely and necessary. I want to highlight the kind of feminist theater that aims for and reaches a broad audience in the new century: the kind of theater created by Sarah Ruhl and this selection of her contemporaries. These women have boldly claimed a spot at the center of American theater, against the odds, and the characters they craft, the stories they tell, the questions they pose, and the ideas they materialize have the potential to shape the cultural imagination of a large group of theatergoers as a complex new era unfolds. These expansive contributions demand the same kind of rigorous and sustained critical attention that alternative feminist theater received from scholars in decades past. Like feminist acts on the margins of the theater world, feminist acts in the center matter greatly to the history of American theater and culture.

Riding Waves of Emotion

The situation faced by most contemporary female playwrights—the lack of production opportunity and the subsequent lack of recognition—makes me angry. Outraged. It's a passion that's drives me from computer to library to theater and back to the computer in a continuous loop of writing, reading, and watching, but I haven't always been sure how (and how forthrightly) to express it.

During one phase of my writing, I felt particularly wary of sounding "too angry" here at the book's start, both because I didn't want to make it easy to dismiss my points as ranting, thus giving readers an easy excuse to put the book down before they'd even begun, and also because I wanted to celebrate the work that I had found so moving both on the page and on the stage. No matter how angry the numbers make me, these plays thrill me. I want more people to read them and to produce them; I want more audiences to experience all they have to offer. So to mask the anger that was part of my reaction, I tried to trace out networks of possibility that linked the writers in my study—things like graduate school experience, mentorship in the profession as well as the academy, awards, and strong artistic partnerships—that gave them the edge to get noticed and produced. These things matter, and they are well worth discussion. But try as I might something was always percolating beneath the surface that made the descriptions seem no more than dutiful and the argument flimsy. That something was the emotion that this positive framework didn't contain or honor.

Sara Ahmed's work in *The Cultural Politics of Emotions* has been pivotal in helping me parse and claim my emotional response to the scene of contemporary women's playwriting and to these plays in particular. Ahmed writes eloquently about feminism's relationship to anger, wonder, and hope and the way these emotions can be related.

First, she helped me embrace my feeling of emotional connection while letting go of my fear that this connection was irrational, and hence, unscholarly. She writes, "The response to the dismissal of feminists as emotional should not then be to claim that feminism is rational rather than emotional. Such a claim would be misguided as it would accept the very opposition between emotions and rational thought that is crucial to the subordination of femininity as well as feminism. Instead we need to contest this understanding of emotion as 'the unthought,' just as we need to contest the assumption that 'rational thought' is unemotional, or that it does not involve being moved by others."[19] She helps her reader reclaim emotional reaction as a reasonable response and reason as something intertwined with emotion. And in regard to anger in particular she writes, "Anger is creative; it works to create a language with which to respond to that which one is against, whereby 'the what' is renamed, and brought into a feminist world."[20]

Ahmed also helps me locate wonder in my reaction. She writes, "Wonder is about learning to see the world as something that does not have to be, and as something that came to be, over time, and with work."[21] When I wonder at unbalanced numbers and the prospect of strong voices unheard and compelling stories untold, I can imagine something else and do something with that imagining. If the 80/20 split was made, not natural or inevitable—because there are plenty of trained, talented professional women writers writing plays worthy of staging—it can be made another way. I start to hope for something better for all the writers in this study and the many more who aren't here.[22] As Ahmed clarifies for me, "Hope is crucial to the act of protest: hope is what allows us to feel that what angers us is not inevitable, even if transformation can sometimes feel impossible . . . The moment of hope is when the 'not yet' impresses upon us in the present, such that we must act, politically, to make it our future."[23]

In her introduction to *Theatre Journal*'s 2008 special issue, "Feminism and Theatre, Redux," Catherine A. Schuler wrote, "Although in the interests of 'equity' our [the University of Maryland, College Park] season generally includes one female-authored play, the season selection committee is often stumped after its members run through the usual suspects: Caryl Churchill, Wendy Wasserstein, and Marsha Norman . . . Bardolatry endures, and it is still the job of the women on the faculty to know the literature by women. In my youth, a prematurely optimistic Virginia Slims ad asserted, 'You've Come a Long Way, Baby'—but what was the destination, and are we there yet?"[24] It is my hope that this book will start chronicling the way the other half of the nation's stories were told at the start of the new century, begin mapping the road to the destination longed for by feminist theater scholars like Schuler, and work toward filling a gaping hole in theater scholarship. College faculty, male and female, simply do not know the range of women are who are writing contemporary American drama, because in-depth analysis beyond production reviews and the occasional article-length inquiry on most of the writers I plan to study does not yet exist. By now, they know Sarah Ruhl. Her work—most particularly *Eurydice* and *Dead Man's Cell Phone*—has been produced on college campuses across the country. But Ruhl is hardly the only female writer telling provocative stories and shedding light on concerns important to men and women. The story of her success shouldn't obscure the broader picture.[25] In addition to Ruhl's plays, the work of Lisa Loomer, Diana Son, Jenny Schwartz, Joan Didion, Bathsheba Doran, Quiara Alegría Hudes, Kate Fodor, Young Jean Lee, Lynn Nottage, and Kia Corthron demands rigorous consideration. While Nottage and Didion are well known, most of the other writers have received scant academic attention, and these playwrights most certainly have not been grouped together and compared in a sustained scholarly investigation. When faculty don't know new work thanks to a dearth of academic criticism, students—the next generation of artists and audiences—don't know it either, because the work isn't being studied comprehensively and it isn't being produced. A true appreciation of the field today, and a meaningful goal for the theater in the future, is impossible without this crucial area of knowledge. Looking at a high-profile author in concert with the constellation of writers, famous and not-yet-but-should-be famous, who share her nonwhimsical concerns is just the beginning, but it is an important place to start. It is a project of protest—and one full of hope.

The Methodology and Structure of the Study

This is also a feminist project. Angela McRobbie has recently argued, "What feminism actually means varies, literally, from one self-declared feminist to the next, but this does not reduce its field of potential influence, quite the opposite."[26] My definition of feminism, my perspective and my agenda, have much in common with liberal feminism. In *Feminist Theories for Dramatic Criticism*, Gayle Austin writes, "Liberal feminism developed from liberal humanism, stressing women's parity with men, based on 'universal values.'"[27] She also notes that liberal feminism "works for success within [the] system" and that it advocates "reform, not revolt."[28] While I may not share the same notions of "universal values" that some liberal feminists have espoused[29] (my embrace of emotion via Ahmed is one indication that traditional bifurcations of reason and emotion are not acceptable to me), I am fully convinced that women deserve equal opportunities to see their work produced on the nation's most prominent stages—on Broadway, Off-Broadway, Off-Off-Broadway, and in regional theaters from coast to coast. I think it is vitally important that they work within the system of mainstream theater to achieve reform of current production practices that have featured limited participation by women, so that they can bring their work to a wide audience. A privilege that has been claimed by men should be sought by women.

In addition to my interest in parity, I'm concerned with how female playwrights achieve parity. In "Supremacy Ideology Masquerading as Reality: The Obstacle Facing Women Playwrights in America," Sarah Schulman offers a scathing critique: "Most plays that receive mainstream production and approval in the United States do so because they represent very rigid ideological perspectives about power. The more mainstream the venue, the more politicized the choices. Plays that assume that the story of the white male is the most central and important story of our culture are the plays most likely to be produced and rewarded. Because of the obsessive repetition of this point of view, it has become so familiar as to be mistakenly confused with quality."[30] And lest the reader have any doubt whether Schulman is addressing female playwrights who find production in the same mainstream venues that male playwrights do, she says, "Plays by women and people of color are often produced and rewarded to the extent that they reflect these values."[31] Through the course of the study, I will argue that the plays I have chosen to analyze do not uncritically mirror hegemonic cultural values. On the contrary, I intend to prove, they offer rigorous and creative critique of these values from a rich variety of female perspectives, even if these plays appear on mainstream stages.

My interest in mainstream stages and in working within established systems of production (cultural and economic) to bring voices that do not mimic hegemonic attitudes, does, if we return to the quotation from Jill Dolan, align the study with third-wave feminism as well as liberal feminism. While the parameters of liberal feminism are relatively stable at this point, the same can't be said for third-wave feminism, which is perpetually (re)defined against the architects and ideas of second-wave feminism, the phase usually situated in the 1960s and 1970s during which liberal feminism surged. In *Not My Mother's Sister: Generational Conflict and Third-Wave Feminism*, Astrid Henry outlines three interrelated features of third-wave feminism that contribute to the term's motility. First, she observes, third-wave feminism implies "generational age," as it is sometimes understood as being "the feminism practiced and produced by men and women born after the baby-boom generation."[32] At first this seems rather straightforward: third wavers are the generation following the second wave, or those born between 1961 and 1981. Many of the writers I study were born in this period (everyone, in fact, but Loomer and Didion), and I join them in this date range linking my perspective with theirs. But as Henry also notes that term suggests youth; other writers have defined the outer limits of the age of third wavers as being 35, so people born between 1961 and 1981 are quickly aging out of the movement if it is defined thus. Of the writers in this study only Quiara Alegría Hudes was still under 35 at the time of the book's publication.

Henry notes a second characterization of the third wave, one based in ideology instead of chronology. She explains, "In this understanding of the term, the third wave represents a shift within feminist thought, moving it in a new direction by blending aspects of second-wave feminism with other forms of contemporary critical theory, such as queer, post-colonial, and critical race theories."[33] Several texts associated with second-wave feminism have been critiqued for emphasizing the conditions and concerns of white, heterosexual, middle-class women. The third wave has learned from this critical discussion, and it actively tries to engage a wider variety of human experience. Likewise, while Ruhl, a white, heterosexual, privileged woman is at the study's center, I place her work "beside" women outside her immediate demographic circle—those who identify as Asian American, African American, and Latina—so hers is not the sole voice heard. I emulate Eve Sedgwick's use of the term *beside* in *Touching Feeling*: "Beside is an interesting preposition also because there's nothing very dualistic about it; a number of elements may lie alongside one another, though not an infinity of them . . . Beside comprises a wide range of desiring, identifying, representing, repelling, paralleling, differentiating, rivaling, leaning, twisting, mimicking, withdrawing, attracting, aggressing, warping, and other relations."[34] The writers beside Ruhl have the kinds of complicated relationships with her and each other that Sedgwick's list of gerunds describes.

Henry's third meaning is the one most directly referenced by Dolan, one that is applicable to all the authors and their work. Henry explains that the third meaning is a response to current lived experience "and the realities of the current historical moment, 'a world of global capitalism and information technology, postmodernism and postcolonialism, and environmental degradation as [Rory] Dicker and [Alison] Piepmeier write in *Catching a Wave*. 'We no longer live in the world that feminists of the second wave faced.' Third wave feminists, they continue, 'are therefore concerned not simply with 'women's issues' but with a broad range of interlocking topics."[35]

This conception of the third wave's historical situation and its theoretically based response to "lived messiness," as third wavers Leslie Heywood and Jennifer Drake have phrased it,[36] underpins the way I've devised and structured the study. The challenges facing people in the early twenty-first century grow out of current lived conditions and are distinctive and multiple. It is no wonder that these vital dramatists are eager to render these conflicts in theatrical form. The issues in the plays very much concern women's lives, but they are not exclusively "women's issues."

After a first chapter that marks the contours of Ruhl's earliest professionally produced plays and the dialogue she had with two of her literary predecessors, Virginia Woolf and Anton Chekhov, I establish the pattern that will hold until the book's conclusion. I pair one of Ruhl's plays with two plays that are authored by other female authors who share similar cultural concerns, that are in relatively to very near chronological proximity within the decade, and that benefit from a particular feminist analytic lens. Because of the diversity of issues that occupy Ruhl and her contemporaries, no single methodology will serve all the plays in the study. I intentionally bring a variety of perspectives to bear on these texts because the writers give shape to a multiplicity of viewpoints onstage. Heywood and Drake inspire me with this thought: "Even as different strains of feminism and activism sometimes directly contradict each other, they are all part of our third-wave lives, our thinking, our praxes: we are products of the contradictory definitions of and differences within feminism."[37] In this spirit I draw on feminist interpretation and analysis of emotion as I analyze *Eurydice*, Joan Didion's *The Year of Magical Thinking*, and Jenny Schwartz's *God's Ear* in Chapter 2. In the third chapter I explore the fields of feminist economics and care ethics as I read *Clean House* in concert with Lisa Loomer's *Living Out* and Diana Son's *Satellites*. In the fourth chapter I use feminist theology to help me read *Passion Play* beside Young Jean Lee's *Church* and Kate Fodor's *100 Saints You Should Know*. In Chapter 5 feminist analyses of space, place, and technology help me navigate the terrain of *Dead Man's Cell Phone*, Bathsheba Doran's *Kin* and Quiara Alegría Hudes's *Water by the Spoonful*. In the final chapter, ecofeminism helps me respond to *In the Next Room* as well as Lynn Nottage's *Ruined* and Kia Corthron's *A Cool Dip in the Barren Saharan Crick*.

In "Re-Runs and Repetition," her study of the contemporary penchant cultural recycling, Ruhl wrote, "For artists who conjure the historic and contemporary invisible, for artists who make a thing that is essentially incapable of being owned, for artists who experiment with wild fancy and then invite *everyone* to the table to partake—to you I give my undying loyalty and love."[38] At various moments, Ruhl herself, and her contemporaries, conjure similar forms of magic, refuse commodification, and undertake similar populist aesthetic experiments. For this I offer them and the reader my protest, my serious and varied critical feminist consideration, and my hope for a different future.

CHAPTER 1

Educating Sarah Ruhl

In a 2006 essay, Sarah Ruhl recounted the experience of an aggravated dramaturg who was struggling to placate her theater's subscribers: "The subscriber said, 'I'm sick of seeing plays that I've seen before. And I'm also sick of seeing plays that are totally unfamiliar to me.' The theatre had no choice but to throw up its hands in frustration." Ruhl's own thoughtful response to the quandary went as follows: "And yet—what if this audience member was making a deeper point? Maybe what's missing in the American theatre is a kind of primal familiarity wedded to the newness of soaring insight."[1] As she launched her playwriting career, it seems that Ruhl had the plight of both the dramaturg and the audience member in mind. In her early plays, Ruhl turned to classic texts, not merely to reframe them, but to animate them with her own particular, developing theatrical insights.

At the time she was writing "Re-Runs and Repetition," her play *Eurydice*, a retelling of the classic Orpheus and Eurydice myth from the female character's perspective, was, after 13 readings, finding its way to the stage in regional theaters—at the Madison Rep, Berkeley Rep, and Yale Rep—before its New York debut at Second Stage in 2007. But two of her even earlier plays, *Orlando* and *Lady with the Lap Dog* provide a map for the ways some of her later work will develop. For that reason, I will analyze these early plays before I put Ruhl's most popular plays into conversation with the work of other female playwrights who are her contemporaries.

As she reflected back on her work adapting these texts as *Orlando* was heading for its New York City premiere in 2010, Ruhl said,

> I am not really interested in doing an adaptation of a writer who I don't bow down to in my head. So working on Chekhov or Woolf is like being a student and kneeling at the feet of a master. I mean, it's just getting their language in my head and trying to be clairvoyant and trying to think about what they were thinking and what their intentions might have been. So I'm really not trying to put a

stamp on it as much as I am trying to think how to make it live theatrically in this particular moment in time—and in English in the case of Chekhov. But I don't really approach it the way I would approach my own original work.[2]

While she may approach adaptation in a way that differs from original composition, these adaptations, and the "masters" who taught her in the process, did, I will argue, have a major impact on the work that would make Ruhl famous within the next five years. As she got their "language in her head" and performed them as writers—she uses the language of the actor when she talks about "intention"—she reinforced elements of her own emerging style.

The Piven Theatre and Joyce Piven

In 1998, the Piven Theatre Workshop produced Ruhl's adaptation of Virginia Woolf's *Orlando*, and then in 2000 the Piven included her adaptations of the Chekhov short stories "The Lady with the Lap Dog" and "Anna Around the Neck" in *Chekhov: The Stories*. Since one company was so crucial in propelling Ruhl to the stage early in her career, I'd like to look at the importance of the Piven Theatre in forging Ruhl's dramatic persona and of planting the language of the actor in her head, before I analyze two of the plays.

Ruhl's study with the Pivens began more than a decade before the premiere of *Orlando*—in her childhood. She grew up in Wilmette, Illinois, not far from Chicago and even closer to Evanston, where the Piven Theatre Workshop is located. That a quiet, bookish child like the young Ruhl found herself in acting workshops is due in large measure to the inspiration of her mother, Kathy Ruhl. Before she gave birth to Sarah (in 1974) and her sister Kate, Kathy Ruhl was an actress in alternative Chicago theaters, performing early work by David Mamet and Maria Irene Fornes, the mentor with whom her younger daughter would one day work. As she discovered the need to combine mothering with performing, Kathy Ruhl shifted her attention to community theater (and channeled her creativity into doctoral study and teaching as well). Both Ruhl and her mother mention in interviews and essays that as a child, Sarah often accompanied her mother to rehearsal; before she could write, Sarah was making and giving notes to her mother's cast mates.

In his interview with Ruhl for *Dead Man's Cell Phone*, Playwrights Horizons artistic director Tim Sanford asked Ruhl about this past experience of taking notes on her mother's work and being in the theater with her. He asked if that was how she knew "how actors and texts are supposed to interact." She replied, "Yes, that feels very natural to me . . . I'd also studied at the Piven Theater Workshop with Joyce Piven from a young age." Her comment led him to the following realization: "When I used to think you were a poet-turned-playwright, I wondered how you had developed such finely tuned antennae about shaping moments with the actors. But now it all makes sense to me. It's inside of you."³

The theatrical sensibility inside Ruhl (that coexists with the poetic sensibility she cultivated as an undergraduate at Brown University prior to meeting Paula Vogel, whom I will discuss later in the chapter), is the direct result of her mother's influence and Joyce Piven's particular style of improvisational work.

The Piven Theatre Workshop was founded by husband-and-wife collaborators, Byrne and Joyce Piven. After graduating from the University of Chicago, they cofounded The Playwrights Theatre Club with Paul Sills—who later cofounded Second City. At the Playwrights Theatre Club and then at the Piven, the ideas of Viola Spolin were at the heart of what they call "The Work."

In a piece for *Northshore Magazine,* Peter Gianopulos interviewed Joyce Piven, Ruhl's classmate and frequent collaborator, Polly Noonan, and Ruhl herself about what "The Work" entails. Both Piven and Ruhl refer to "The Work" using the term *ritual.* Ruhl explains further, "I grew up watching the rituals of the [Catholic] church, which are very theatrical. The rituals of the theater are sacred in the same way."⁴

Through Spolin-inspired improvisational work, Ruhl and her classmates were asked to experience in the present moment in its multidimensional fullness, to feel in their bodies what it meant to play and to transform, and to translate the everyday into remarkable ritual. One of the key coaching calls the Pivens would use was the phrase "Explore and heighten!" Noonan adds further of Ruhl, "When I see her plays or am part of her plays . . . I see the kind of play and impulse taught at the Piven workshop. That lightness, the effortlessness, the humor, the discovery."⁵

As influential as Joyce Piven has been in developing the lightness in Ruhl, she has also had an effect on the darker counterpoints in her work. In her introduction to her 2009 adaptation of *The Three Sisters,* Ruhl talks about how important conversations over tea with Piven were in helping her create this recent adaptation. Ruhl describes Piven's work in the 1960s with the Russian acting teacher, Mira Rostova. Rostova introduced Piven to idea that speech might be developed into five melodies, or "doings." She goes on to explain that for Rostova and Piven "the defy," in addition to "the lament," "looms large."⁶ Though she is speaking specifically of the *Three Sisters,* this sentiment applies much more broadly to Ruhl's work: "To look for the act of defiance in the sisters rather than the elegy; to find the philosophical lament with humor rather than the complaint . . . this was my hope in the translation, and also my hope with the actors who ultimately do the production."⁷

Bringing professional actors into Ruhl's process is another crucial gift that Joyce Piven gave Sarah Ruhl. After she earned her undergraduate degree from Brown University—which occurred with interruption due to the death of her much-beloved father from bone cancer when she was twenty years old.[8]—Ruhl stayed in Providence for a year, briefly teaching at Wheaton College there. After that, she moved back to Chicago. Ruhl says, "I went back to Chicago and wrote an adaptation of *Orlando* for Joyce, and that was my first production outside of college . . . She commissioned it, and I said sure. She'd been my teacher, so that was big leap, to go from her being my teacher to sitting in the room collaborating with her."[9] The work with Piven and her actors, even if it wasn't critically embraced, and even if it had moments of difficulty,[10] helped her gain crucial experience with professional production. Shortly thereafter she returned to Brown to study again and in greater depth with Paula Vogel as well as Mac Wellman and Nilo Cruz, and there she started writing the plays for which she would soon become famous.[11]

Adapting and Studying Woolf

When *Orlando* was remounted by New York City's Classic Stage Company in 2010, many reviewers commented on Ruhl's faithfulness to Woolf's text.[12] Charles Isherwood's remarked in *The New York Times* that Ruhl had in fact been too faithful: "If Ms. Ruhl's 'Orlando' does not escape all the pitfalls of transforming a work of deeply imagined prose into a fully animated play, she cannot be accused of taking any undue stylistic or thematic liberties. In fact, the production's main flaw is a reliance on third-person narration to denote much of the action, which derives directly from Woolf's description-rich, dialogue-light book."[13]

And while Ruhl herself notes that she omitted "huge swaths and chunks"[14] from the book—such as the literary allusions that Woolf uses to characterize each section, the critic Nick Greene who like Orlando crosses centuries, and colorful episodes such as Orlando's sojourn with the gypsies, I'm most interested in neither the parts of the book that Ruhl preserved in their original form nor the parts she excised entirely. Instead, I will use the elements of Woolf's "fairytale-a-clef"[15] that Ruhl transformed and theatricalized, in a dramatic analogue to Piven's theatrical games, to explore how the adaptation of the book trained Ruhl for the major plays she would compose later in the decade.

It must be noted that transformation and if not theatricalization precisely, then its close relation performativity, undergird Woolf's *Orlando*. The first thing Woolf transformed was genre. Woolf titled the book *Orlando: A Biography*, but it is hardly typical of that form. While Woolf does tell the story of the daily life and wild adventures of the noble Orlando and claims through her first chapter to have fulfilled "the first duty of a biographer, which is to plod, without looking to right or left, in the indelible footprints of truth,"[16] Orlando travels from male to female and lives in the sixteenth, seventeenth, eighteenth, nineteenth, and twentieth centuries. Orlando is not a historical figure (though she occasionally encounters the likes of Queen Elizabeth, William Shakespeare, and Alexander Pope). She is instead an amalgamation of bits and pieces of Woolf's lover, Vita Sackville-West, to whom Woolf dedicated the book. Photographs supplement the text at various points in the manner typical of biography, but three of these are Sackville-West snapped on random occasions but labeled as Orlando in various time periods. Woolf hardly limits herself to the tone of biography either. Through Orlando's failed literary aspirations—her poetry travels with her throughout the centuries without ever improving dramatically—she satirizes the literary and social manners of each age while she also dramatizes the gendered boundaries of existence, for her title subject "knew the secrets, shared the weaknesses of each"[17] sex.

It is in her treatment of gender and its parameters that Woolf's performativity and postmodernity appear—like Orlando herself—out of time,[18] since the book was published in 1928. As Laura Marcus has observed, "*Orlando* is . . . postmodern in its production of performative identities, and its radical undermining of fixed gender identities."[19] And Christy L. Burns writes, "The effects of Orlando's transformation through the ages—marked especially by his/her changes in clothing—execute a parodic deconstruction of essentialist claims tentatively offered in the text . . . Woolf plays on a twentieth-century conception of truth, derived from the Greek notion of alethea, unveiling. In her novel truth is destabilized and turns into parody through an emphasis on period fashions, cross-dressing, and undressing of 'essential' bodies."[20] When Orlando is lamenting the gender he has left, or testing the gender she has found, clothing does serve to reveal more than it conceals. For example, as she's sailing to England, the narrator muses, "It is a strange fact, but a true one that up to this moment she had scarcely given her sex a thought. Perhaps the Turkish trousers, which she had hitherto worn had done something to distract her thoughts . . . At any rate, it was not until she felt the coil of skirts about her legs and the Captain offered, with great politeness, to have an awning spread for her on deck that she realized, with a start the penalties and privileges of her position."[21] The skirts are like coils of rope, binding her and constraining in the way her breeches and Turkish trousers never did. While the skirts may be modest, revealing little of her new physical shape, they make clear to Orlando what the social consequences of that shape will be. They help her perform her role as woman and reinforce the codes associated with that role at the same time.

Woolf's genre and gender bending presage the compatibility she would have with Ruhl some seventy years after *Orlando* was published. And while Ruhl does perform these aspects of Woolf's writing as she's developing as a writer—adaptation for the stage in and of itself is a kind of genre bending, and gender bending will reemerge in *Passion Play* as the same performer plays Queen

Elizabeth, Hitler, and Reagan—she also plays with conventional understandings of time (a device that will appear again later, most obviously in *Passion Play* but also in *The Clean House* and *Dead Man's Cell Phone*) and shares Woolf's "incandescent" use of language.[22] But Ruhl is at moments a rebellious student. Even as she's penning this first adaptation, from a writer and work she's admired since her youth,[23] she intervenes in the text at key moments, finding ways to enhance Woolf's theatricality and in so doing to nurture her own emerging independent style and persona as a writer.

In both Woolf and Ruhl, a shared language ignites the intimacy between Orlando and Sasha, the Russian princess who would both capture and break his heart. But in Woolf, the language is actual French. When Sasha speaks French to the young courtiers around her at a banquet table, it is only Orlando who can understand her and respond. She then asks impertinent questions about those around her—including the king and queen. Orlando answers her with equal brazenness and "thus began an intimacy between the two which became the scandal of the court."[24]

Ruhl maintains the shape of the scene, but where she differs is in what comes out of the mouths of Orlando and Sasha. Her stage directions in the scene read, "Sasha speaks gibberish French to Orlando; it sounds like a sexual invitation . . . Orlando speaks gibberish French to Sasha; it sounds like a sexual invitation . . . Orlando looks at her, bewitched."[25] Here Ruhl experiments with the unintelligible and the effect that might work on her audience. She returns to and amplifies the technique in *The Clean House* when she opens her play with Matilde, a Brazilian maid who refuses to clean her employer's house, telling a joke in Portuguese. Since that language is less commonly understood in the United States than French, she uses actual Portuguese, but the effect is the same. The play opens, in fact, with the following stage directions: "Matilde tells a long joke in Portuguese to the audience. We can tell she is telling a joke even though we might not understand the language. She finishes the joke. She exits."[26] In an interview, Ruhl described the impulse behind her opening scene: "When I wrote that, I didn't intend it to be funny particularly. I was just interested in the question of translation, and would you know if someone was telling a joke in another language, would that be formally communicated."[27] Ruhl thus opens her play by asking her audience to apprehend meaning without the benefit of words. They must read body language while they listen to the rhythm and timing of the actress's delivery; they must meet the performer on the plane that Piven's exercises cultivate. The gibberish French scene in *Orlando* allowed Ruhl to experiment with this technique so that she might advance it later on.

After the scene with French launches Orlando and Sasha's relationship, the two begin exploring the world beyond the court. One adventure finds them watching a company of players perform *Othello*. Woolf includes but a snippet of the play in her book: "Methinks it should be now a huge eclipse / Of sun and moon, and that the affrighted globe / Should yawn."[28] Here Othello laments the violence he has done to Desdemona in his speech to Emilia. Ruhl, however, includes several more lines from Shakespeare's play, and instead of quoting the aftermath of Othello's passion, she uses the part of the play showing the height of that passion—when Desdemona denies giving Cassio the handkerchief and begs for her life, and Othello smothers her anyway. She keeps Woolf's lines "Tears streamed down Orlando's face. The frenzy of the Moor seemed to him his own frenzy,"[29] but she chooses to show that frenzy far more directly. This move toward an expanded metatheatricality is an important step for Ruhl, because metatheatricality is a device upon which two of Ruhl's later plays, *Passion Play*, which traces the movement of that dramatic form through the Elizabethan era, World War II Germany, and into the 1980s in Sioux Falls, South Dakota, and her 2011 play *Stage Kiss*, which explores the effect of playing intimacy onstage, will turn.

On a far more subterranean level, the expanded reference to Shakespeare in Ruhl's play permits a reference to another of Ruhl's deep influences. Shakespeare plays an important role in several of Woolf's works, not just in *Orlando*. He is also referenced in *A Room of One's Own, Mrs. Dalloway, To the Lighthouse*, and *The Waves*. Beth Schwartz has argued that as Woolf pursues her project throughout these texts of "re-gendering Shakespeare and transforming him into a maternal muse, she challenges the heterosexual conventions of the poet-muse relationship—as well as worrying essentialist constructions of gender."[30] Woolf's referencing of Shakespeare allows Ruhl to connect to one of her maternal muses as well, though her poet-muse relationship is different in terms of gender.

Ruhl studied under Paula Vogel at Brown University, as already noted, as both an undergraduate and a graduate student. Though Ruhl has written of the impact of Vogel's *Baltimore Waltz* on her dramaturgy (she's called it "a Rosetta stone"[31]) instead of her Shakespearean deconstruction, *Desdemona*, Ruhl no doubt knows that play, too. Riffing on this particular play of Shakespeare's allows her to make a very subtle reference to a woman who is at once mentor and muse and who, like Shakespeare for Woolf, explodes the notion that the muse-poet relationship is an inherently heterosexual construct. In her contribution to *The Play That Changed My Life*, Ruhl wrote,

> And I think there was something about meeting Paula, and having been so affected by her work, that made it possible for me to write. This is to say, I always wrote—as a young child I wrote poems and stories and plays—but that meeting Paula made it possible for me to take up what is known rather ponderously as the writing life. I wonder if one precondition for taking on writing as an absolute vocation is to realize that the great works you so admire were written by living

people—not given to Moses on the mountaintop, not flung down onto parchment from great heights, but written by people who eat cookies or offer cookies or talk on the telephone. And not only written by people in general, but yes, written by women.[32]

In her play with Shakespeare and how it figures in and for Woolf, Ruhl's intertextuality becomes complex and pointed. She creates a genealogy of female creativity that exceeds and extends the narrative in the play.

Ruhl's treatment of Orlando's adventures in the seventeenth and eighteenth centuries are quite straightforward, but when she reaches the nineteenth century two points in the adaptation merit analysis. In both cases Ruhl transposes Woolf's verbal imagery into a new sensory mode. Ruhl labels her first scene in act 4, The Nineteenth Century, "On the Preponderance of Wedding Rings." As Orlando is trying to accommodate herself to the new age, she experiences an odd physical sensation: "her arms sang and twanged; her hairs seemed to erect themselves."[33] This "vibration" eventually centers itself on her ring finger. The scene reads

> **ORLANDO:** The vibration seemed, in the oddest way, to say:
> **CHORUS:** No that is not enough!
> **ORLANDO:** Life! A lover!
> **CHORUS:** And the spirit of the age would always reply: No, Orlando. Life, a husband!
> **ORLANDO:** Until Orlando felt positively ashamed of the second finger of her left hand without in the least knowing why.[34]

Orlando then seeks to try her maid's ring, but the maid refuses. Orlando apologizes saying, "I'm sorry Grimsditch. I didn't realize. Heaven help us. What a world we live in. What a world to be sure."[35]

Ruhl has conserved Woolf's lines of dialogue and narration very faithfully to this point, simply breaking it up for the various speakers and here, as throughout the play, she has characters refer to themselves as they speak of their feelings, providing a kind of distance while enhancing the effect that this is text being read. But then Ruhl offers a fantastic stage direction: "Orlando takes up her umbrella and walks, surveying the streets of London. Wedding rings are dropped from the sky on strings. They dangle above her."[36] This the first of many stage images with which Ruhl instigates a collision of the literal and the poetic. (Following on the heels of the rings would be a room made of string in *Eurydice*, a host of fish images in *Passion Play*, dirt and apples littering a pristine white living room in *The Clean House*, and floating paper houses in *Dead Man's Cell Phone*.) Wedding rings are everywhere in Victorian London, symbolizing and enforcing the heterosexual marriage contract. But they were not raining from the sky, threatening and taunting Orlando when she ventured beyond her domestic space. There is a joyfulness and jokiness to these moments, not unlike the spirit created by Piven in her improvisational games, and not unlike Woolf when she used photographs of Sackville-West to illustrate *Orlando*, thereby thwarting conventional biographic form. As Helen Wussow explained in "Virginia Woolf and the Problematic Nature of the Photographic Image," "the joy provided by Orlando is not the joy of recognition (of Orlando, Sackville-West, or the self-as-subject) but rather the acknowledgment of the supreme joke of the text and its images, a jest which serves to dislocate codes of perception and meaning."[37] So too does Ruhl interrogate the ways her audiences perceive and make meaning. She makes a familiar symbol of marriage strange through her uncanny, physicalized imagery.

Two of the most resonant theories of aesthetic estrangement emerged in the early twentieth century: Bertolt Brecht's *Verfremdung*, or "alienation," and Viktor Shklovsky's *ostranenie*, a less widely known idea about how art can make ideas and habits unfamiliar. Perhaps the most often cited passage of Shklovsky's, from his *Art as Technique*, is the following:

> Habitualization devours works, clothes, furniture, one's wife, and the fear of war. "If the whole complex lives of many people go on unconsciously, then such lives are as if they had never been." And art exists that one may recover the sensation of life; it exists to make one feel things, to make the stone *stony*. The purpose of art is to impart the sensation of things as they are perceived and not as they are known. The technique of art is to make objects "unfamiliar," to make forms difficult, to increase the difficulty and length of perception because the process of perception is an aesthetic end in itself and must be prolonged.[38]

It is Shklovsky, rather than Brecht, who Ruhl and Vogel claim as influential on their dramatic thought, and it is perhaps due in part to her claimed association that form or style is often privileged over idea in analysis of Ruhl. *Ostranenie* is sometimes, in distinction from *Verfremdung*, perceived as apolitical and ahistorical in its formal concerns. But Silvija Jestrovic helps us relocate the political in *ostranenie*, and by extension Ruhl's chosen approach to image: "Shklovsky's approach indirectly suggests that aesthetic choices are always in a way political, ideological, or ethical choices as well . . . the choice to defamiliarize reality and art through aesthetic means is a political position in itself."[39] Ruhl's particular brand of estrangement, which is sometimes labeled whimsy, progresses through imagery to often profound ethical statements in her future plays.

Ruhl's most intense intervention into Woolf's text happens in the play's final moments. Here she scripts a scene between Orlando and the dead Queen Elizabeth that does not occur in the book; she continues to use Woolf's words in other parts of the scene, but she rearranges them significantly, combining the final pages of the book with an earlier section; she exchanges Woolf's final image for one she uses earlier; and she uses a sound cue to extend the narrative into the present. What emerges from these multiple changes is a picture of the future Ruhl, no longer performing Woolf, but taking the stage herself—the one who will be able to play boldly with canonical figures and the texts in which they reside. The groundwork is laid for *Eurydice* and *Passion Play*.

By far the largest section of invented material occurs in the play's final scene. Ruhl plays off a section of text on Woolf's penultimate page: "All was phantom. All was still. All was lit as for the coming of a dead Queen . . . A Queen once more stepped from her chariot. 'The house is at your service, Ma'am,' she cried, curtsying deeply. 'Nothing has changed. The dead Lord, my father, shall lead you in.'"[40] Ruhl divides this text between Orlando and the Chorus and then proceeds to stage a scene between Orlando and the Queen that does not exist in the book. Here Orlando fully confronts her existential dilemma regarding the authenticity of a single or multiple selves:

> QUEEN: You don't seem like yourself.
> ORLANDO: I'm not sure that there is such a thing, Your Highness.
> QUEEN: Don't be silly, Orlando. You are many things, to many people. To me, you are a boy with delightful legs in silk stockings—apparently you have changed. But no matter. The dead have wonderful memories.
> ORLANDO: I would like, Your Highness, at the present moment, to feel as though I am only one thing.
> QUEEN: Poppycock! Don't be a bore, Orlando. You were never a bore in silk stockings.[41]

Orlando next reveals her longing for death. As the Queen dismisses this, reminding her that she had always been "bursting" with life, a wild goose enters the garden. In Woolf's *Orlando*, the wild goose signaled literary inspiration and here, too, the coming of the goose both serves that purpose and draws Ruhl back into Woolf's words, only in reordered form.

As she creates her play's final scene, Ruhl borrows from a part of Woolf's nineteenth-century section and combines it with her chronicle of Orlando in the present—1928. Throughout the book, Orlando has struggled to write her poetry. After her marriage—she did in fact give into the spirit of the age, which Ruhl made plain with her dangling rings—Orlando wonders what effect marriage will have on her writing and vice versa: "If one still wished, more than anything in the whole world, to write poetry, was it marriage?"[42] She decides to take her own dare, and as the chorus reports, "She plunged her pen neck deep in the ink. To her enormous surprise, she wrote. The words were a little long in coming, but come they did . . . And so—she wrote. And wrote. And wrote." At last Orlando cries, "Done! Done! It's done!"[43]

Woolf places the completion of the poem much earlier. She also has Orlando publish it, receive sparkling reviews, and contemplate burying it on her family estate near the book's end. Instead of staging the aftereffects of Orlando's act of creation, Ruhl stages the act itself, thus emphasizing that moment and connecting literary creation to the defining of selves that Orlando had so recently pondered. Ruhl leaves us with the sense that Orlando has chosen a self—the writer who is also a wife.

It is worth interjecting here that Ruhl too has chosen both the life of the writer and the life of a wife and mother. By the time *Orlando* premiered in New York in 2010, she'd been married for five years (after a seven-year courtship) to child psychologist Tony Charuvastra. He was the reason for her four-year sojourn to Los Angeles. Ruhl says of this time, "I went kicking and screaming, saying, 'This is the death of my career, there's no theater in L.A.!' And every year I kept trying to come back, but, you know, I loved Tony, and he had to be there for four years [for his medical residency], so . . . I think maybe as a result I ended up doing a lot of regional theater."[44] As it turned out, the development opportunities and exposure in the regional theaters—including the Madison Rep, the Berkeley Rep, the Yale Rep, the Arena, and the Goodman—were (and continue to be) extremely productive for Ruhl. Rather than hindering her nascent career, they launched it. Many a new playwright, male or female, would kill for opportunities like these. Usually Ruhl is exceptionally gracious and humble in interviews—this is a rare comment that troubles that image.

The couple now has three daughters—the younger two are twins. In interviews Ruhl regularly speaks of what she observes in her children and how they affect her work. Of the oldest child in her infancy she said, "This is why I love having a baby. Anna laughs at things, even though she doesn't understand language. I think that at the most primal level, the intention to be funny, to share wit, is beyond language."[45] Rather than seeing motherhood as something that stands in the way of her creative work, Ruhl finds ways to use that part of her life to help her understand her craft anew.

Ruhl rejoins Woolf's chronology again, having Orlando call out for Shelmerdine, who comes at her bidding, only to disrupt it a final time. Woolf's Orlando sees the goose again as the clock strikes midnight and the book comes to an end. Ruhl's Orlando against a soundscape of "the faint sounds of the modern world—a muffled airplane, a computer, a telephone" declaims, "I can begin to live again. The little boat is climbing through the white arch of a thousand deaths. I am about to understand."[46]

Ruhl's final image is multilayered and difficult to unpack without precise knowledge of earlier moments in Woolf's text. Woolf had introduced the image of a toy boat standing in for Shelmerdine's brig on the sea back in the nineteenth-century section. After Orlando has left a bookseller in a dizzy state, she goes to Hyde Park where she sits under a tree, with critical journals spread around her, trying to divine how to write in order to please those she is reading. She becomes distracted by the sensory pleasures of the park and muses, "Life? Literature? One to be made into the other? But how monstrously difficult!"[47] And then she realizes as she gazes on ordinary things around her that the imagination can make them into something else entirely. Her realization resonates with Piven's improvisation and with Shklovsky's *ostranenie*: "The thing one is looking at becomes, not itself, but another thing, which is bigger and much more important and yet remains the same thing. If one looks at the Serpentine in this state of mind, the waves soon become just as big as the waves on the Atlantic; the toy boats become indistinguishable from ocean liners."[48]

The realization she reaches—the "ecstasy"—is that the strictures of critical opinion or custom do not define art or artistic process. Instead "it's something useless, sudden, violent; something that costs a life; red, blue, purple; a spirt [sic]; a splash; like those hyacinths (she was passing a fine bed of them); free from taint, dependence, soilure of humanity or care for one's kind, something rash, ridiculous, like my hyacinth, husband I mean Bonthrop: that's what it is—a toy boat on the Serpentine, it's ecstasy, ecstasy."[49] Orlando begins to perceive a reality beneath the surface order of things, as the text whirls lyrically about until it—and the nineteenth century—grinds to a halt when Orlando delivers her son.

Woolf and Orlando reclaim the image of the boat on the waves in the twentieth century. When Orlando feels faint at the sight of a carpenter's missing thumbnail, her mind roams, her senses seek, and working with "the innumerable sights she had been receiving, composed them into something tolerable, comprehensible." With this realization she declares what will become the final lines in Ruhl's play: "I can begin to live again . . . the little boat is climbing through the white arch of a thousand deaths. I am about to understand."[50]

Thus the power of the mind—in strange concert with the body and its senses—can transform experience, rendering it aesthetic. Ruhl surrounds this realization with the noise of life beyond Woolf's present of 1928. She keeps the sound of the airplane—which Woolf uses at book's end—but adds the computer, which transports the audience and Orlando into the present. As she revises Woolf, building off her images and ideas but extending beyond them through her reordering and her contemporization, Ruhl propels Orlando's artistic ambitions, which no doubt echo Ruhl's own, into the new century.

Adapting and Studying Chekhov

In "The Passion of Sarah Ruhl," Peter Gianopulos tells of the conflict that accompanied *Orlando*'s premiere production at the Piven. When actors demanded of Ruhl that she change lines in the play, Byrne Piven tried to negotiate a compromise, but Joyce Piven remembers, "Sarah Ruhl said, 'I'm not changing that line.' And she did not change that line."[51]

These growing pains did not dissuade Piven from commissioning and producing more work by Sarah Ruhl. In 2000, the Piven Theatre produced her short plays, *The Lady with the Lap Dog* and *Anna Around the Neck* as part of their *Chekhov: The Stories*. Since Ruhl's attraction to Chekhov was sustained until the decade's end—her adaptation of *Three Sisters* premiered at Cincinnati's Playhouse in the Park in 2009 and had its West Coast premiere at The Berkeley Rep in 2011—it also provides an excellent vantage point from which to begin viewing Ruhl's work. I will analyze her work on *The Lady with the Lap Dog* as it represents her strategies in both works.

The links between *Anna Around the Neck* and *The Lady with the Lap Dog*, the other play Ruhl adapted for *Chekhov: The Stories*, are numerous. Both of Chekhov's stories, composed in the latter phase of his literary career, concern young women in loveless marriages who seek respite from the tedium of such domestic arrangements and ultimately exercise control over their own sexual desire. But *The Lady with the Lap Dog*, which is the more popular of the two stories, is also the more complicated. Critics have long seen in the story a conversation with Tolstoy about *Anna Karenina* and the novel's depiction of adultery. Lyudmila Parts writes, "One scene in particular is crucial in sustaining and making obvious the intertextual link between Chekhov's and Tolstoy's texts, as well as the two authors' different stances regarding adultery. It is the seduction scene, in which both Annas experience excruciating guilt and grief for their lost moral integrity. In this scene Chekhov brings Tolstoy's theme to its culmination and also turns away from Tolstoy in order to concentrate on his own artistic and philosophical goals."[52] It is significant that Ruhl, who again has been very faithful to the major plot points, language, and essence of characterization in Chekhov's story in the first scenes of her play, chooses to diverge from Chekhov in the seduction scene to concentrate on her own artistic and philosophical goals.

At several moments during this crucial scene, Ruhl chooses to inflect her word choices without the religious allusions that flavor Chekhov's narration, and she chooses to omit what Parts reads as a significant detail. In Chekhov's story, when Anna wakes and is overwhelmed by sadness because the intimacy she and Gurov have just shared has thrown the emptiness of her ordinary life into high relief, the text reads as follows: "The attitude of Anna Sergeveyna— 'the lady with the dog'—to what had happened was somehow peculiar, very grave, as though it were her fall—so it seemed, and it was strange and inappropriate. Her face dropped and faded, and on both sides of it her long hair hung down mournfully; she mused in a dejected attitude like 'the woman who was a sinner' in an old-fashioned picture."[53] Ruhl changes "fall" to "downfall," a less freighted and slightly more secular term, and as she too imagines Anna framed by her hair and pictorially rendered, she writes, "She looked like a sad adulteress in an antique painting."[54] While viewing her as an "adulteress" still names her through transgression, the image is softer than that of a "sinner," perhaps because it is more specific. Meanwhile switching "old-fashioned" for "antique" further displaces the moral judgment in time and implies a quaintness that is no longer in style. Ruhl's interest in morality runs throughout all the plays I will evaluate later in the study, but transformed religious imagery appears most strikingly in *Passion Play* and *In the Next Room*.

Next Chekhov's text reads, "There was a water-melon on the table. Gurov cut himself a slice and began eating it without haste. There followed at least half an hour of silence." Ruhl excises the mundane detail of the watermelon and cuts the excruciating silence that accompanied it.

Ruhl also down plays the notion of forgiveness, speaking of making excuses instead, but she does have Anna refer to herself as a "wicked, fallen woman." Ruhl then follows Chekhov, repeating the key points of Anna's declaration:

> It isn't my husband I've deceived, but myself. And not only now—I've been deceiving myself for a long time. My husband may be a good, honest man, but he is also a flunky! I don't even know what work he does, but I know he is a flunky.
>
> When I married him, I was only twenty. I was burning with curiosity. I wanted to live! I swear by God that I was no longer in control of myself. I told my husband I was ill, and I came here . . . And now I'm nothing, but a low, common woman, and anyone may despise me!

Like Chekhov, Ruhl has Anna articulate the ways her life has been curtailed by her marriage. While she has been unfaithful to her husband, she has also been unfaithful to herself. Parts's reading of Chekhov and Tolstoy is again helpful: "Gurov's ultimate response is emblematic of Chekhov's response to Tolstoy's view of morality in general. Chekhov renders Tolstoy's moralistic and social message ineffective by assigning inherent value to love . . . He operates with a moral code wholly different from Tolstoy's—certainly it is devoid of the traditional religious element; it is rather one according to which marriages for money or convenience, like those of both Annas and Gurov, is truly immoral, more immoral perhaps than the adultery that results from such marriages."[55] Ruhl takes Chekhov's response to Tolstoy a step further. The last vestiges of religion are completely excised in Ruhl's version. Her characters must make their own moral code and negotiate the ways they fit within it. A key component of it is being faithful to one's own potential as an individual, and specifically as a woman: Ruhl will return to this idea several times in all her future plays included in this study.

Ruhl works to articulate this emerging credo through the rest of the play by improvising off this kernel of an idea in Chekhov's story. As he watches Anna's dismay, Gurov begins to feel frustrated, and Chekhov writes of Gurov, "but for the tears in her eyes, he might have thought she was jesting or playing a part."[56] Chekhov ultimately dismisses the performative quality of Anna's emotion, but Ruhl chooses to amplify it as she moves her characters toward the story's end. Women's experience and expression of emotion will reemerge as one of Ruhl's dramatic preoccupations in *Eurydice*.

As Gurov aims to soothe and reassure Anna when she fears that he has lost respect for her, he says in Ruhl's play, "You're not a low common woman. You're a Lady. You're the Lady with the Pet Dog." Gurov thus takes Anna back to her performance at the beginning of the story. Her character is thus determined not by her private behavior, but by her public construction. She created her character as she walked along the esplanade. The Lady with the Pet Dog—who onstage carries a stiff lead that suggests the animal without its physical presence—is the reality.

Gurov's tactics are successful, and Anna is calmed. The two leave her room and go out to the sea once again. In Chekhov's story, Gurov's thoughts turn philosophical, and we come to Chekhov's articulation of his story's moral: "Sitting beside a young woman who in the dawn seemed so lovely, soothed and spellbound in these magical surroundings—the sea, mountains, clouds, and open sky—Gurov thought in reality everything is beautiful in this world when one reflects: everything except what we think or do ourselves when we forget our human dignity and the higher aims of our existence."[57] Chekhov's Gurov thus gives voice to the need to focus on a higher human calling.

Ruhl's Gurov articulates a different idea: "Gurov thought that everything in the universe, if properly understood, would be entirely beautiful." Though the notion of beauty reappears, here Ruhl leaves the specifics of proper understanding either unvoiced or unapprehended by Gurov, even as he comments on his own thought process. But this is not the end of the scene. Ruhl sculpts earlier narration from Chekhov: "So it sounds now, and it will sound as indifferently and monotonously when we are all no more. And in this constancy, in this complete indifference to the life and death of each of us, there lies hid, perhaps, a pledge of our eternal salvation, of the unceasing movement of life upon earth, of unceasing progress towards perfection."[58] Ruhl gives Anna a chance to reflect on the power of nature and how human values might be extrapolated from it, a nascent ecofeminist impulse that will be fully realized in *In the Next Room*.

Anna says of herself, "Anna thought about the sea's indifference. It rumbled whether or not she heard it. She thought she's found the secret to salvation—an unceasing, indifferent movement toward perfection."[59] What the self-aware Anna learns from the sea is that it does not require an audience. It doesn't need her to observe it, and it does not change based on her narration and judgment. Because Ruhl has Anna speak these lines after Gurov's meditation—instead of placing it before as Chekhov did without assigning the thoughts to Anna—she emphasizes the ideas' power and the mental force of the female character who articulated them. She frees Anna to take control of her self-construction, regardless of how others might judge it and her. Ruhl has learned a valuable lesson in how to construct the ethical outlook of her central female characters.

After changing little about Anna's return to her hometown, Gurov's experiences back in Moscow, and their eventual reunion in a provincial theater, Ruhl also intervenes significantly in Chekhov's ending. Earlier in the story and play, Gurov had been struck by Anna as image—the sad adulteress in the antique painting. He has an analogous confrontation with his own image when he catches sight of himself, rapidly aging, in the mirror. Where Ruhl diverges from Chekhov is in allowing Gurov to speak of his self-realization to Anna and to articulate another dismissal of the conventional roles that bind them. Gurov says to Anna, "I don't understand why I have a wife, and why you have a husband—I don't care—I love you the way a husband loves his wife; I love you the way two friends from childhood love—Fate has intended us for each other."[60] He, too, seems primed to construct himself beyond the demands of the culture and morality that are his audience.

Propelled by Gurov's declaration, Ruhl's lovers venture outside to walk and clear their heads. In Chekhov, the lovers don't leave the room. They are trapped in their private space. But Ruhl's Anna and Gurov are not—presaging a transformation of space powerfully realized in *In the Next Room*'s closing moments. Furthermore, as they walk, they imaginatively restage their surroundings. Man 2 says, "They walked along the streets of Moscow, slowly, as though they were at Yalta, on the esplanade," and Woman 2 adds, "they could almost hear the sea."[61] As they walk, the stage directions indicate that they are "holding the leash of the little dog."

Ruhl sticks close to Chekhov's final, much-analyzed line of the story,[62] though she gives it directly to Anna, who says, "It was clear to both of them that the end was still far off, and the hardest and most complicated part was only just beginning."[63] But this, too, Ruhl embellishes with a hopeful theatricality. The opening stage directions called for "the sound of a simple melody played on the piano, far off, then broken off—the wrong note."[64] Her final directions read, "The sound of the sea. The sound of a simple melody played on the piano, far off, completed. The end."[65] As Ruhl allows the lovers to redesign their setting with their definitive prop in hand, she takes them back to the scene of their romance. Sensual, natural Yalta overwhelms cold, urban Moscow thanks to their performance. She permits the lovers completion and a happy rather than ambiguous ending.[66] Ruhl's optimistic worldview shines through, refined by her tutelage from Chekhov.

Ultimately Woolf and Chekhov proved to be excellent teachers for Ruhl. Adapting their scripts, under commission from Joyce Piven, one of her earliest theatrical mentors and inspirations, forced Ruhl to work closely with these masters' styles, performing their voices and ideas, but with subtle yet significant alterations that make these plays very much Ruhl's own. *Orlando* and *Lady with a Lap Dog* showcase several traits of Ruhl that we will see deepen and intensify in the chapters concerning her mature and most popular plays: language will move beyond discursive sense to forge a new kind of audience-performer connection; images and icons of the past will be transposed and reinvigorated; objects and sounds will be made strange so audience perception can be recharged; and an optimism will emerge from sadness, prompting the possibility of spiritual and moral renewal.

CHAPTER 2

Emotional Journeys

At the start of the new century, Americans had much to grieve. From September 11, 2001, to the Gulf War, to Hurricane Katrina, to the BP oil spill, to a variety of less-publicized or smaller-scale events, the chances for mourning have been many. This is not to say that grieving and mourning have been widely encouraged in American culture. On the contrary, grieving and mourning have been carefully regulated. Take for example the Bush administration's censorship of photos of flag-draped coffins bearing the bodies of American soldiers killed in Iraq and Afghanistan or the general dearth of graphic photographs showing soldiers killed in these conflicts.[1]

This is the context for the first of Sarah Ruhl's mature plays, *Eurydice*. *Eurydice* received a world premiere at the Madison Repertory Theatre in 2003, after workshop productions in 2001 at Brown University's New Play Festival and at The Children's Theatre Company in Minneapolis. When the script played at the Yale Rep in 2006, Charles Isherwood connected the play to its social and historical context writing, "It may just be the most moving exploration of the theme of loss that the American theater has produced since the events of Sept. 11, 2001, although Ms. Ruhl began work on the play before that terrible day."[2]

By the time *Eurydice* arrived at Second Stage in New York City for a June 12, 2007 opening, it was not alone in dealing with grief and loss. Joan Didion's adaptation of her bestselling memoir, *The Year of Magical Thinking*, opened on Broadway at the Booth Theatre on March 29, 2007, and Jenny Schwartz's *God's Ear* opened at New Georges on May 2, 2007, then reopened at the Vineyard on April 17, 2008. In each of the plays, a woman grieves an intimate loss—of a father, a husband, or a son. Elissa Marder reminds us of how typical a figure the grieving woman is across the centuries: "The history of western culture is saturated, inundated, drenched with the tears of mourning women. And, with very few exceptions (notably mothers who sometimes mourn for daughters) the most famous mourning women are those women who mourn for men . . . Moreover, Nicole Loraux reminds us that in the ancient world mourning was uniquely a feminine activity. It was only practiced by women and, like the women themselves, mourning was kept inside the home (oikos) and away from the public, political space (agora) of the City."[3] While Ruhl and her contemporaries may begin to explore grief from a familiar starting point, that is not where their plays finish. In each text, the female mourners at the center of the narrative test cultural expectations about the nature and form of mourning. In all three cases, the writers chart journeys to the underworld, and they deploy various repetitive structures as they explore the capacity of language and image to contain and convey grief as they reconfigure popular images of the female mourner. As they do so, they replace a transformed vision of grief in public life, recuperating it as a valid force on contemporary, and potentially political, expression.

Before we launch into the plays themselves, it is helpful to explore emotion generally and grief particularly. In *American Cool: Constructing a Twentieth-Century Emotional Style*, Daniel Stearns argues that one of the passions that was dampened on the way to constructing the emotional control valued by Americans in the twentieth century was grief. Etiquette guides were one of his sources for judging the shift. He writes,

> Whereas Emily Post [in the 1920s and 30s] had readily allowed the emotion to overcome all rational or altruistic capacity for a time, not so Amy Vanderbilt and her peers in the 1950s. Grief simply must not be intense . . . Whatever went on inside should be kept firmly under wraps. Vanderbilt went on to note, in recognition of the more general culture, that wartime had taught people to restrain their grief because it damaged morale and gave comfort to the enemy. With this, the focus of etiquette shifted largely from appropriate sorrow and condolence to emphasis on restraint and upbeat mood.[4]

The desire to contain grief was not spent in the mid-twentieth century. It returned in the early twenty-first, coupled with an injunction to redirect grief into action in the aftermath of the September 11 attacks. On September 21, 2001, as Judith Butler summarizes, "President Bush announced . . . that we have finished grieving and that now it is time for resolute action to take the place of grief."[5] Butler urges her reader to take another course—rather than rushing to displace grief with (aggressive) action, we might allow it to live among us, for a productive end. She suggests, "To grieve, and to make grief itself into a resource for politics, is not to be resigned to inaction, but it may be understood as the slow process by which we develop a point of identification with suffering itself."[6]

Part of the rush to disarm grief—in the aftermath of 9/11 and in the public sphere more broadly—is the cultural perception that emotion generally, and grief particularly, is feminine. In *The Cultural Politics of Emotion*, Sara Ahmed writes,

> It is significant that the word "passion" and the word "passive" share the same root in the Latin word for "suffering" (passio). To be passive is to be enacted upon, as a negation that is already felt as suffering. The fear of passivity is tied to the fear of emotionality, in which weakness is defined in terms of a tendency to be shaped by others. Softness is narrated as a proneness to injury. The association between passion and passivity is instructive. It works of a reminder of how "emotion" has been viewed as "beneath" the faculties of thought and reason. To be emotional is to have one's judgment affected: it is to be reactive rather than active, dependent rather than autonomous. Feminist philosophers have shown us how the subordination of emotions also works to subordinate the feminine and the body (Spelman 1989; Jaggar 1996). Emotions are associated with women, who are represented as "closer" to nature, ruled by appetite, and less able to transcend the body through thought, will and judgment.[7]

If emotion is, as Ahmed describes it, generally suspect for causing one to be passive and irrational, grief is particularly dangerous because of Freud's early linking of hysteria with mourning. In "Hopeful Sentences: Gender and Mourning Language in Two Contemporary Narratives," Jodi Kanter reminds readers that in his first lecture in America, Freud connected the development of psychoanalysis with Joseph Breuer's treatment of hysteria. Likewise in "Mourning and Melancholia," Kanter reports, "Freud defined melancholia as a neurotic need to hold on to lost objects, but conceded that its symptoms almost entirely coincided with those of normal mourning work. Although Freud later even further normalized his assessment of protracted mourning, much later work in psychiatry implicitly built on his association of grief and neurosis, providing even greater impetus to both feminize and pathologize mourning."[8]

If emotion is passive and irrational and grief hysterical and pathological in the cultural imaginary, then Ruhl, Didion, and Schwartz had much reconstructive work to do in reclaiming grief as an effective cultural tool, but careful analysis and close reading of the plays will show that in many ways, they succeeded in doing just that.

Eurydice

The first step toward understanding Ruhl's recuperation of grief is to appreciate that *Eurydice* is a point of transition from her early work adapting Woolf and Chekhov to her work later in the decade. As with that early work, Ruhl began with a preexisting story, or more precisely, a collection of stories and texts. She told Wendy Weckwerth in *American Theatre* that the Orpheus and Eurydice tale has always stayed with me, more than any other Greek myth. I'd seen so many beautiful retellings from Cocteau to *Black Orpheus*, but rarely does anyone look at Eurydice's experience. I always found that troubling . . . There's an exception, a beautiful 1904 Rilke poem called "Orpheus. Eurydice. Hermes." Rilke looks at Eurydice's experience at the fullness of her death when Orpheus arrives, with a kind of ambivalence . . . I'm also compelled by the questions the myth raises about music and language. Mainly, though, I was caught with this idea of memory and language and the idea of Eurydice going into the underworld and meeting her father there. The play is really dedicated to my father, who died when I was twenty and he was fifty-five. *Eurydice* is a transparently personal play.[9]

While Ruhl's early work on Woolf and Chekhov was largely in the mode of faithful adaptation, she intervenes unabashedly into conventional understanding of this myth, driven as she is by a deeply personal connection to the material and her own lingering grief. She boldly shifts the dramatic focus from Orpheus to Eurydice (positioning both as mourners and travelers) and in so doing she creates wholly new story elements while she repurposes a classic dramatic device: the chorus.

There are, as Ruhl indicates, many variations on the Orpheus and Eurydice myth, but common features include the following: Orpheus, a famous musician, is so overcome by grief at the death of his wife that he travels to the underworld in hopes of bringing her back to life. The music he plays is so powerful that Hades agrees to grant his request—on one condition. He must walk ahead of Eurydice as he leads her out of the underworld, never looking back to check that she is behind him. Orpheus is unable to keep his end of the bargain. He looks back at Eurydice on their journey, and when he does so, he loses her forever.

Ruhl begins her rescripting of the myth by granting her audience a peek into Orpheus and Eurydice's relationship before their wedding. At points it is charming—as they frolic by the sea at play's opening—but it is hardly a mythically perfect love. Orpheus is obsessed with creating music. It's almost always playing in his head, and he seems to revere creation above other human activities. Eurydice, meanwhile, is a reader. She wants to know "if other people—like dead people who wrote books—agree or disagree with what you think."[10] Orpheus responds, "Maybe you should make up your own thoughts. Instead of reading them in a book."[11] When she defends her thinking and opinions, rather than apologizing, Orpheus instructs and bribes, "Don't be mad. (pause) I made up a song for you today."[12] Ultimately Ruhl crafts her lovers with fundamentally different ways of creatively perceiving the world that would probably render them incompatible after the first blush of romance faded.

Ruhl also positions Eurydice not just as the mourned and thus static, as she is in most versions of the classic tale, but as the mourner and as one who is active and mobile. And though Ruhl creates a traditional grieving figure—a woman who mourns a man—her creation isn't only traditional since she implants this reconceived figure into one of the West's most famous stories. Eurydice's grief, her desire to reconnect with her dead father by reading a letter from him, is what sends her to the underworld on her wedding day, not the serpent's bite on her ankle as she's crossing a field with a band of naiads that appears in several versions of the tale. In the play's third scene we find Eurydice at a water pump, having just escaped her wedding party. She misses her father on this special day and opines, "A wedding is for a father and a daughter. They stop being married to each other on that day."[13] As she quenches her thirst at the pump, the Nasty Interesting Man, or the Lord of the Underworld, appears. He lures her to his apartment with promise of further satisfaction: that she can read a letter from her father on the occasion of her wedding.

The Nasty Interesting Man's plan works. Eurydice goes to his high-rise apartment where he tries to seduce her. She succeeds in getting the letter, addressed by a familiar hand, but then vertigo overwhelms her, and she pitches down six hundred stairs, following the tumbling letter that escapes her grasp as it floats back down to the underworld from whence it came.

Ruhl also breaks away from many versions of the tale by dramatizing Eurydice's experience in the world of the dead. Soon after she arrives via raining elevator, the imperfect romantic love of Orpheus is juxtaposed with the love of her father through string. Orpheus tied string around Eurydice's finger to make an impromptu ring when he proposed to her; the Father constructs a room out of string to house Eurydice when she discovers there is no shelter in the underworld. Sara Ahmed's comments on the etymology of emotion and how it can obscure our understanding of emotional connection are evocative here: "We should note that the word 'emotion' comes from the Latin, *emovere*, referring to 'to move, to move out.' Of course, emotions are not only about movement, they are also about attachments or about what connects us to this or that. The relationship between movement and attachment is instructive. What moves us, what makes us feel, is also that which holds us in place, or gives us a dwelling place."[14]

The father's binding ties, which give Eurydice a place to dwell, are on a scale that dwarfs Orpheus's. It is also well worth considering how the Father defies conventional gender roles. While he does play the masculine part of providing his family's shelter, he is also Eurydice's sole caregiver in this strange place. He attends to her emotional needs as faithfully as he does to her material ones. It is no wonder that Eurydice mourned his loss and that she might put her love of her father ahead of her love of her husband.

When she first arrives in the underworld, Eurydice is bereft of memory, language, and emotional expression. Her father helps her reclaim her memory of Orpheus and her life with him, but the images she recovers are at best bittersweet. She reveals, "This is what it is to love an artist: The moon is always rising above your house. The houses of your neighbors look dull and lacking in moonlight. But he is always going away from you. Inside his head there is always something more beautiful."[15] If it weren't for the power of centuries of myth, it would otherwise come as little surprise when Eurydice rejected Orpheus when she had to choose between life on earth with him and life in the string room with her father. Rather than staying quietly behind him as they trek away from her father, she calls Orpheus's name. He turns around, and they must part.

But this is not the point of greatest devastation in Ruhl's tale. Rather than Orpheus's loss of Eurydice—traditionally just before they come to the end of their journey—the true climax comes with Eurydice's second loss of her father. When the father assumes he's lost Eurydice to life and to Orpheus, he mourns by dipping himself in the river of forgetting and resigning himself to oblivion. When Eurydice returns, her string room is gone and her father lies mute on the ground. Eurydice, rather than submitting to marriage with the king of the underworld, writes Orpheus a letter that releases him to find a new love, and then dips herself in the river too. Orpheus returns again, but like Eurydice, he finds his love transformed into still silence.

Another kind of repetition and revision Ruhl employs is her reclaiming of the Greek chorus. Her Chorus of Stones attempts to regulate grief in the underworld. How we interpret it provides a legend to Ruhl's map of mourning. When asked by Wendy Weckwerth about her use of the chorus Ruhl responded, "Mac Wellman talks about ransacking theater history for forms to dredge up and reuse. That fascinates me. Why do we reuse forms? When is it subversive and when is it a cliché? . . . I don't tend to write in a realist mode. I'm interested in things that automatically dig you out of that impulse."[16] Ruhl's use of a three-member chorus, and not just any chorus, but a chorus of Stones (Big, Little, and Loud), emphatically divorces the text from realism without divorcing it from significant cultural issues.

When Eurydice arrives in the underworld, bereft of speech, the Stones first tell the audience how to react: "Pretend that you understand her or she'll be embarrassed," and "Listen to her the way you would listen to your own daughter if she died too young and tried to speak to you across long distances."[17] This is the Stones at one of their most empathetic moments, and they encourage empathetic response in the audience. It is also the only time that they break the fourth wall, addressing the audience directly. During the rest of the play, they are part of the scene rather than a connection between the world of the play and the world of the audience, but their inherent theatricality prevents them from functioning as conventional, psychologically motivated characters. Instead they are external psychological appendages motivating other characters.

As the play progresses the instructional tone they took with the audience becomes more intense with Eurydice and the Father. Suggestions become rules. They direct, "You have to speak in the language of stones."[18] "THERE ARE NO ROOMS!"[19] and "NO ONE KNOCKS AT THE DOOR OF THE DEAD!"[20] Perhaps their most meaningful instruction, the one that encapsulates most of the others, is "Being sad is not allowed! Act like a stone."[21] In Greek tragedy the chorus often provides the moral framework for the play, establishing the rules by which the audience might judge the play's action. As Ruhl's chorus legislates behavior and attitude for the characters, the audience can evaluate this external mechanism for regulating character behavior and how they might judge nontheatrical entities that attempt to do the same thing.

While the Stones want to prohibit sadness, they also want to inhibit an excess of positive emotion. They demand from Eurydice and her father a kind of stoicism—an apatheia, or indifference to emotion. When they are in the process of reconnecting, and when Ruhl is still in the midst of showing how Eurydice's bond with her father is deeper than her bond with Orpheus, the two attempt to sing. Unlike Orpheus, they are not master musicians. They've forgotten the words to the song, so they do their best with "Da da Dee Da."[22] These single syllables call to mind a child learning the name for her father—Da Da. They also call to mind Freud's "fort-da" theory. Freud came up with his theory about the subject's desire symbolically to control the disappearance of the mother while watching his young grandson play a game of his own invention. The child threw a spool with attached string from his crib, saying "fort" when the spool disappeared, and "da" when it returned. This effort to control and connect is made all the more resonant for Eurydice and her father since it is done in the example provided by Freud, with string.[23]

The Stones interrupt them:

THE STONES: WHAT IS THAT NOISE?
LITTLE STONE: Stop Singing!
LOUD STONE: STOP SINGING!
BIG STONE: Neither of you can carry a tune.
LITTLE STONE: It's awful.
THE STONES: DEAD PEOPLE CAN'T SING![24]

Not only do the Stones police emotional equilibrium in the underworld, but they also aim to protect the tale as it most widely known, perhaps because familiar cultural tropes are a force for maintaining emotional equilibrium: when audiences know how a story is supposed to go, they are calmed and reassured as the plot unfolds as they expect. But as Eurydice prepares to follow Orpheus out of the underworld, she has second thoughts. Little Stone tells her, "You can't go back now, Eurydice."²⁵ And when she says she wants her father, Loud Stone reminds her, "You're all grown up now. You have a husband."²⁶ In traditional versions of the myth, the one who wants to turn back, to check and confirm despite the rule of the gods, is Orpheus. Here it is Eurydice who wants to turn back, to engage in sacrilege, not by disobeying the gods but by returning to the comfort of her childhood relationship and forsaking her adult one.

The Stones very nearly convince her to play her conventional part in the tale through their own uncharacteristic acceptance of emotional excess:

> **LITTLE STONE**: Orpheus braved the gates of hell to find you.
> **LOUD STONE**: He played the saddest music.
> **BIG STONE**: Even we—
> **THE STONES**: The stones—
> **LITTLE STONE**: cried when we heard it.²⁷

Nevertheless, Eurydice refuses instruction. She will make her own role. She claims not to recognize Orpheus or hear his music. With a single word—"Orpheus?"²⁸—she changes her storyline.

When Eurydice tries to return to her father, she is angry when she finds her room destroyed and her father curled in a ball like a semihuman stone after his self-baptism in the river of forgetting. She tries to reteach him her name and to speak in the language of the Stones, but nothing works. The Stones then intervene in Eurydice's grieving with their greatest force:

> **LOUD STONE**: Didn't you already mourn for your father, young lady?
> **LITTLE STONE**: Some things are left well enough alone.
> **BIG STONE**: To mourn twice is excessive.
> **LITTLE STONE**: To mourn three times a sin.
> **LOUD STONE**: Life is like a good meal.
> **BIG STONE**: Only gluttons want more food when they finish their helping.
> **LITTLE STONE**: Learn to be more moderate.
> **BIG STONE**: It's weird for a dead person to be morbid . . . Learn the art of keeping busy!²⁹

The Stones prescribe a form of grieving that is cool, controlled, and non-repeatable. Catherine Lutz helps us interpret what the "rhetoric of control" in regard to emotion might entail. She argues that it "reproduces an important part of the cultural view of emotion (and then implicitly of women as the more emotional gender) as irrational, weak, and dangerous."³⁰ She notes that control of emotion is about policing the boundaries between the inside and the outside and about constructing "a set of roles—one strong and defensive and the other weak but invasive."³¹ She goes on to observe that in the interviews she conducted, when women talk about emotional control, "they identify their emotions and themselves as undisciplined and discipline both through a discourse on the control of feeling. The construction of a feminine self, this material might suggest, includes a process by which women come to control themselves and so obviate the necessity for more coercive outside control."³²

The Lord of the Underworld appears shortly after the Stones provide their legislation. He assumes that Eurydice's decision to return to the underworld means she will be his bride. His wedding preparations, along with the Stones' emotional edicts, propel Eurydice's choice to become a stone herself. She would rather control her emotions by becoming stonily stoic than submit to this marriage, a version of coercive external control like that described by Lutz.

In the context of an analysis of grieving and its gendering, Eurydice's choice is fascinating. She does not mourn a second time or gluttonously feed her grief; instead she rejects it and claims some degree of autonomy, but in so doing, she disciplines herself into annihilation. Ruhl reduces an argument for emotional control and feminine self-disciplining to the ultimate absurdity. Witnessing Eurydice forsake emotion and weighing the consequences of the act—as we watch Orpheus standing on a heartbreaking letter that he can't read in desolate silence—we know they extend beyond the feminine individual, and we can glimpse what grief expressed might mean in our lives. Charles Isherwood wrote of the Second Stage production, "Perhaps more than anything else, the eerie wonderland of 'Eurydice' evokes the discombobulating experience of grief and loss, the desperate need to move on and the overwhelming desire never to let go—to turn and look back just one more time,"³³ while John Lahr observed, "Somehow this subtle production works the trick of imagining the unimaginable."³⁴ Ultimately Ruhl shows us a Eurydice (and a female mourner) whom we've never seen before. Eurydice's grief is epic in scope, but she has to let go of that grief in order for us to grasp it. Her absurd control and the tragic silence that ensues help us reconsider an experience that cultures political and social have encouraged us to renounce and forget. As we accept this invitation to remember the potential of grief, we realize we are also experiencing a dramatist coming into her full artistic power.

The Year of Magical Thinking

Near the end of her 2005 memoir, *The Year of Magical Thinking*, Joan Didion writes, "I realize as I write this that I do not want to finish this account. Nor did I want to finish the year. The craziness is receding but no clarity is taking its place. I look for resolution and find none."³⁵ Perhaps because that resolution was lacking—even after her memoir (the thirteenth book she had published in her long and illustrious career) chronicling the death of her husband of nearly forty years and the concurrent traumatic illnesses of her daughter had become a national bestseller and the winner of the National Book Award—when producer Scott Rudin suggested she make the memoir into a play, she (eventually) said yes.

Didion recounted her initial reluctance in her *New York Times* essay describing the play's journey to Broadway's Booth Theatre. Didion writes of her lack of playwriting experience and the overwhelming promotional tour for the memoir that she was in the midst of, but even more important was the death of her daughter, Quintana, in August of 2005. Though the book, *Year of Magical Thinking*, had not yet been released at the time of Quintana's death, Didion did not revise her text or reference this second devastating loss in the jacket copy or in an afterword. When questioned about this omission during promotional interviews, Didion said the book was "finished" at the time of Quintana's death.[36]

But clearly Didion was not finished—her statement within the memoir that I quoted was far more accurate than her interview reply. After initially rejecting Rudin's proposal, she changed her mind. She writes, "At some point in the days that followed I was seized by the idea that the fact that I had never written and did not know how to write a play could be the point, the imperative, the very reason to write one. My husband had died, our only child had died, I was no longer exactly the person I had been."[37] Judith Butler's thoughts on grief are instructive here:

> But maybe when we undergo what we do, something about who we are is revealed, something that delineates the ties we have to others, that show us that these ties constitute what we are, ties or bonds that compose us. It is not as if an "I" exists independently over here and then simply loses a "you" over there, especially if the attachment to "you" is part of what composes who "I" am. If I lose "you" under these conditions, then I not only mourn the loss, but I become inscrutable to myself. Who "am" I without you? When we lose some of the ties by which we are constituted, we do not know who we are or what we do.[38]

Butler is working her way toward a reconstruction of grief as a political force, one that establishes a new kind of community and ethical obligations, but her remarks also precisely describe the kind of loss Didion experienced. Though Didion's exploration of her own grief is not specifically directed toward the ends Butler had in mind, her willingness to show us the process of grieving nevertheless demonstrates its identity-defining potential, personal and political.

Given the redefinition of self that grief forges, it therefore makes sense that even a very successful and highly regarded memoir might be reworked and transformed to accommodate that change and to cross genres. While Ruhl revised millennia of versions of the Orpheus and Eurydice story, Didion had a differently onerous task—revising herself as she was in the process of change. Didion comments further, "I could see right away that writing a play could not be a simple matter of adapting the book: I had written the book, I had no interest in rewriting it, a play would need to go deeper, come from a new perspective, tell me what I did not know when I wrote the book."[39] What she didn't know when she wrote the book was how quickly the death of her child would follow on the heels of the death of her husband. This provides a new perspective, and a new version of the author, her identity, and the ties that constitute her that is very much evident in the play.

As she prepared the work for the stage, Didion reduced, compressed, and rearranged her text, paring the twenty sections of the book down to nine. As she whittled down the memoir to its dramatic essence, her general attitude toward emotion remained intact. Her first line of the play is "This happened on December 30, 2003." From that barest statement of fact, she moves ahead to tell the audience how John Dunne, her husband of almost four decades, suffered a massive coronary in their living room—while she was preparing their dinner—and died. Afterward she checked all the facts surrounding the event: "Within what I now know to have been exactly five minutes, two ambulances came. The crews worked on the living room floor for what I now know to have been exactly forty-five minutes. I know these facts because I obtained the documents. I obtained the Emergency Department Nursing Documentation Sheet. I obtained the Nursing Flow Chart. I obtained the Physician's Record. I obtained the log kept by the doormen in our Building. 'Paramedics arrived at 9:20 PM for Mr. Dunne, the log read. Mr. Dunne was taken to the hospital at 10:05 PM.'"[40] Didion recounts her facts with such precision, with such insistent ritual repetition of the formality of "I obtained," that the auditor soon becomes a little suspicious of her mental state, preceding the awareness of the other figures in the text. When the social worker leads Didion from the insurance line into an empty room and introduces her husband's doctor, Didion recalls, "I hear my own voice. What I hear it saying is this: 'He's dead, isn't he.' The doctor looks at the social worker. 'It's okay,' the social worker says. 'She's a pretty cool customer.'"[41]

From these first recounted moments, the audience sees that Didion is doing everything in her power to maintain at least the illusion of control. Her reaction to her traumatic loss is not, however, the typically gendered manifestation of sadness. Robyn Fivush and Janine P. Buckner write,

> What does it mean to be sad? Certainly sadness involves loss. But for females, sadness is a loss of self-in-relation, whereas for males, sadness is a loss of self-in-control. Obviously this is an overly extreme characterization; the experience and

expression of all emotion, including sadness, is multiply determined and complex, and there are as many similarities between the genders as there are differences. However, females and males discuss sadness with others in different ways, and through these gender-differentiated discourses, females and males construct different understandings of sadness. To be sad is an inevitable part of life; how one is sad is part of being male or female.[42]

Didion resists a typically female expression of sadness as she discusses the end of her husband's life, even as she works through her definition of herself without her essential relationships. Her narrative emphasizes a desire to take control and maintain control that is, at least according to these theorists and researchers in addition to Catherine Lutz, more typically male.

Jeroen Jansz explains further the linking of emotional control, or "restrictive emotionality," and masculinity. He condenses the findings of several studies and identifies four attributes characteristic of contemporary masculinity: autonomy, achievement, aggression, and stoicism. He focuses on stoicism and the effects it can have on men. He finds "the inhibition of feelings is a focal characteristic of masculinity, but it is also detrimental in its effects on health and social interaction. The paradox cannot be solved easily, because restrictive emotionality is linked inextricably to the construction of a masculine identity in traditional families. The gendered nature of emotional communication creates a context of interaction in which boys and (young) men do not learn to talk about or act upon emotions that imply vulnerability. As a result, men tend to deny their experience of this class of emotions, and conceal their expression."[43]

Again in sharing her experience of transforming the memoir for the stage, Didion wrote in *The New York Times* of her reaction to the notes from her producer and her experience seeing her image onstage, refracted through character and Vanessa Redgrave's performance. She saw onstage a vulnerability that she had denied to herself, masking it behind restrictive emotionality and control: "*'This is about the speaker discovering that she is completely powerless, that the control she so prizes is nonexistent.'* This was for me, even as I wrote it, novel information. I had never before thought of myself as a person prizing control. Only when I saw the play performed did I see that character clear, and I also saw her in the mirror."[44] And while she refers to her character as feminine, her editing of the memoir and a specific change to the play also highlight a masculine quality in the projected stage image.

Didion excises much of the memoir as she creates her play, but in the context of a comparison to *Eurydice* and gendered expression of emotion, her omission of a discussion of *Alcestis* is particularly intriguing. Just past the halfway point in the memoir, Didion discusses her rereading of Euripides's ancient play. She writes, "I remembered the Greeks in general but *Alcestis* in particular as good on the passage between life and death. They visualized it, they dramatized it, they made the dark water and the ferry into the mise-en-scene itself."⁴⁵ She goes on to recount the plot of the play, reminding her reader that Admetus, king of Thessaly, has been condemned to die, but thanks to the intercession of his friend, Apollo, if he can find someone to die in his stead, his own life will be spared. Neither his friends nor his parents will take his place, but his young wife, Alcestis, will. Though she in fact dies for him, as Didion says, Admetus, ravaged by guilt and self-pity, "behaves badly in every way," claiming that none suffers more than he. Didion doesn't name the "remarkably clumsy (even for 430 B.C.) deus ex machina that facilitates Alcestis's return," but come back she does, thanks to a rescue by the adventurous Hercules. Upon her return she is not allowed to speak for three days until she has been purified.

Didion says this is not the way she remembers the tale. While Euripides provides a happy ending, Didion's "editing" as she calls it leaves an ending "that could not be construed as happy." Instead of a religious injunction preventing Alcestis's speech, Didion remembered it as her choice—a response to Admetus's failings. Didion writes of her version, "In some ways this is a better (more worked out) story, one that at least acknowledges that death changes the one who had died, but it opens up further questions about the divide. If the dead were truly to come back, what would they come back knowing? Could we face them? Who allowed them to die? The clear light of day tells me that I did not allow John to die, that I did not have that power, but do I believe that? Does he?"⁴⁶ In the memoir and through her revision of Euripides, Didion casts herself as Admetus. She sees herself as the one who failed emotionally and ethically but also as the one to whom the loved one, however silent, might return. By the time she gets to the stage play, Admetus and Alcestis are gone. In their stead are hints of Orpheus and his failed attempt to return his love to the land of the living. In the stage play, Didion recasts herself as Orpheus.

In Euripides's *Alcestis*, there is a reference to Orpheus that has inspired debate among scholars and, as we will see when we get to the discussion of *God's Ear*, intrigued many dramatists. Admetus says, "Oh, if I had the tongue, the music of Orpheus, so I could charm Persephone and Hades the king, her husband, bringing you back from Hades, I would journey down. Hades' hellhound would not stop me, nor the Deliverer of Spirits, Charon, till I restored your life once more to light."⁴⁷ But this is a rare instance suggesting that Orpheus could be successful in his quest; John Heath argues that this passage does not indicate that there was a tradition in which Orpheus was successful. Instead he reads it as ironic: "This response, however, is conditioned primarily by our expectations of Admetus. If he is an ingenuous, an 'un-ironic' speaker, then we will take his wish at face value. But in fact the grieving husband's speech is anything but straightforward. It is filled with extreme and inappropriate, not to mention bizarre elements. Taken in its context—and it is the context that is missing in most discussions of the references to Orpheus' descent—it is just this sort of ironic remark that we come to count on from the self-absorbed protagonist."[48] So despite Didion's prior attention to *Alcestis* and her admitted tendency toward rewriting, we may still reasonably assume that she would regard the movement from Admetus to Orpheus as a shift from the successful journey to the underworld and back to the unsuccessful.

In her essay "Sideswiped," Patricia Foster writes of Didion's memoir, "*The Year of Magical Thinking* uses Freud's idea of 'digging over' the same ground, and in Didion's case going back again and again to December 30, 2003, the night John Dunne died, combing her specific memory of that last evening . . . for any data that might clarify 'what happened' with the belief that the narrator could go back and 'fix' it. That's the pathological conceit in Didion's mind: information is control, knowledge is curative. If she knows enough. She can control what happens, even though it's already happened."[49] In the book and in the stage play, Didion not only repeats the events, "digging over the same ground," but she also repeats imagery. Throughout both the stage and book version of *The Year of Magical Thinking*, water motifs abound. The play contains this passage, which very nearly echoes a passage in the book,[50] in which Didion reflects back on her final exchange with the social worker at the hospital after her husband's death. He asks how he can help her. When she requests a cab to take her back to her apartment, he asks if she has "the fare." Later she says, "To myself I am invisible, incorporeal. I have crossed one of those rivers that divide the living from the dead. I feel for the first time the power in the image of the rivers, the Styx, the Lethe, the cloaked ferryman with his pole. I saw the ferryman I heard the ferryman speak. It was the ferryman who asked if I had the fare."[51] From this instance early in the play, Didion draws the connection to the rivers of the underworld—though from this reference alone it is not yet clear that she bears a closer relation to Orpheus than Admetus.

While the imagery is thematic, conveying her venture into the land of the dead, it is also structural, thanks to the logic of the repetition. As Sandra Gilbert writes, "Clearly Didion has learned what most grievers learn, and clearly, as the style and structure of her book reveal, she has learned, too, the bitter repetitiveness of grief, with its recycling of magical hopes and its reiterations of terrible memories."[52] The water repetition shows the obsessive thinking of the griever, and the experience of having grief wash over one in waves. The water imagery logically conveys the illogic of griever.

Didion clarifies her thinking further, again using water imagery: "To keep her alive I need to focus. I need to avoid noticing anything that might lead me back into the past. Going back has trick currents, unrevealed eddies, you can be skimming along on what looks like clear water and suddenly go under.

Get sucked down. Get caught in the vortex and let go of her hand. Lose control. Lose her. Feel the water take her."[53] Here we begin to discern that she is Orpheus and not Admetus. She is the one on the journey—she has no hero like Hercules at the ready to send in her stead. And it is she who might let go of the hand, lose her charge, fail to meet the terms of the agreement that might save the beloved.

As Quintana's death approaches, the imagery becomes even simpler and the words even sparer. When she describes the morning that she arrived in her daughter's hospital room, finding a team of doctors and nurses taking desperate measures, she says plainly, "I watched the river as it happened."[54]

And as she tries to make peace with the events, to succumb to the inevitably of what is past, and to find a way to move ahead herself, she says, again referencing the water, "We all know that if we are to live ourselves there comes a time when we must relinquish the dead, let them go, keep them dead . . . Let go of them in the water. Knowing this does not make it any easier to let go of them in the water."[55] Nor does it make it easier to journey from the a masculine experience of sadness as loss of self-in-control—the one who chooses to let go—back to the feminine experience of loss of self-in-relation—the one who loses the connection that helps define her.

In this final section of the play, the speaker also reminds the audience, "I told you I wrote a book." She has the book in her hand and she reads some of the text. As the Broadway show closed, the audience saw a larger projected version of the image on the back cover of the published memoir. It is a black and white photograph of Didion, Dunne, and Quintana in Malibu in 1976. They are on the raised deck of a beach house, overlooking the beach and the ocean. It is an eerie scene. Quintana and her father are very close together, over to left side of the image, gazing directly at the photographer while Didion stands apart from them, just off center, looking enigmatically at them instead of us. We have the sense that already they were drifting away from her, and we see her starkly depicted once again as feminine in her predestined sadness.

In recounting the notes from Scott Rudin as she was thinking about creating the play, Didion reports on his structural advice to her: "'*SR sees the form as six or eight 'sections,' or 'chunks'—call them movements*,' my notes read that day. '*The movements should build sequentially, repeated refrains taking on new meaning as they build. The speaker is urgent, driven to tell us something we don't want to know. She is reporting, bringing us a dispatch from a far country.*'"[56] Indeed this is the thought I have at production's end. Like Orpheus, the speaker has been to the place of grief that we have been conditioned to fear, and she now realizes she might have seen it coming a long way off. Like the movement of the waves at the ocean front, its coming is inevitable, and no restrained, restricted, gendered performance of sadness will keep it at bay. We will all, male and female regardless of our self-casting, pay the fare if we are blessed and cursed with a long life's journey.

God's Ear

The characters in *God's Ear* bear a close relationship to those in *Eurydice* and *The Year of Magical Thinking*, because like Orpheus and Eurydice and the speaker who relates Didion's experience of grief, Mel, Ted, and Lanie all travel to hell metaphorically after the death of a loved one. But unlike Ruhl and Didion, the dramatic tale Schwartz tells was not forged in the crucible of personal experience. She has said the genesis of the play came when she wrote the line, "Why is it that everyone you talk to has a dead son?"[57] From this starting point, Schwartz created unique language and imagery that transported her audience along with this bereaved family across the terrain of loss and into an altogether unique realm of dramatic expression.

Before recounting the bereft family's experience of grief and the innovative language structures Schwartz crafted to convey it, I'd like to recount Schwartz's journey with the play. As Sarah Stern, associate artistic director of the Vineyard Theatre explained, "The Vineyard invited Jenny to develop *God's Ear* in an ongoing process that spanned two seasons. *God's Ear* was then produced by the acclaimed downtown theatre company New Georges last April, and now comes full circle to The Vineyard stage in an enhanced production in association with New Georges."[58]

And while this wasn't Schwartz's first play—her *Cause for Alarm* debuted at the New York International Fringe Festival in 2002, and she had collaborated with The Civilians early in the decade as well—*God's Ear* brought her a whole new level of attention. In a *New York Times* article titled "New Dramas, New Voices Below 14th Street," Jason Zinoman grouped Schwartz together with Anne Washburn and Adam Bock as the strongest in a bumper crop of new, naturalism-eschewing dramatists and singled them out as writers who provide "hope for the American play."[59]

Hope, however, is a long time coming for the characters in *God's Ear*. As the play opens, the audience learns from Mel about the condition of her son: he's in a coma with little chance of survival. When Ted, Mel's husband asks, "Did they mention hope?" Mel replies, "They asked us to consider organ donation. Gentle, they were gentle, with a, hand on my shoulder, they were, gentle." Mel doesn't tell us yet why she tells the doctors, "I do not deserve gentle;" it takes her until play's end to share this crucial part of the story.

In the meanwhile, neither plot nor storytelling is of central importance to *God's Ear*. Instead of patterns of event or story, the audience must wend its way through a tangle of sound. This shift, at once simple and radical, reframes character and emotion. Jeffrey M. Jones summarizes critical trends in regard to the play and also introduces how Schwartz uses language:

> Virtually everyone who's written about Jenny Schwartz's marvelous play has noted how the dialog has been built out of clichés (I'm going to use the term "catchphrase" instead, to avoid the other meaning of clichés as "stale and formulaic description.") Many often point out that the dialog is rhythmical too—almost musical. But, in fact, Schwartz has developed this highly-structured language and syntax—a kind of verse really—as a radical way to depict, and recreate, the experience of grief. And as with any verse, listening requires a shift of appreciation that include[s] the rhythm and pattern as much as the literal sense of the words themselves.[60]

Jones goes on to explicate brilliantly Schwartz's use of repetition, from the simple to the "loop" involving complex patterns of alternating phrases. Perhaps one of the most memorable speeches in the play is delivered by Mel, shortly after Ted says to her, "No, but I really missed you. Those are just words to you, but I mean it." Her dizzying speech tests what it means to be "just words" and how we can mean through words. A fraction of Mel's speech reads as follows:

> And we'll cross that bridge.
> And bridge that gap.
> And bear that cross.
> And cross that t.
>
> And part that sea.
> And act that part.
> And turn that leaf.
> And turn that cheek.
>
> And speak our minds.
> And mind our manners.
> And clear our heads.
> And right our wrongs.[61]

The three representative stanzas, which occur in the middle of the long 25-stanza monologue, play off each other in fascinating ways. Jones helps us with the first quoted stanza, noting "the second term in the lead phrase moves to the first term in the flowing phrase." In addition, the terms flip flop from verbs to nouns: "cross" is first a verb and "bridge" is a noun, but then "bridge" becomes a verb and "cross" becomes a noun. Terms vacillate between action and functioning as objects. In the next stanza, "part" echoes the pattern; in the third stanza "mind/minds" does likewise. But we also see the repetition of the cross, which is further amplified in the next stanza with the biblical imagery of parted seas and turned cheeks. This reverberates further as we're left to consider how and if we might be capable of righting our wrongs. Mel's monologue is at once bereft of sense and overflowing with it.

As is the case in these specific utterances, Mel's speech generally tends toward excess and outpouring; Ted tends to respond rather than initiate, and his utterances are generally much shorter. Through Lanie, their six-year-old, we are asked to measure degrees of sadness:

> **LANIE:** Who's sadder? You or Dad?
> **MEL:** Shh.
> **LANIE:** Who's sadder? Me or You?
> **MEL:** Shh.
> **LANIE:** Who's sadder? Me or Dad?
> **MEL:** Shh.
> **LANIE:** Who's sadder? Me, you, or Dad?[62]

While effusiveness has been colored feminine and reticence masculine by the various researchers and theorists of emotions I've previously cited, Schwartz doesn't let her characters or her audience off that easily thanks to Lanie. One mode of expression is not allowed to trump the other or to indicate a more intense experience of emotion.

Schwartz also disrupts her own patterning, forcing the audience to keep reasoning about grief and gender. An exception to the pattern of Mel and Ted's utterances comes when Ted is on an airplane, speaking with a transvestite stewardess who initially holds a gun to his head. (Stage directions indicate that the same actor plays the stewardess and G. I. Joe.) When the stewardess asks, "Is there anything you want?" in one of his two longest speeches of the play, Ted replies,

> I just want my son to outlive me by a million and three years.
> I just want my tears to roll up my face instead of down my face.
> I just want my tears to defy the laws of gravity.
> I just want my son to defy the laws of nature.
> I just want another drink.[63]

Ted wishes desperately that he could defy the laws of nature and bring his son back to life. In an echo of *Alcestis*, the flight attendant commiserates: "Had I the lips, the tongue, the mouth, the song of Orpheus, I'd go beneath the earth and bring him back, and sing him back, I'd sing him back."[64]

We begin to understand—after Ted asks multiple times whether he is dead and the stewardess tells him he is stunned—that he has taken a trip to the underworld. In the next scene, two airport bar patrons, Guy and Leonora, sing, "CNN. Here in the underworld./ It makes me feel/ It makes me a feel/ It makes me feel as if/ I makes me feel as if/ I could call someone back from the dead."[65] Writing of her influences for "The Program," Schwartz said that Anne Bogart "showed me that what characters are saying on stage doesn't necessarily have to match up with what they are doing. Although this can at first seem illogical or counterintuitive, the dissonance can ultimately create poetry and resonance, and surprisingly, can bring us closer to capturing and expressing something real." So while it might seem that drunk airport lounge patrons watching cable news aren't likely to be testing their metaphysical powers, within the world of the play, this actually feels real and sensible—more sensible than the loss of a child.

At two other key points, Schwartz also pairs the banal and fantastical to create emotional realism through dissonance. While Mel and Lanie wait for Ted to return from his business trip two specific and common events in households with young children occur—Lanie loses a tooth and Mel steps on a G. I. Joe toy. (Mel does take the rather unconventional action of burying the errant figure afterward.) Jeffrey Jones observed that these two occurrences have unusual consequences: "they are responsible for the appearance of the two non-human characters in the play." Jones explicates the importance of the tooth and action figure further: "It is significant that one is lost, taken away, and cannot be returned while the other is buried, but magically 'escapes,' not only coming back but coming to life. Substitute child for object and the meaning becomes self-evident."[66]

Coming to terms with the characters spawned by these significant objects, the Tooth Fairy and G. I. Joe, is an essential point in Mel's process of grieving. Early in the play Lanie loses her tooth, and the Tooth Fairy hovers around the action of the play almost until the end. Despite some moments of cheerfully nonsensical early utterance, most of the wisdom the Tooth Fairy dispenses is serious, and on several occasions, Mel repeats it. While her lines may be clichéd, they still merit repetition because of the truth obscured by the too-familiar surface. In regard to dealing with the past she says, "You can run, but you just can't hide"[67] and "No backsies."[68]

Mel in fact must stop hiding from her past, and eventually she must confront it. Jones reads G. I. Joe as a fantasy of rebirth for the buried son, but I read him as a memory that will not stay repressed. Mel repeatedly asks G. I. Joe (with slight variations), "Didn't we bury you?" to which he replies, "I escaped."[69] When Mel stepped on the toy, she felt pain. Even though she buried the offending object, the pain returned and grew to several times its original size. Until she is able to unearth what she's submerged, to tell the story of Sam's death, and internalize its consequences, G. I. Joe will come back.

Cathy Caruth's theorization of trauma in *Unclaimed Experience: Trauma, Narrative, History* reverberates powerfully with G. I. Joe's function in the play. Caruth writes,

> Trauma is not locatable in the simple violent or original event in an individual's past, but rather in the way that its very unassimilated nature—the way it was precisely not known in the first instance—returns to haunt the survivor later on . . . Trauma seems to be much more than a pathology, or the simple illness of a wounded psyche: it is always the story of a wound that cries out, that addresses us in the attempt to tell us of a reality or truth that is otherwise unavailable. The truth, in its delayed appearance and its belated address, cannot be linked only to what is known, but also to what remains unknown in our very actions and our language.[70]

Schwartz transubstantiates Mel's trauma as a life-sized, unburiable G. I. Joe that cries out to her.

Eventually Mel does tell G. I. Joe and the Tooth Fairy how Sam drowned. She describes Lanie's reluctance to have sunscreen applied at the lake and her meticulous attention to every inch of Lanie's skin in retribution. They did battle. Mel says, "'You win,' I said. 'I quit,' I said. 'Go be someone else's daughter . . . Get yourself another mother . . . I don't want you anymore.' And so she gave up. Because she had no choice. And she sat still. Because she didn't have a choice . . . I didn't miss a spot. And when I finished. When I finally, finally finished. I stood up. Pleased. And I looked around. Proud. And he was . . ." Mel can't finish this crucial sentence, so Ted finishes it for her: "He's gone."[71]

Mel's story is at once exposition and dramatic climax. It sets the audience in motion to take a journey of character and shows the audience that we have reached the point of highest intensity. The story will not continue to progress, as loose ends will be tied up and we will soon conclude our journey. This moment of simultaneous progression and stasis, the lurching forward and staying put, is the recognition and acknowledgement of loss as physical reality. The telling of Mel's story, the crying of the wound, allows the Tooth Fairy and G. I. Joe to disappear and it allows Ted to come home from his strange trip. Mel, Ted, and Lanie will be a family again, albeit a very different one.

When Ted returns, Mel physically registers a surprise that they have difficulty naming—they catalogue jumping, flinching, shuddering, cringing, grimacing, gasping, and wincing—before, according to the stage directions, "She wails. Long and loud . . . She wails again. Longer and louder."[72] Mel finally vents her emotion, breaking free from language in her cry. Ted immediately returns to language, not so much to undermine her expression, but to reshape it.

TED: It was subtle.
Just a flash of pain.

>
> Panic.
> A pang of grief.
> Anguish.
> A twinge of agony.
> Despair.
> And then . . .
> MEL: And then?
> TED: A glimmer of hope.
> MEL: A glimmer of what?
> TED: And then . . .
> MEL: And then?
> TED: Normal.[73]

Though Ted's wish to defy the physical laws of nature—to bring his son back—can't be granted, at long last, the characters in the play find hope and the promise of normalcy through simple linguistic expression. At play's end, the Tooth Fairy and G. I. Joe have left for Beirut, and Mel falls asleep quickly. Ted's last lines are unadorned, cliché free, and while they bear the trace of the repetition that has trapped the characters in their grief throughout the play, Mel has finally escaped physically and emotionally: "Do you want ice? Mel? Do you want ice? Mel? Are you sleeping? You're sleeping. That was quick."[74]

Like Ruhl's Eurydice, Mel is also silent and asleep at play's end, but her sleep is different. She hasn't been required to annihilate gender and self to claim this peace. Grief has not defined Mel in the way it defined Eurydice. I'm reminded here of Teresa Brennan's distinction between feeling and affect: "Feelings are not the same thing as affects. Putting it simply, when I feel angry, I feel the passage of anger through me. What I feel with and what I feel are distinct."[75] Grief has passed through Mel. The audience is left with a sense of hope that grief, as important as it is for a time, can pass. A female mourner has the power to be something else as well.

Women writers staged grief in provocative ways in the early twenty-first century. Their audiences were surrounded by anguish—large-scale and more personal—outside the theater, and if there were many injunctions against expressing that pain offstage, Ruhl, Didion, and Schwartz permitted their viewers an opportunity to explore how grief might be felt and shown onstage. They neither mimicked hegemonic versions of emotion nor simply echoed each other. Reading *Eurydice* beside *The Year of Magical Thinking* and *God's Ear* showcases the differences that mark these powerful plays.

If we return to Judith Butler, we might consider how this project could be extended by future writers. In her recent work, Butler has written passionately about who is grievable, and the ethical demand to extend who is grievable to include others whose faces do not mirror ours. She says, "Those who remain faceless or whose faces are presented to us as the symbols of evil, authorize us to become senseless before those lives we have eradicated, and whose grievability is indefinitely postponed. Certain faces must be admitted into public view, must be seen and heard for some keener sense of the value of life, all life, to take hold. So, it is not that mourning is the goal of politics, but that without the capacity to mourn, we lose that keener sense of life we need in order to oppose violence."[76]

None of the writers considered here achieves Butler's goal. They provide us with mourners who do not challenge us to identify with someone beyond our culture. But what they do achieve is an ability to bring grief and mourning back into a public forum in multiply transformed ways. They disarm conventional gendered expectations of the look and sound of grief while they show how important it is not just in the lives of dramatic characters but in the lives of those in the audience who hurt with them. They allow us to acknowledge the precariousness of the ties that bind us to others and our sense of ourselves, and they give us license to mourn openly or with a sense of control, within the bounds of gender or without, when these essential bonds are broken.

CHAPTER 3

Caring Labor

The Clean House, Ruhl's 2004 play[1] that launched her into the national spotlight with its Susan Smith Blackburn win and its designation as a Pulitzer Prize finalist, contains a constellation of characters who do domestic, caring work. Lane, a doctor, employs Matilde, a young woman from Brazil to clean her house. But it is ultimately Lane's sister, Virginia, who does that work without pay. Meanwhile, Lane eschews common contemporary medical practice to care for her husband's lover, Ana, in her home as she's dying of breast cancer.

Ruhl is not alone in concern for the issues that surround women's caring labor, paid and unpaid, within the home. Among the list of her contemporaries who treat similar issues are Lisa Loomer, whose 2003 play *Living Out* explores the pressures facing Ana, a Salvadoran nanny who has one child living in the United States with her and another back in her native country, and Nancy, the lawyer who employs Ana; and Diana Son, whose 2006 play *Satellites* shows the conflicts that arise when Nina, an architect, attempts to work from home on a major project after the birth of her baby with the help of a nanny who shares her Korean heritage, Mrs. Chae. Looking at *The Clean House* in context with *Living Out* and *Satellites* leads to a deeper understanding of all three plays and the culture in which they reside.

As I analyze these plays, I'll use feminist economic philosophy as a lens through which to view them. Drucilla Barker and Susan Feiner help define what such a lens can do:

> Feminist economists read economic texts to discover, name, and valorize the many productive economic activities performed by women and other subordinated peoples. Economic analyses informed by such suspicions are able to uncover what dominant narratives repress. Even when women are confined to the household, they still perform the lioness's share of the world's work; the activities of reproduction (both biological and social) and provisioning are incredibly valuable yet

consistently devalued. Conflict is as likely to characterize economic processes as are harmony and mutually beneficial voluntary exchange, while power, class position, and status—not the workings of the invisible hand—are key determinants of who gets what.[2]

With such principles in mind, it comes as no surprise that a major subfield within feminist economic analysis concerns the labor of care. Caring labor often includes the care of dependent peoples like children, the sick, and the elderly and care within the home and is traditionally undertaken by women, most particularly women who are in subordinate class and racial positions. While it may be paid or unpaid in pecuniary form, it is also assumed to carry with it recompense beyond money. And therein lies part of the interest and problem with care labor from a feminist economic perspective: while care labor is essential to the function of society, it is consistently undervalued in economic terms.

Nancy Folbre, one of the most prominent feminist economists who has studied caring labor, summarizes the multiple, conflicting responses her colleagues have voiced to the problem of the socialization of care labor as feminine activity, the undervaluing of care labor, and the subsequent penalizing of women who participate in it: "A feminine norm of care may be a kind of trick imposed by men who use it to extract extra care for themselves. Or norms of care may be socially necessary, but imposed primarily on women as means of lowering costs to men. Caring preferences may be an almost incidental result of the social organization of childrearing or the larger sexual division of labor. Or they may actually be a by-product of subordination, in which an end of subordination would bring an end to caring labor."[3] Folbre explores what the feminist response to these issues might be. She observes that there are two classic feminist responses, regardless of context—demanding equality or asserting difference—and that both are problematic in this complex situation if, as she suggests, women's caring labor has significant value to the economy. She urges her reader to reject polarities of thought and to engage in "a more systematic discussion of the ways that caring labor should be valued."[4]

This is precisely what Ruhl, Loomer, and Son do, albeit in theatrical form. The grouping of *The Clean House*, *Living Out*, and *Satellites* does several important things. First, it makes clear the variety and nuances of caring labor. Caring labor is defined multiple ways in economic texts and in these dramatic texts as well. While the plays share certain elements—perhaps most notably the employment of women of color by affluent professional class women to do various kinds of labor—there are significant variations on this theme that emerge as the dramatic narratives unfold. Forces highlighting the differences are the affluent women's feelings about demands on them to provide care as well as their partners' roles in creating this demand. Also important is how space is conceptualized in the four plays. The ways the playwrights create and deploy domestic space has significant influence on the conclusions the audiences are most likely to draw about the issues in the plays. And finally, each play is at least partially comic. The parameters of genre also help shape the issues in the plays. These shared dramaturgical factors permit Ruhl and her contemporaries to look at the ways caring work shapes character and to propose a revaluation of caring work and principles.

The Clean House

In *The Clean House*, Matilde has come to the United States from Brazil after the death of her parents. Though Lane, a doctor, employs her to clean her house, she refuses to do that work. Lane takes Matilde to the hospital and has her medicated, but Lane declares, "She still wouldn't clean. And—in the meantime—I've been cleaning my house! I'm sorry, but I did not go to medical school to clean my own house."[5] Ruhl has explained in several interviews that she was motivated to write the play thanks to a real conversation that she overheard at a party in Providence. She says of the conversation, "I couldn't stop thinking about this. Not only about what she said, but the transparency with which she said it, as though there were nothing wrong with her statement. As though her cleaning woman were just for cleaning . . . Politically it freaked me out, and the assumptions about race and gender freaked me out. And class . . . Does class get us beyond the obligation to clean for ourselves, to care for our own dirt in a daily way? Does medical school supersede our gender? As women are we supposed to clean up after other people?"[6] Ruhl explores these questions not just through Lane and Matilde, the employer and the employee, but also through Lane's sister, Virginia. Virginia tells the audience in monologue that she knows that her sister has given up the "privilege" of cleaning her own house: "Something deeply personal—she has given up."[7] So Virginia goes to Lane's house and aims to get to know Matilde and discover the root of the young woman's sadness. When Matilde tells Virginia that cleaning makes her sad,[8] Virginia extols the virtues she sees in cleaning: "Cleaning my house—makes me feel clean."[9] Matilde points out a key difference in their situations, "But you don't clean other people's houses. For money."[10] So Virginia offers Matilde a deal: she will clean her sister's house, but they can't tell Lane.

For a while the bargain seems to be working for all involved. Lane is pleased that her house is now very clean; Matilde has the psychic energy to concentrate on her jokes—comedy is her true vocation; and Virginia is finding satisfaction in cleaning. But when Lane discovers that her husband, Charles, is having an affair with one of his cancer patients, she comes home early and finds Virginia and Matilde engaged in their own brand of domestic subterfuge. As she's forced into a painful insight about her marriage—"He didn't want a doctor. He wanted a housewife"[11]—she also begins to understand why her house has been so clean. As Lane and Virginia confront each other about the unconventional arrangement that had made all three women happy, Virginia admits that she was gaining a kind of profit:

> VIRGINIA: I wanted something—big. I didn't know how to ask for it. Don't blame Matilde. Blame me. I wanted—a task . . . Let me . . . take care of you.
> LANE: I don't need to be taken care of.
> VIRGINIA: Everybody needs to be taken care of.
> LANE: Virginia. I'm all grown up. I DON'T NEED TO BE TAKEN CARE OF.
> VIRGINIA: WHY NOT?
> LANE: I don't want my sister to clean my house. I want a stranger to clean my house.[12]

Clearly Virginia sees her labor as caring. Her first attempt to deny having any motive suggests a classic perception about women's work in the home—that it should be selfless, altruistic. Caring labor is not about individualism, but rather its opposite. The very act is gendered female, and it provides Virginia with the "big" satisfaction she lacked.

Lane's reaction to caring is complex when it comes to gender, but not to class. Lane defines herself as a doctor—and she sees this as oppositional to being a housewife. Her caring is professionalized, socially valorized, and it takes place outside the home. If she lets a woman of her class assume caring, and in her view feminine, functions within her home, her displacement will be complete. But if she lets a woman of a different class (and ethnicity as well) do this work, that does not threaten her. A "stranger's" class status will not upset the new gendered system she has created.

Lane's first reaction to what she's discovered is to fire Matilde. In this regard Matilde is typical—like her offstage caring labor counterparts, she has few legal protections in her working life. She gets no severance, and she has no rights. But she is also unlike real-life caregivers in that she can see what Lane imagines. As she walks in with her suitcase, asking Lane if there's anything she can do before she goes, she spots a couple. When she asks who they are, Lane replies, "My husband and the woman he loves. Don't worry. It's only my imagination."[13] This is the most emphatic visual clue that Ruhl has provided in the play up to this point that this is not a typical or realistic exploration of a social issue. I will return to the ways Ruhl exceeds realism when I discuss her use of stage space.

Almost immediately thereafter, Charles and his lover, Ana, are supposed to arrive at the house. Ana, much to Lane's chagrin, wants to employ Matilde after she enjoys a joke Matilde tells in Spanish. Ana, who is Argentinean, immediately connects with Matilde. Though they don't understand each other perfectly because of the differences between Portuguese and Spanish, they quickly forge a bond that has eluded both Anglo women in their relationships with Matilde. Ana's different attitude toward Matilde is revealed as soon as she bothers to pronounce Matilde's name correctly. Ruhl offers her readers a note on pronunciation before beginning the play. She writes, "'Matilde' is pronounced by the Americans in the play as 'Matilda.' It is pronounced by Ana as 'Matilda' at first, until Ana realizes that Matilde is Brazilian. And it is pronounced by Matilde, and the more observant characters in the play, 'Ma-chil-gee,' which is the correct Brazilian pronunciation."[14] The characters who can correctly pronounce Matilde's name are also the ones who can comprehend jokes. Lane and her sister Virginia routinely mispronounce the name while Ana seeks to learn it. When Matilde tells her second joke of the play in the presence of Lane, Charles, and Virginia, it is only Ana who laughs. She comprehends the joke and then shows her appreciation in Spanish. Ana is more interested in employing Matilde for her jokes than her cleaning.

Lane and Virginia both become reluctant to let Matilde go, but for different reasons. Virginia uses an emotional pull to convince Matilde to stay. She says, "Matilde is like a sister to me . . . We clean together. We talk, and fold laundry, as women used to do. They would gather at the public fountains and wash their clothes and tell stories. Now we are alone in our separate houses and it is terrible."[15] Lane claims love for Matilde and for the first time attempts to pronounce her name correctly, but then quickly shifts gears and offers a raise. The cumulative effect of these manipulations work: Matilde decides she will work in the homes of both Lane and Ana.

The next scene, after Ana and Matilde have returned from apple picking, takes place on Ana's balcony, which the stage directions indicate is directly above Lane's perfect, white living room. Ana and Matilde survey their bounty of apples, take a bite of each apple, and as the stage directions say, "if they don't think it is a perfect apple they throw it into the sea. The sea is also Lane's living room. Lane sees the apples fall into her living room."[16] Ana makes good on her promise from the scene before: Matilde's chief occupation with her will be telling jokes—her caring function has thus completely transformed. As they eat the apples, Matilde tells Ana of her quest for the perfect joke and her fear that finding it will kill her since her mother died laughing because of one of her father's jokes. Earlier in the play, the actress playing Ana has also played Matilde's mother while the actor playing Charles has played her father. When Matilde imagines her dead parents, they are embodied thus. The doubling of the parts, which Ruhl outlines very specifically in a note before the play starts, "should create a full circle for Matilde, from the dead to the living and back again."[17]

Ruhl requests that this part of the scene be played in a combination of Spanish and Portuguese if the actors playing Ana and Matilde are able. Elsewhere in the play, jokes and their aftermath are in a foreign language, while the rest of the dialogue is in English. Ruhl suggests subtitling the scene in English so that the important information will not be lost—something she does not propose in regard to the play's opening joke. In this strange and lovely scene, with brightly colored apples punctuating the sea of white, Ruhl forces us to attend to our hearing in the theater. We can either give up the discursive mode and listen to the rhythms of speech, or we can see speech on the projection screen, but in either case, we must notice our intimate, sensual connection to the story. We must pay attention to people in a new way. Through Matilde's joke, Ruhl forces us into a new kind of caring. At the end of the scene, Ana offers Charles the very best apple, and they exit to the bedroom. Matilde says in English, "The perfect joke is the perfect music. You want to hear it only once in your life, and then, never again."[18] When she finishes the line, the projection screen should read, "Matilde tries to think up the perfect joke."

Though Matilde is no longer forced to clean in a literal sense, jokes are repeatedly connected to cleansing and thus we see another kind of care. The subject of cleaning is intimately bound to the jokes Matilde tells, and Ruhl begins juxtaposing the two ideas midway through the first act. Matilde says, "I am sad when I think about cleaning. But I try not to think about cleaning while I am cleaning. I try to think of jokes. But sometimes the cleaning makes me mad. And then I'm not in a funny mood. And that makes me sad."[19] Ruhl positions cleaning and jokes as opposing forces for the spiritually vibrant Matilde. Virginia's attitude toward laughter is the polar opposite of Matilde's. Virginia, who loves to clean, says simply, "I don't like to laugh out loud."[20] At this point in the play characters who clean don't laugh, and characters who laugh don't clean.

Ruhl complicates the idea by playing with the concept of the "dirty joke." Matilde says, "A good joke cleans your insides out. If I don't laugh for a week, I feel dirty. I feel dirty now, like my insides are rotting."[21] While jokers and jokes may not clean houses, they do clean people, and thus cleaning and cleansing are marked as different forces. The best kinds of jokes, those that are the most cleansing, are the dirty ones. Matilde tells Lane, "Love isn't clean like that. It's dirty. Like a good joke" (47). Matilde follows this line by telling Lane a joke in Portuguese. Lane doesn't laugh; she cries. Though this is not the way most people react to a good dirty joke, it makes sense for the character. She has an intense reaction on a visceral level. She cleans her insides out, and as she does so the crying becomes laughter. The stage directions read, "Lane cries. She laughs. She cries. She laughs. And this goes on for some time."[22]

The cleansing power of the dirty appears twice more late in the play. In the scene immediately following Matilde's discovery of her perfect joke, Lane and Virginia confront each other about cleaning. Lane is tired of Virginia's cleaning and yells, "I DON'T WANT ANYTHING IN MY HOUSE TO BE CLEAN EVER AGAIN! I WANT THERE TO BE DIRT AND PIGS IN THE CORNER. MAYBE SOME COW MANURE SOME BIG DIRTY SHITTY COW SHIT LOTS OF IT AND LOTS OF DIRTY FUCKING SOCKS—AND NONE OF THEM MATCH—NONE OF THEM—BECAUSE YOU KNOW WHAT—THAT IS HOW I FEEL."[23] After her tirade, Lane exits, leaving Virginia alone. Virginia responds to an Italian aria only she can hear on Ana's stereo on the balcony and, as the stage directions describe it, makes "a giant operatic mess in the living room" by dumping a plant on the ground and spilling the dirt all over the white floor. When Matilde asks if she is OK, Virginia declares, "I feel fabulous."[24] Though all the characters' lives are still in chaos, the externalized mess is more palliative than the false, obsessive cleanliness that existed early in the play.

The mess is a catalyst that gives Lane a chance to offer care and do cleansing work. When she sees the mess, she also sees something is wrong with Matilde. When Matilde says, "It's a mess," she's not referring to the living room but to Ana and Charles. Ana's cancer has returned, but she refuses to go to a hospital. Charles has set off, pickaxe in hand, to find a yew tree to cure Ana. Earlier in the play, Charles has talked of loving to the point of invention and, apparently driven by the romantic instead of the practical, has set off on epic quest while leaving his lover, much in need of care, alone. As Ana says, "I want him to be a nurse and he wants to be an explorer."[25]

Though Virginia has accused her sister of lacking compassion, Lane at last shows it. She is not just willing to make house calls on Ana; she ultimately decides to move the sick woman into her home and care for her. She changes the space of care and her role within that space. Instead of operating within the boundaries of the impersonal institution that has been privileged within contemporary culture—the hospital—she has returned care for the dying to the home. She steps back from her role of doctor as she does so. Her care is neither compensated nor socially sanctioned, but it is not without benefit. The restaging of care and the recasting of her role forces Lane to acknowledge that she will need her sister's caring help. She is thus given the valuable opportunity to renegotiate their sororal relationship.

Near the end of the play, Ana, Matilde, Lane, and Virginia enjoy homemade chocolate ice cream together. Upon the conclusion of what will be Ana's last supper, the stage directions carefully indicate "No one cleans up."[26] The mess stays out as Ana asks Matilde to help her end her life with a joke. After the joke and Ana's death, the play's most moving cleansing occurs. At first, despite Lane's profession, she is discombobulated. She says, "I've never seen someone die in a house before. Only in a hospital. Where they clean everything up."[27] She and Virginia need Matilde to tell them what to do. Matilde says, "They close the eyes . . . And they wash the body . . . You say a prayer, Virginia. A prayer cleans the air the way water cleans the dirt."[28] In most contexts prayers and jokes might seem to be opposing forms of utterance, but not in *The Clean House*. Both are powerful cleansing agents. While Matilde thought of the perfect joke, it seems that Virginia found the perfect prayer, short but eloquent. She prays, "Ana. I hope you are apple picking."[29] Virginia thus wills a return to the scene of perfectly translated being, sensual and present, on the balcony.

Jokes in *The Clean House* ultimately work toward erasing the boundary that some perceive between women and comedy. Early in the play, Matilde notes the consequence of this misperception: "My mother once said to me: Matilde, in order to tell a good joke, you have to believe that your problems are very small, and that the world is very big. She said: if more women knew more jokes, there would be more justice in the world."[30] This aspect of joking—creating justice—reveals it as a central component of another kind of caring. In an interview Ruhl said,

> I remember hearing the critic John Lahr speak about humor and aggression, and I thought his ideas were so sexist, because he kept saying that humor was masculine and aggressive, that comic metaphors were masculine. You know, "stick it to him." He was talking about all these sexualized metaphors for why comedians make people laugh, and that it was an act of masculine sexual aggression. But I think comedy can be quite the opposite. You're taking something in and accepting it as true, and that can be funny. Life is funny, because it's both tragic and bizarre. Laughter is a kind of acceptance.[31]

A feminine comic aesthetic is still a subversive idea—even in the first years of the new century. The substitution of acceptance for aggression is cleansing, provocative, and powerful. In *The Clean House*, Ruhl thus shows her audience many dimensions of care.

Living Out

Lisa Loomer's *Living Out* is a very near contemporary of Ruhl's *The Clean House*. *Living Out* was a finalist for the 2003–4 Susan Smith Blackburn Prize; *The Clean House* was the winner that year. Loomer's play premiered at the Mark Taper Forum in January of 2003 and then opened at Second Stage in New York in late September 2003. In both versions of the show, Zilah Mendoza played Ana, one of the two main characters.[32] When *The Clean House* premiered in its full-length form at the Yale Rep in September 2004 (it won the Blackburn Prize earlier based on readings at New Jersey's McCarter Theatre, the Seattle Rep, and the Women's Project in New York City), Mendoza was back onstage, this time in the role of Matilde. But similarities between the two plays aren't limited to years of production or Ms. Mendoza's stellar presence. Like Ruhl, Loomer tests the parameters of caring labor, but she does so from the perspective of child care.

Before analyzing particulars of *Living Out*, it is first useful to explore Loomer's background. Loomer is one of the most-produced Latina playwrights working today, yet little academic scholarship exists on the work of this important and prolific writer.[33] She is of Spanish and Romanian heritage, and though she grew up in New York, her parents moved to Mexico when she was in her late teens. She has cited these experiences as shaping her work as a playwright: "Maybe part of the reason I'm not as linear, logical or naturalistic as some is that I did spend a lot of time in a culture that was not driven by linear expectations, where the boundaries between life and death, between the literal and the fanciful, are a lot looser."[34]

She studied at Brandeis and NYU but spent summers and holidays in Mexico. Her first professional pursuit was acting, but after finding a lack of good female, and especially Latina roles, she began writing one-woman pieces for herself (under the pseudonym Jane Da Vinci) and doing political stand-up at such venues as Manhattan's West Bank Cafe. In 1985, she studied at International Arts Relations, Inc. (INTAR) under Maria Irene Fornes. She has said of her mentor, "Irene felt that the problem with most theater is that it had already been chewed and digested for you . . . that you 'got it' within the first few minutes. That it was neither original nor surprising. She had a low tolerance for 'jokes.' She did not teach 'structure.' Rather, she had a way of getting you to hear and to use your own voice. Playwrights who have worked with her tend not to lose that 'voice'—which is what makes one's work unique."[35] Loomer does in fact have a unique voice, one that has been challenging American theater audiences since her breakthrough play, *The Waiting Room*, was staged in 1994. That script, which looks at the effects of body modification in an effort to meet social standards of beauty in three centuries and cultures as the women involved wait to see a doctor—an eighteenth-century Chinese woman is suffering from the effects of foot binding, a Victorian English woman has been corseted too tightly, and a contemporary American woman faces a cancer diagnosis stemming from her breast implants—won the Jane Chambers Playwriting Award and was a finalist for the Susan Smith Blackburn. When Ben Brantley reviewed the Vineyard's 1996 production of the play, he noted the text's similarities to Churchill's *Top Girls* and Kushner's *Angels in America* because of the fluidity of time. Though he didn't think *The Waiting Room* was as strong as those plays, he did find that Loomer had "distinctive knack for turning scientific statistics and historical data into loopy but well-honed tools for making characters breathe."[36]

Loomer herself has said of her writing, "I tend to be moved to write when something bugs me. I seem to have written a lot about balance or the need for balance—the balance of masculine versus feminine, nature versus science, Anglo culture versus Latino culture, the powerful versus the powerless, life versus art." The next thing that bugged her that she was able to transpose into issues for characters who breathe was the battle some couples undergo to conceive a child. Her play on this subject, *Expecting Isabel*, opened at the Arena in 1998.

Before *Living Out* premiered, Loomer experienced major success in Hollywood in 1999. She was one of three screenwriters credited on the adaptation of Susanna Kaysen's *Girl, Interrupted*, for which Angelina Jolie won an Oscar. And she had previously written for the 1990s television series *Hearts Afire*, starring John Ritter and Markie Post. In addition to noting differences in process between theater and television or film (she finds that the latter forms demand a more linear approach), she also found a difference in the content of the media— that theater allowed her to address the kind of controversial issues for which she feels a passion: "I don't think these issues will be dealt with on television, and sometimes even the movies steer away. The theater does offer that freedom to deal with issues that aren't talked about on television and film."[37]

But even if she found shortcomings in television and film work, that experience (coupled with the birth of her son) was no doubt significant in her crafting of a tale chronicling the perspectives of two working mothers in *Living Out*—the entertainment lawyer, Nancy, and the nanny, Ana. Loomer herself has employed a nanny, but her real inspiration and research for the play came from taking her son to their neighborhood park: "I have a young child and I spent a lot of time in the park, talking, listening, sometimes eavesdropping. My son had a nanny for a while, and through her I got to know a few women quite well. I also did one or two formal interviews. And my family lives in Mexico so I know several people there who are not nannies but do go back and forth to the U.S. for work."[38] Loomer's close connection to both employer and employee clearly shows in the play; both viewpoints are fully represented.

Before analyzing the text it is also well worth reviewing Caridad Svich's and David Roman's brief statements about the play. I am not the first critic to consider *The Clean House* in relation to *Living Out*—Svich did so first. She writes,

> With an almost cavalier shrug, the put-upon, comic, foreign-born, usually but-not-exclusively Latina maid has been seen in as disparately-lauded theatrical works as Lisa Loomer's *Living Out* (2003), Sarah Ruhl's *The Clean House* (2004), Paul Weitz' *Privilege* (2005), and Rinne Groff's *Inky* (2005), as well as in James L. Brooks' film *Spanglish* (2004) and the J. Lo starring vehicle *Maid in Manhattan*

(2002). In almost all these examples the retro-fit notion that the maid is present simply to serve the growth and maturation of non-Latino characters is exercised. Ostensibly politically-correct and wrapped in well-intentioned pedigrees of progressiveness, these pieces, which are symptomatic of a creeping trend, reinforce the position of the Latina/o as whimsically Other.[39]

I would argue that Matilde is neither the agent of retrofit notions nor primarily whimsical (and neither is the play in which she resides). She refuses the role of maid early in the play, passing her duties to Virginia, while drawing attention to the power dynamics inherent in the role that she finds unacceptable. She does aid in Lane's transformation, but so do Ana and Virginia. Matilde ultimately becomes a creative force through her unique versions of joking and spirituality that very much exceed cultural expectations of domestic comedy. But if some readers insist that there is a lingering whiff of othering about Matilde's function in *The Clean House*, surely the same cannot reasonably be said of Ana in *Living Out*.

David Roman's perspective on *Living Out* is very different from Svich's. After witnessing a workshop production in Los Angeles, he wrote about this play in the context of Latino theater that has been deeply important to him:

> Now clearly, I am not a Latina *domestica* nor am I a white woman trying to raise an infant, but I loved this play for its bold and bitter representation of these intricate and volatile relationships. This is a play, ostensibly a comedy, about the failure of race relations among people who are making the effort to build connections across difference.... In the talk back after the performance ... Many of the spectators wanted to universalize the experience of the Latina at the heart of the story, an effort to dilute the particularities of her experience, a recommendation to the playwright that I found troubling. I was arguing for the specificity of her experience—as a Latina, as an immigrant, as a worker—which I thought Loomer has presented effectively.[40]

My reading, as will become evident, is much closer to Roman's. Ana is a domestic care worker, but the costs and value of that care are intelligently critiqued, not taken for granted and blindly represented without comment, and her experience is central to the play. There is nothing remotely whimsical about Ana's character.

As the play opens, we see Ana interviewing for a job. Before she meets Nancy, the woman who will employ her, she meets two of her neighbors, Wallace and Linda. To both these women Ana admits that she herself has a young child, and the interviews end almost immediately. As Linda, the more kind of the first two interviewers puts it, "I'm sorry Ana. I need someone who can make my kids a priority."[41] By the time she gets to her third interview with Nancy, Ana knows how to present herself to a prospective employer. She tells Nancy, "I have two boys. (Long beat.) But they are both in El Salvador."[42] In fact, only her older son is in El Salvador—her six-year-old lives with her in Los Angeles.

Both women excitedly tell their husbands, Bobby and Richard, the news of the relationship that has been formed. This is the first chance the audience gets to see how the stage space will work. Geographical space is more specific in *Living Out* than in *The Clean House*. In her stage directions, Ruhl designates place as "a metaphysical Connecticut. Or, a house that is not far from the sea and not far from the city." Loomer's designation is far shorter, "Los Angeles," though this will get more complex as two spots in Los Angeles are depicted—the more urban and diverse Huntington Park and the more suburban and white Santa Monica. Loomer describes her set thus: "The set is a living room, a kitchen and two children's areas—flexible enough so that the play can go back and forth between an expensive home on the Westside of Los Angeles and a modest apartment on the Eastside. It's essential that the Anglo couple and the Latino couple occupy the same stage space. So sometimes the living room is Ana and Bobby's, and sometimes it's Richard and Nancy's."[43] This is a crucial move on Loomer's part. In *The Clean House* we see Lane's home and Ana's balcony, but Matilde has no space of her own. She is never at home. Loomer shows us two homes and two interconnected worlds.

Loomer's living room also morphs into a park, and again we see two worlds. The Anglo mothers come to the park with their children and discuss their nannies, while the nannies come, same strollers in hand, and discuss their employers. In the version of the script published by Dramatists Play Service, the scenes featuring the nannies in the park contain a considerable amount of Spanish. A note at the beginning of the text offers translations of these scenes (and those between Ana and Bobby)—entirely into Spanish so that the Spanish-speaking characters can be completely immersed in that language. Minneapolis's Mixed Blood Theatre took Loomer up on this offer in 2004. But whether the scenes are entirely or only partially in Spanish, language works differently in *Living Out* than it does in *The Clean House*. While Ruhl is interested in translation or its failure as a formalist device for making perception strange, Loomer uses language more naturalistically. It is color and texture that can both separate and link Loomer's two worlds. *New York Times* reviewer Margo Jefferson commented about the Second Stage production, "We're caught up in an insistent beat, like a march. Whether the voices are Anglo or Latino, the rhythm of the dialogue is the same. (Even when the characters speak Spanish, one feels pushed toward this march tempo.)."[44]

Another difference between *The Clean House* and *Living Out* is the pressure exerted by the men on what happens in the play. In Ruhl's text, Charles plays a relatively minor role. His relative indifference to most of what happens can be seen when Ana aims to hire Matilde. She asks him, "Charles? Do you like things to be clean?" He replies, "Sure. I like things to be clean." We also see him wandering upstage, axe in hand, looking for a yew tree to save Ana. Throughout a significant portion of the play, he is lost. Richard and Bobby are far more active players. Both men are at best ambivalent about their wives' need and desire to work.

The women in the play are ambitious—they are eager to work for a better standard of living for themselves and their children. For Nancy this means owning a home in Santa Monica; for Ana it means earning money to pay for an immigration lawyer to secure her own citizenship and to get the money to bring her older son to the United States. Both women need to negotiate with their husbands regarding the child care that will make their working possible. At the beginning of the play, it is clear that Richard only nominally supports Nancy's decision to return to work. While she is concerned with making partner at her firm to earn money for their mortgage and the best preschool, Richard counters with "You always say the job's unrewarding" (she corrects him—"I said it's unfulfilling") and says, "I completely support whatever decision you make, Nance . . . I'm only questioning the timing. You're still breast-feeding, honey."[45] Richard subtly suggests that biology should keep his wife at home—at least temporarily.

Very little is actually required of Richard to make the nanny relationship work. This is not true of Bobby. For Ana to work, he will have to assume care responsibilities for his son. For a time he does this grudgingly and with only moderate skill. When Ana learns that he fed their son nothing but fries for dinner, the following argument unfolds:

> **BOBBY:** That's what he ask for! Just fries! And who's picking him up in the truck while you working late?
> **ANA:** You think I want to work late?
> **BOBBY:** I don't know . . .
> **ANA:** Sure, Bobby! Sure I rather be washing their underwear than yours! Sure I rather be sweeping their floors! And I rather be taking care of their kid than my own son![46]

In addition to showing the differences between Bobby and Richard, the scene also shows a difference between Ana and Nancy. When Nancy comes home from work, Ana has cleaned her house; when Ana gets home, she starts her "second shift."

When Bobby gets better work, he is no longer able to pick up their son. The "nanny chain," as Arlie Hochschild has called it, gains another link when Bobby's 18-year-old sister is now put in charge of looking after Santi. Nanny chains or global care chains have, according to Hochschild, been proliferating. She writes,

> A typical global care chain might work something like this: An older daughter from a poor family in a third world country cares for her siblings (the first link in the chain) while her mother works as a nanny caring for the children of a nanny migrating to a first world country (the second link) who, in turn, cares for the child of a family in a rich country (the final link). Each kind of chain expresses an invisible human *ecology of care*, one care worker depending on another and so on. A global care chain might start in a poor country and end in a rich one, or it might link rural and urban areas within the same poor country. More complex versions start in one poor country and extend to another slightly less poor country and then link to a rich country.[47]

The care chain in *Living Out* does in fact begin in El Salvador. Ana's older son, Tomas, is living in their native country and is being cared for by his grandmother. This link partially frees Ana to work for Nancy for ten dollars an hour, a higher rate of pay than she would make in her native land. Meanwhile Santi's care must come from someone other than his mother—first his father and then his young aunt.

One of the problems that Hochschild identifies in this globalization of love and care is the displacement of affection from one child to another. The first-world child—in her example the one who is being cared for in Beverly Hills—gets the love that would belong to child of the nanny had she not chosen to immigrate for work. Hochschild writes,

> This displacement is often upward in wealth and power. This, in turn, raises the question of the equitable distribution of care. It makes us wonder, is there—in the realm of love—an analogue to what Marx calls "surplus value," something skimmed off from the poor for the benefit of the rich?
> ... Is time spent with the first world child in some sense "taken" from a child further down the care chain? Is the Beverly Hills child getting "surplus" love, the way immigrant farm workers give us surplus labor? Are first world countries such as the United States importing maternal love as they have imported copper, zinc, gold, and other ores from third world countries in the past?[48]

The displacement of care has very serious consequences in *Living Out*. At first Ana merely feels guilty—for not getting home before Santi falls asleep and for missing his soccer games. Between watching Nancy's baby Jenna and commuting across the greater Los Angeles area, there simply are not enough hours in the day. But when an emergency happens, Santi's aunt is not prepared to deal with it effectively and tragedy ensues.

Before we get to the tragedy, the tone of the play is comic. Among the many humorous moments are the nannies talking of subverting their employers' dietary demands for tofu with donuts, their fantasizing about the Americanos' inability to handle what would happen if all service employees stayed home one day, and Richard's threatened destruction of the nanny cam–embedded teddy bear in the microwave. But a comic world is a protected one—slights are many and pointed barbs fly, but redemption through the promise of regeneration is the final outcome. Loomer's very point in the play is that the protected world of comedy is a class-specific world. Nancy can't even imagine what has happened to Santi. When she calls the hospital and hears that he is no longer a patient, her assumption is that he has been discharged and all is well. It doesn't occur to her that he has died—that when Bobby's sister took Santi "to the nearest lousy clinic before getting to a real hospital"[49] when he had an asthma attack, that ill-informed decision might be fatal.

Loomer, like Ruhl, talks about comedy and the gendered ways it sometimes works. Loomer speaks particularly about "the aggressive game" of sitcom writing: "Where if you were in a room of male businessmen, they might be talking about how much money they made or where they vacationed, in a room of comics, they've got those jokes going loud and fast . . . That's their way of being men and comics at the same time." She also distinguishes male comedy from her own comic style: "It's not my nature. I'm not that kind of funny."[50] While both Ruhl and Loomer may reject a masculine approach to comedy, their feminine strategies are different. Like Ruhl, Loomer and her jokes require the audience to take something in and accept it as true, but she is more pointed in urging the audience to see the socially insane that's underpinning the comic. For example, when Nancy is wallowing in the guilt she feels about Santi's illness (again not realizing that he actually died), she and Richard have the following exchange:

RICHARD: You were paying her to work late—
NANCY: She was doing me a favor—as a friend!
RICHARD: No, honey, you were working. Ana was working. For all we know she was paying the sister-in-law to take care of her child. Everyone's working a paying someone else to take care of their child—it's insane! It's insane people even have to leave their families to come to this country—
NANCY: Well, we funded the war in El Salvador—
RICHARD: We personally?
NANCY: We pay taxes—
RICHARD: So in a couple of years we can hire a nanny from Iraq.[51]

At play's end, there is no redemption. Ana has learned a lesson. When she decides Tomas is better off in El Salvador than in Los Angeles, Bobby tries to convince Ana otherwise, but Ana's retort showcases her painful realization:

> **BOBBY:** A grandmother is not a mother—
> **ANA:** Sometime . . . a mother is not a mother, Bobby.[52]

In both of these late-play exchanges, Loomer drives her message home. The global nanny chain is unending and is the product, if not the profit, of US foreign policy. There are real human consequences to this situation. When love is unplaced and displaced, the family—at least at the beginning of the chain—suffers. Loomer offers her characters and audience no solution, only a clear-eyed view of the problem of care.

Satellites

While *The Clean House* and *Living Out* sprung from overheard conversations about care, *Satellites* came from a direct talk Diana Son had with a friend, the actress Sandra Oh, about the writer's block she'd experienced for several years after giving birth to and caring for her first child:

> Sandra told me, "I think you've been surprised by how single-mindedly devoted to your son you've been. You write for TV, but that's just work you do for your family. You can contain it. When you're in a rehearsal room with a play, you love every minute of it. I think that must feel threatening to the mother in you because, since you had your son, you haven't really let anything compete with that." I felt very liberated; no one had said that to me before. So, I thought maybe I should write a play about how a working mother tries to engage in her work while remaining devoted to her child.[53]

Despite this story about the play's genesis and some coincidences with Son's personal details—she is a Korean American mother, she moved to Brooklyn, her husband works in computers, and her mother is dead—Son does not want audiences to read the work as autobiographical. She told *The New York Times*, "I resent the assumption because people assume that women could not write about experiences that they didn't have themselves," she said. "Do people ask Neil LaBute if he dates a fat woman?"[54]

Son in fact skillfully shows that she can write about people very different from herself in *Satellites*: the play has a very specific cast with complex racial ties. Though Nina and the nanny she hires, Mrs. Chae, are of Korean descent like Son, Miles, Nina's husband is an African American, who was adopted as an infant by a Caucasian family. His brother, Eric is a secondary character in the play, as is Nina's business partner, Kit, another Caucasian. Finally, Reggie, a longtime resident of the rapidly gentrifying Brooklyn neighborhood into which Nina, Miles, and their baby Hannah have just moved, is African American.

The choice to create characters with very specific racial backgrounds integral to the play's plot was a specific one. The stage work for which Son is best known is the 1999 play *Stop Kiss*.[55] In the play, two young women fall in love. Sara, a school teacher just arrived in New York from St. Louis, is brutally beaten in a park when her assailant observes her sharing a first kiss with Callie. None of the characters has a specific racial background. Son said she wrote this and her other early plays this way because she wanted "the casting to be open, so that actors of many races could be considered for all the roles."[56] But despite her invitation to open casting, few productions took the opportunity. Son elaborates: "I had an awakening with *Stop Kiss*. No matter how emphatic I was about the casting, most regional productions would still be all-white. So with my two new plays, I've chosen to write race-specific characters. I had felt very strongly before that I would just write characters; anybody could play them. But I have shifted in response to my disappointment."[57] As she wrote *Satellites*, she had not just the frustration with regional productions of *Stop Kiss* in mind but the success of the Public Theater production in New York. There, Sandra Oh played Sara and Kevin Carroll played George, Sara's boyfriend from home. She wrote Nina for Oh and Miles for Carroll.

In *Satellites*, race is not the sole marker of identity. Working in tandem with race is language. Nina wants to hire a nanny when she is overwhelmed by the pressures of her work as an architect. But she doesn't just want any nanny—she is particularly interested in a Korean nanny who will speak Korean to the infant Hannah. Nina says, "I can't speak Korean, so she's not going to learn it from me."[58] This culturally specific kind of caring is important to her. At first she's very moved by Mrs. Chae's Korean lullabies and cooing endearments, but when Mrs. Chae refers to Miles as "clean" and commends his adoptive family for taking in a black baby and when she thinks Mrs. Chae doesn't want her infant granddaughter to play with Hannah because she's biracial, she fears Mrs. Chae's lessons will move beyond word identification and instilling an appreciation of kimchee and sea weed soup to "poison[ing] my baby with racist thoughts."[59]

Both Mrs. Chae and Nina relate to giving and receiving care differently than the characters in *The Clean House* and *Living Out*. Both women want the care relationship to replace one missing within their biological families: Mrs. Chae wants a second daughter and Nina wants a second mother. From their first meeting, the mother-daughter relationship shapes their interaction. When Mrs. Chae inquires about Nina's mother's pride in the new baby, Nina tells her that her mother is dead. Mrs. Chae replies, "Tsk tsk tsk. You take care of baby, your mommy supposed to take care of you."[60] Mrs. Chae quickly moves to fill this role, cooking and cleaning for Nina in addition to looking after the baby. At one point in the play, Mrs. Chae literally spoon-feeds Nina some soup while Nina's hands are full.[61] But as Mrs. Chae's racist attitudes begin to emerge, Nina discovers there is a line she doesn't want Mrs. Chae to cross: Nina bristles when Mrs. Chae calls herself "halmoni," or "grandma."[62] Mrs. Chae's attitude toward African Americans troubles Nina deeply, and she wants part, but not all, of who Mrs. Chae is. As Miles observes late in the play, "It's like you hired Mrs. Chae to be your mom. And you're firing her because she's not."[63] Nina is new at parenting and anxious about her new responsibilities. She longs to be cared for again, before she can negotiate her own identity in relationship to giving care. She needs a maternal figure, but she also needs to define herself against Mrs. Chae as she moves toward forging her own code of familial values.

While Nina is forthcoming about the absent maternal presence in her life, Mrs. Chae is more secretive. Initially she tells Nina that she is not taking care of her daughter's child because Kyung Soon, who is a lawyer, has day care in her office building. Much later she reveals the truth: her daughter employs two nannies, one British and one Tibetan, because "she don't want grandson to speak the bad English like Mommy."[64] And when Nina presses her about the lie, Mrs. Chae says, "I tell you the truth now. Before I want[ed] you to hire me, I see nice family, two good parents—happy baby . . . I wanted to be in this house, I want[ed] to be in this [family]."[65]

Mrs. Chae does not seem to be primarily motivated by payment. Instead she wants emotional compensation. She wants to be able to define herself in relationship to a family unit who accepts her. Caring is not so much a choice activity as a constitutive activity in the sense described by labor philosopher Margaret Jane Radin. Radin writes, "Laborers experience their labor as separate from their real selves. Workers make money but are also at the same time givers. Money does not fully motivate them to work, nor does it exhaust the value of their activity. Work is understood not as separate from life and self, but rather as a part of the worker, and indeed constitutive of her. Nor is work understood as separate from relations with other people."[66] Caring for people is part of who Mrs. Chae is; monetary payment seems to be an incidental by-product.

Also unlike *The Clean House* and *Living Out*, we see the person who employs the caregiver in her own work environment. We certainly hear about Lane's hospital, but we don't see her doing that work; we hear Nancy negotiating with her boss on the phone, but we don't see her at her firm. In *Satellites*, Nina's work space is located on another floor of the Brooklyn brownstone she and Miles are renovating. The scene shifts regularly to the basement where Nina and her business partner Kit are working to complete a model for part of their proposal to design an Arts Center in Barcelona. The choice of architecture for Nina's profession is an inspired one. The audience gets to see her struggling to put together a small physical world made from the details she's dreamt. As we see her hands literally full, gluing and holding the physical manifestation of her fragile, idealized vision, we get a striking physical metaphor for her life in general.

But while Nina's work life appears to hold great potential, Son balances this promise with the sheer physicality of motherhood—a force that complicates turning care over to someone else, no matter how much a woman succeeds in her chosen work environment. In much economic theorizing there is an emphasis on the socially constructed nature of caring roles. As Gillian Hewitson explains, "women are the careers in the home because of a socially defined feminine gender identity and not because female biology dictates that it be so. That this care and connected feminine selfhood is an outcome of women's socially defined role in mothering is central to the conceptual frameworks of many feminist economists."[67] Son challenges this idea by reminding her audience that there are biological aspects of this relationship that exert a powerful force on women.[68] There are two prime examples in the play. In the first, Nina tries to explain why she is feeling so distracted:

> NINA: I hear her. Being a mother has given me superhuman powers. And Hannah—Hannah can smell me from twenty feet away.
> KIT: You measured?
> NINA: I read it and I tested it. And her crying—it triggers my milk. I was in the bathroom yesterday and she started crying, and milk shot out of my nipples. Smacked right into the back of the door. Sometimes my milk attacks her.[69]

In the second, she apologizes for standing Kit up for her fortieth birthday dinner. She tells her friend, "I shouldn't have done that. It's just—I never . . . it's like this feral—this animal drive to take care of my daughter. I can't even apologize for it, it fucking feels right."

By making the competing forces of work and the physicality of motherhood vividly clear to the audience, Son shows what a difficult position many contemporary women find themselves in. It is hard to craft a definition of self and role in this context. When Son explained in an interview the idea behind her title, she points to this idea: "I titled the play *Satellites* because all of the characters are free-floating. A satellite is an entity that orbits around a larger entity; all of the characters lack a defining thing within their lives, so they end up colliding into each other." In addition to layering this idea into the production through character development, Mark Wendlund, the set designer of the New York production, gave the idea visual life through his moving set pieces. As Ben Brantley described it in his review in *The New York Times*, "Rooms slide sideways, backward and forward in this study of big-city identity crises . . . A seemingly solid structure splits again and again into a house divided, as distinctions between outdoors and indoors, between public and private, melt and dissolve . . . It feels absolutely right that the ground should shift so literally beneath the feet of Ms. Son's wandering, wondering characters."[70] Within this evocative set, there was a particularly important element: a large window. Near the end of the play, Kit reflects back on Miles and Nina's first night in their new home: "I think that first night when your window got smashed, the ghost of all the neglected communities past—who couldn't get the city to fix their sidewalks or keep their electricity going on hot days, let alone provide them with a local organic source of half-and-half—wafted in here and tried to spook you into leaving."[71] But by play's end, Nina, Miles, and the extended family they've built around them are sticking it out. Bringing the action, and the soundscape, back to the beginning, window glass breaks again. But this time instead of a brick causing the damage, it's the workers who are installing a new window. Nina and Mrs. Chae both head to comfort Hannah when the sound of broken glass frightens her, but for the first time, Miles gets there first. The end of the play reads as follows:

> MILES: I got her . . . "Hush little baby don't say a word. Papa's gonna buy you a mockingbird. If that mockingbird won't sing, Papa's gonna buy you a diamond ring . . ." You want me to teach you the rest of the words?
> NINA: Yes.
> MILES: If that diamond ring turns brass . . .
> NINA: Turns brass.
> MILES: Papa's gonna buy you a looking-glass.
> NINA: —looking-glass.
> MILES: If that looking-glass gets broke—(*They stop at the window. They look out into the street for a while. We start to hear the sounds of the neighborhood. Indeterminate voices in conversation. A basketball being bounced, music from a car stereo.*)[72]

Son's stage directions here drive home the connection between the glass of the window and a mirror. The window and its permeability help Nina and Miles see themselves and their place in the world more clearly. The scene concludes,

> NINA: (*Looks out*) You know what I think this hole in our window's for?
> MILES: No, what?
> NINA: To let out all the dust and ghosts that have been trapped in here.
> MILES: There's too many old stories floating around.
> NINA: It's our house now.[73]

While *Satellites* is the least funny of the three plays discussed here, it has the most hopeful and comic ending because a new social order that promises regeneration is established by play's end. It requires a mother, a father, a paid caregiver, a business partner, extended family, and neighbors. The whole cast comes together at the end of the play as Nina claims her house and her life. It is certainly an order full of complications, but it is a new order nonetheless.

In this book's introduction, I quoted Sarah Schulman's "Supremacy Ideology Masquerading as Reality: The Obstacle Facing Women Playwrights in America." She argues that plays that appear on mainstream stages and are subsequently honored reproduce hegemonic stories and perspectives and that the familiarity of this perspective is mistaken for quality playwriting.[74] While Schulman's diagnosis of the illness afflicting American theater may too often be correct, in the case of these three plays, it is not. Ruhl, Loomer, and Son have all received (varying yet substantial degrees of) mainstream production and approval, but it is not because they repeat stories of white male privilege. They tell provocative, original stories about women while using theatrical space and generic conventions imaginatively and strategically. Their dramatization of caring labor reveals new dimensions of contemporary lived experience—across the spectrum of gender, race, and class—to their wide and varied audiences. In *The Clean House*, *Living Out*, and *Satellites*, Sarah Ruhl and her contemporaries shift dominant, conventional perspectives and in so doing, they overcome a significant obstacle in American theater.

CHAPTER 4

Theatrical Devotion

In her introduction to the 2010 published version of *Passion Play*, Sarah Ruhl wrote,

> More and more, it seems to me that the separation between church and state is coming into question in our country. We are a divided nation. And the more divided we are, the less we talk about what divides us. The left is perceived as anti-religious, ideological secularists; the right as religious zealots. But whatever happened to the founding fathers' rationale for separating church and state? More devotion was possible, and more kinds of devotion would be possible, the less the state controlled religious rhetoric. More devotion and more conversation about devotion, would be possible with that freedom. I miss that conversation, and I think theater is a good place for it.[1]

Ruhl was not alone in these sentiments. Several other contemporary female playwrights were interested in expanding the conversation about religious devotion and sought to place that conversation in the theater.[2] Included among these writers were Kate Fodor, whose *100 Saints You Should Know* was produced at Playwrights Horizons in 2007, and Young Jean Lee, whose *Church* premiered at PS 122 in 2007 prior to a 2008 remount at the Public Theater.

Dating Ruhl's *Passion Play* is not easy. As she says in her playwright's note, "I started writing this play fourteen years ago after rereading an account of Oberammergau in the early 1900s." She also frequently refers to *Passion Play* as her first play, as she did in this recent interview: "Paula sneaked my first play, *Passion Play*, into the New Plays Festival at Trinity Repertory Theater and it was that performance that turned me into a playwright. I got into a car accident on the way there, blacked out, arrived, saw *Passion Play*, and thought, 'This is what I want to do with my life.' Perhaps it never really happened. Perhaps my whole life has been a dream since that car accident."[3] But even though she began the play in 1996 while she was Vogel's student, writing the parts of the play chronicling the end of the Passion play form in Elizabethan England and the enthusiasm for the annual Passion play at Oberammergau in Hitler's Germany, she didn't pen the play's third and final section until much later. As she elaborated in her playwright's note, she wrote the first draft of part 3, set in 1969 in Spearfish, South Dakota, before the 2004 election when she was under commission from Washington, DC's Arena Theatre, "with a great sense of urgency." But still the play was not finished. In the version of the play available from New Dramatists before the play's publication by Theatre Communications Group, she follows the passage I just quoted with "Now it's 2007. It's easy to feel powerless as the great political wheels turn, financed by enormous wealth."[4] And 2007 was an important year for *Passion Play*. That year Mark Wing-Davey directed the play and shepherded the rewriting process at Chicago's Goodman Theatre. In an interview contained in the Goodman's audience materials, Ruhl said,

> Molly [Smith, the Arena Theatre's artistic director,] did a beautiful production in Washington, but I didn't have time to quite finish the third act. It was such a huge undertaking, so this production feels so crucial to me in terms of how all three acts fit together. Mark did a reading of all three parts in London which I wasn't able to go to, but then we did a workshop in New York that the Goodman sponsored that was a delight. Mark had the actors doing all kinds of interviews that were related to the play . . . The actors came back and pretended to actually *be* those people. It was all fuel for the rewriting process.[5]

The play had very nearly reached its final form, though it would not be published until 2010, after its New York premiere. The Epic Theatre Company staged the play in the spring of that year to great acclaim, and Ruhl did make some changes to the 2007 script before the 2010 production.

Thus in terms of date of completion, *Passion Play* does stand in very close proximity to *100 Saints* and *Church*, but perhaps more important than chronology is the three writers' shared interest in aspects of feminist theology. Rosemary Radford Ruether outlines the concerns of feminist theologians who bring the strategies and thinking of feminism into their theological work thus: "They question patterns of theology that justify male dominance and female subordination, such as exclusive male language for God, the view that males are more like God than females, that only males can represent God as leaders in church and society, or that women are created by God to be subordinate to males and thus sin by rejecting this subordination."[6] Of particular importance, Ruether argues, is feminist theologians' revision of Christian symbology. They recognize that theological symbols are "socially constructed rather than eternally and unchangeably disclosed from beyond. Those in power construct symbols to validate their own power and the subjugation of women; social relations, such as class, race, and gender, are not eternally given by God as the 'order of creation,' but are social constructs and as such, can be changed."[7]

As Ruhl, Fodor, and Lee expand their theater-based dialogue about kinds of devotion, they upend traditional assumptions and symbology that have subordinated women. They are interested in women's embodied experience and how it can be sanctified; they explore what sin and grace mean in the contemporary world and how they are manifest; they look at leadership (inside and outside the church) and charisma; and they engage new parable structures and new imagery for conveying their messages.

Passion Play

The first part of *Passion Play* is set in spring of 1575 in northern England. Within the first couple of scenes, Ruhl introduces one of the themes that will span all three parts of the play: how playing an iconic role transforms the core identity of the player—a kind of theatrical transubstantiation. As the play opens, the carpenters are fitting John the Fisherman, who plays Jesus in his town's Passion play, to the set's wooden cross. He's grown since the last year—the staging of the Passion is an annual event—and so the key set piece needs to be adjusted to accommodate the star's changing height. John suggests that his cousin, Pontius the fish gutter, might play the role instead since he has stopped growing. But the Second Carpenter responds, "Oh, but he's a limp wee little thing. Gutted his own hand when he meant to gut a flounder. And now his back's as crooked as the road to hell."[8] John meanwhile is praised for his "mighty" and "brawny" arms. Clearly the townspeople want the actors to resemble their roles physically and emotionally.

The fictional audience is not alone in seeking congruence between actor and character. Pontius, who plays Pilate and Satan, says, "All my life I've wanted to play Christ . . . if only, I thought, they put me on a cross, I would feel holy, I would walk upright. And every year my cousin plays the Savior. I want to kill my cousin."[9] Pontius seeks the adulation that comes from playing history's greatest leading role, but he also wants an internal and external transformation to go with it.

The women in the play have feelings about performer and role that echo the feelings of the men. While this might seem a rather small point at first, it is actually a significant move in terms of biblical exegesis. Constructing male and female theological and historical figures and their experience as equal operates within the "hermeneutics of suspicion" famously outlined by feminist biblical scholar and historian Elisabeth Schussler Fiorenza. Fiorenza urges readers not to take androcentric language and texts (historical and scriptural) at face value and to read carefully for bias of omission and commission in regard to women. Ultimately, she says, "by highlighting the often unconscious bias of established so-called objective scholarship as well as the obfuscating functions of androcentric language of biblical sources, a hermeneutics of suspicion is able to recover glimpses of the discipleship of equals in the beginnings of Christianity as a heritage and vision for us all."[10]

When Mary 1, who plays the Virgin, and Mary 2, who plays Magdalene, marvel over John's golden muscles as revealed by his loin cloth during rehearsal, Mary 2 convinces Mary 1 that they ought to change roles. She says, "It's sinful to covet your own son, Mary. It's a sin, a sin against God . . . Perhaps we should switch roles. I think my part has more scenes with John the Fishermen."[11]

This is enough to convince Mary 1, who runs off to seek the permission of the director to recast the roles in a way that would normalize her desire. But the director responds: "You look like a saint (to Mary 1) and you (points to Mary 2) look like a whore. There's no getting around it. (To Mary 2) Look at that beauty mark and that gap between the teeth. And you've got a bit of deformity in the chin—it just wouldn't do for the Virgin Mary to have a bit of deformity in the chin . . . There's no time for all this driveling anarchy."[12] The kinds of anarchy here are multiple. First, it would break down the theatrical hierarchy if actors got to choose their own roles. That is a power reserved for the director, not just in this antique production situation, but in most modern contexts as well. And second, if the women did not play according to their physical type, the visual rules would be broken. Morality, particularly as it applies to sexual availability, should, according to medieval codes, be inscribed on the body—through beauty marks, teeth, and chins.[13]

While the director assumes his word on the matter will be sacrosanct, the women plot a much more significant rebellion. Though Mary 1 has long been attracted to John, she has sex with Pontius, because according to the stage directions, she pities him. When Mary becomes pregnant, she does not want to lose her part in the play. Mary 2 conceives of the idea to save her role. Mary 1 goes to the visiting friar and tells him that something miraculous has happened: "God has impregnated me that I can better play the Virgin Mary."[14] The carpenters doubt Mary's story, and Pontius knows for certain what role he played in the "miracle," but John is a believer and proposes to her, seeking to trade his role as Christ for that of Joseph: "We'll raise the child together as Mary and Joseph did before us."[15] Though Mary has long desired John, the role she has chosen forces her to reject him, saying, "I'm God's bride now."

John isn't the only one who wants to play Joseph. Mary 2 echoes his lines verbatim to Mary 1 when she suggests they run away together. (Earlier in the play Mary 2 had confessed her lesbian dreams to the visiting friar who had suggested various forms of penance to her but absolved her from blame as "it addles a young girl's brain to play the role of a whore from a young age."[16]) But Mary 1 believes she can no longer play the part for which she was cast. She tells Mary 2, "I'm a whore, Mary."[17]

While at first it appears that she is taking up the role that Mary 2 had more or less tricked her into asking the director for earlier in the play, she is making a far more transgressive switch—across genders and into the divine. Mary eventually comes to play Christ, while John takes up an aspect of the Magdalene. For several days, Mary has been missing. In the interim, the Village Idiot has been cast in her stead and Queen Elizabeth has visited the town, threatened to behead anyone who impersonates a holy figure or conceals a priest, and shut down the Passion, thereby providing Ruhl's first example of the state's control of religious rhetoric. While the cast is in the town square handing in their costumes, John appears, carrying the dead body of Mary—she has drowned herself. In Ruhl's play, it is Mary who dies, not Jesus, and it is John who reports the "news," not Mary Magdalene. The stage directions read, "She is dripping wet. Water pours out of her mouth and onto the stage. Water continues to pour out of her and off of her."[18]

Janet Martin Soskice has observed, "The cross with its blood, death, and sacrifice of a Son, is not an easy symbol for feminist theology."[19] She therefore tries to renegotiate these images, bringing them into alignment with "the symbolism of blood, birth, and new life." Soskice's main concern in "Blood and Defilement" is clear from her essay's title. She writes,

> The symbolic of blood and the cross, it would seem, are by no means restricted to punitive and penal readings. Indeed other readings, notably that of blood, birth, and kin, are not only present within historical theology but may well afford better ways into the New Testament texts whose kinship patterns are nearer to those of medieval Europe than of the modern West. Birth as well as death is a type of sacrificial giving. As far as my original plea for flexibility goes, it should be apparent that the symbolic orderings of Christianity are neither obvious nor unchanging. Similarly it is by no means clear that Christ is always and everywhere in the symbolic order a "male" figure. There is abundant sense in seeing Christ as our mother, and his blood as the source of new life—indeed by doing so we recover a proud heritage of patristic theology.[20]

But equally worthy of recuperation along the same logical lines is water—the other liquid that was said to pour from Christ's side when the soldier's lance pierced him. St. John of Chrysostom, a Church Father of the fifth century, famously analyzed the relationship of the two fluids in a text that is still used in the Roman Catholic Church's Office of Readings for Good Friday:

> "There flowed from his side water and blood." Beloved, do not pass over this mystery without thought; it has yet another hidden meaning, which I will explain to you. I said that water and blood symbolized baptism and the holy Eucharist. From these two sacraments the Church is born: from baptism, "the cleansing water that gives rebirth and renewal through the Holy Spirit," and from the holy

Eucharist. Since the symbols of baptism and the Eucharist flowed from his side, it was from his side that Christ fashioned the Church, as he had fashioned Eve from the side of Adam.[21]

So when Mary 1's body pours forth water she has a clear connection to the body of Christ, his birth of a new Church, and the promise of baptism. What we also see, if we return to Soskice's ideas, is the flexibility with which Ruhl plays with Christian symbology. More than a particular message, what is most crucial here, and with all the characters' efforts to play roles others than those for which they seem most likely to be cast, is that it is within the power of the individual to reshape and reinterpret biblical imagery. To use Soskice's language, this imagery is neither "obvious nor unchanging," and it can be reworked as social and historical conditions—such as those moderated by a feminist consciousness—demand.

As she moves into her second act, Ruhl demonstrates the malleability of images in a different time and place, but while she seemed to celebrate that potential in act 1, in act 2 she warns against it. The action has leapt forward—to the town of Oberammergau in Bavaria in 1934. A young man, Eric, has recently been tapped to play the role of Jesus because his father, who played the role to great acclaim for many years, has become too old and sick to perform. But while in the first act two men are eager to play Jesus, in this act no one who is physically fit to play the part wants it. As new carpenters measure the new Jesus for the cross in a direct echo of the first act, they try to engage him in conversation about the difficulty of playing the part. Carpenter 2 says, "Never understood how a man could stomach playing Jesus. Couldn't have any fun. No rolls in the hay, huh?"[22] But Eric doesn't want to chat—he's having trouble memorizing his lines. This is the audience's first indication that something will be wrong with the performance.

A foot soldier has been cast as Pilate in the Oberammergau Passion. It soon becomes clear that Eric is falling in love with the soldier. When Eric complains of the physical toll the part is taking on him, the soldier comforts him by rubbing his arms. Eventually their physical contact will escalate to kissing, but the intimacy is already apparent in this early scene. Eric and the soldier start to play a game called "would you rather." When Eric asks the soldier which of their roles he would rather play, the soldier answers, "Very unpleasant, the nails, the whipping, the blood . . . No one actually wants to *be* Christ, they only want to admire him from a distance."[23] Eric also has a role he'd rather play: "I'd rather play Judas. To be hated, that's easy. To be loved—that's hard."[24]

By act's end, the audience will see that Eric has assumed the role he desired. When Eric forgets his lines while rehearsing the Last Supper, Violet, a young Jewish girl who is referred to by others as the Village Idiot, feeds him lines from under the table. But she changes the text to warn the Oberammergauers of their future. Violet and Eric say together, "And if you decide that there is no God, you will need someone with vision, someone stronger, to tell you what to do? Resist, I say unto you! And finally, I want everyone at this table, eating my blood and my body, to remember that I am a Jew."[25] When the director hears himself mocked in these lines—the stronger man with a stronger vision is the way he described his own work to a visiting Englishman—he punishes Violet by locking her in a bird cage for a week without food. But Eric, perhaps inspired by goodness as he comes back in the evening to rehearse the Mount of Olives speech alone, releases Violet. He is still able to break an unjust rule and think for himself.

But time passes, and Eric changes his role from Christ to Nazi soldier. He finds Violet hiding in the woods, and he has orders to take her with him, because of her "different blood." Violet urges Eric to learn from his own performance in the play. She says, "Do you remember your lines from the play? Many shall come in my name saying, 'I am Christ' and shall deceive the multitudes. For false Christs and false prophets shall rise."[26] But when this tactic fails, she urges him to reject the theatricality of the role he has assumed outside the theater: "Even if they give you a costume and boots and a hat—even then you're not in a play! You're a man. A man must decide for himself what he wants to do."[27] Ultimately because Eric can't abandon the roles he chose for himself, both soldier and Judas, he betrays Violet. The final scene's stage directions read, "The sound of a train speeding across the track. Eric gives Violet a final push forward, into the light. The lights change from red to grey. A terrible silence."[28] The audience will infer both that the history of violence is like a speeding train into whose path Violet was thrown and, more specifically, that Violet rode a train to a Nazi death camp, eventually becoming the smoke from the crematorium filling the sky.

As the play moves from act 1 to act 2, the state's intervention in religion becomes more profound. In the first act, Elizabeth shuts down the Passion play, which we can read, with help of Louis Montrose, as a ploy to direct religious representation herself and to create civic dramas celebrating her divine right to the throne.[29] In the second act Hitler comes to see the Passion play and celebrates how well the performance portrays—and here Ruhl quotes Hitler's actual words from a 1942 speech—"the menace of the Jews."[30] In addition, the performance of the play and the roles associated with it are linked to the actions of the Nazis, fueled by the sentiment that the Oberammergau Passion reinforced, and their victims. By the third act, this clear sense of progression dissipates. We see that Ruhl is not simply showing an escalation of force and violence in the name of religion. Leaders are not merely getting more charismatic and more dangerous. Her sense of time as a stage on which such dramas are played is far more complicated than that.

As the third act opens, the cast is backstage immediately following a performance. P, who plays Pilate, has just played his part for the last time before he will begin his first tour in Viet Nam. He also proposes to Mary 1, who plays the Virgin Mary. As he does so, Queen Elizabeth enters. It is she who places the ring on Mary's finger while blessing P, "Go forth into battle my son, and go with God."[31] From this early moment in the play, it is clear that time is out of joint. Between acts 1 and 2 there were echoed motifs—like measuring for the crucifixion; an evaluation of the arms of the actor playing; and a variety of symbolic biblically derived repetitions, including the sky turning to or from the color red, birds, and fish. But by act 3 the power of these reverberations has intensified to the point that epochs are colliding. In addition to the repetition of images—the fish, boats, and wind of act 1 reappear with a vengeance here, and the bird and sky imagery continues too—whole lines of text repeat, as when Mary 1 tells Mary 2 she is pregnant and when P says of Mary 1, "She is a deer wrapped in brown velvet. She is the air breathing inside the body of a violin."[32] Character and action seem to be at once in the late twentieth century and in the ages of Elizabeth and Hitler as well. This idea is clearly illustrated in an exchange between P and Violet, his young daughter, when he is home from war:

> **VIOLET**: When I was in the war, I was not a pilot.
> **P**: What do you mean, honey? What war?
> **VIOLET**: The war before.
> **P**: Before what?
> **VIOLET**: There is always a war before and a war after.
> **P**: Before this war you were safe, safe in your mother's stomach.
> **VIOLET**: Nope. There was a war before. I died.[33]

Because of this chronological multiplicity and instability, this act also features an intensification of concern in the characters for creating and discerning appearances of reality and the real. While P is away at war, J goes to college where he studies acting. When he comes back to perform in the Passion, he doesn't like the way the director is doing things and has opinions on what should and shouldn't be rehearsed. Trying to understand his point of view, Mary asks him, "You want it to feel real, right?"[34] J's college acting experience of pretending to smell lemons in class that makes him hunger for a particular kind of stage reality, but he doesn't know how to achieve it. Mary, who hasn't been away to college but did watch her father perform this same role for many years, suggests to J that he let his own experiences with betrayal infuse his performance.

Though he has none and must draw on the experience of others (he and Mary just betrayed P in the previous scene), he is still not able to create the emotion:

> J: It wasn't right. I wasn't feeling it.
> DIRECTOR: It was better.
> MARY 1: No! It wasn't better! You're still acting! My father—he never acted—he just told the story. There was no—effort. There was no—acting.[35]

Immediately thereafter the director works with the crew to tech the ascension. Never before have the Passion producers had this much technology at their disposal to create a fantastic illusion. In act 2, Eric was concerned with making his face glow for the audience through his own acting skill. But in act 3 the director can demand, "More light! No we want it back-lit! On the scrim! More smoke! (to J) Are you rigged? Are you strapped in? Now lift him up. Now the clouds part. The clouds part. Now look up at Him! . . . Now everyone freeze! And—blackout."[36]

P's time away from home teaches him a very different set of lessons, and his reintegration into the cast eventually proves impossible. First, he questions the way the text portrays Pontius Pilate. When he gets to the scene in which the crowd urges him to condemn Jesus and he bends to their will but says he washes his hands to avoid the guilt, instead of water, P sees blood everywhere and asks, "Is this fake blood or real blood?"[37] He also sees Hitler, who stands between him and the director. He tries to continue and to play the part as all those around him desire, but it is impossible. He says, "I, Pontius Pilate, at the desire of the whole Jewish people, condemn—Wait. The Jews are saying: kill Jesus! But they're religious men, right? And Pilate was a bad guy, a tyrant. How come they want to kill him and I'm being all heroic—like—no, no, I can't kill him?"[38] Eventually the conflict culminates in P hitting the director. Mary has to beg the director to reinstate her husband, but P has some hesitation about reclaiming his role. He says, "I don't want to be in the play anymore . . . I don't believe in God anymore,"[39] suggesting that genuine belief is necessary for playing these parts. But he goes to another rehearsal anyway, where he creates yet another tumultuous scene. He, the director, and J fight about how to play the reality and "humanity" of the scene for an audience of six thousand in an amphitheater. In order to make it "just real—two men talking," J suggests they be miked. J also admits he doesn't like P's performance. P responds, "You want real? . . . This nail is real . . . This wood is real . . . And my hand is real. You want to know about real sacrifice? It's in the body."[40] He then proceeds to drive the nail through his own hand. P's anger forces him into his body, out of his role and into J's, and away from his home and family.

Time passes. We don't see many of P's wanderings in the wilderness, but we do see his visit to a Veterans Administration (VA)[41] psychiatrist. He tells him, "I'll play Pontius Pilate the way he was meant to be played . . . Like a hung-over politician in a God-forsaken province who took stupid orders on a really bad fucking day."[42] And thus P is driven home again, where it turns out a benefit performance of the Passion will soon be played in honor of Ronald Reagan, who is in South Dakota campaigning in 1984. When P shows up at Mary's house, he's eager for a shower and a shave because "Pontius Pilate didn't have a beard. He was a Roman. He was clean shaven."[43] When Mary tries to explain that a professional actor now plays the part, P says, "Can he show what it's like to give orders to kill a man? Unless he's been there and seen what it's like up close— . . . I killed people—for that man—and no one wants to give me a fucking bar of soap."[44] Mary and P proceed to discuss political charisma. P says, "A likeable man becomes a tyrant just like any other man. In a democracy—likeability is tantamount to tyranny."[45]

When Mary aims to distinguish between this kind of charisma and evil, P says, "I can tell you, you don't feel the difference, when everyone gets zipped up in a body bag, and no one says anything about it, they just say, 'ZIP!' Because when there are guts—where skin should be—and skin, where guts should be—there's no difference between a nice guy and an evil guy who sent you out to kill. One of them is photogenic and the other one isn't—they both take you out and they go ZIP."[46] Again we feel the force of eras colliding because P repeats lines of Pontius's self-loathing from act 1. We hear the biblical, the Elizabethan, the mid-twentieth century, the late twentieth century, and surely the early twenty-first century as well bouncing off each other. We hear the voice of madness and of truth simultaneously.

So in the next scene, when Reagan comes to give the curtain speech and we see P confront him, we are tempted to expect the worst dramatically, even if we know how history actually played out. The themes of the entire play swirl together in this scene, forming what feels like a dangerous vortex. The Ronald Reagan character speaks of history, politics, and religion using metaphors drawn from the stage and acting in ways that the audience knows will only provoke P. P says, "This big stage this stage of history, this little block of wood separates you from your most terrible fantasies—it's important, this piece of wood, this stage, between you and it—." But before he can work through articulating the healing power of the stage, Reagan continues to spin his thoughts on baseball (earlier he had talked about calling the games on the radio and moving the fans though he himself couldn't see the game). P demands that the play be stopped. After P and Reagan salute each other, Reagan says, "I never did serve in the military, but I feel as though I did. I made training films for soldiers during the war. It was one of the happiest times of my life. What's the matter, son? Dontcha have a part in the play?"⁴⁷ P says he does not—and this feels like it should be the catalyst for tragedy. The mind races back into the pages of history, stopping at John Hinckley Jr. who also was an insane man without a part, though he was eager to recast himself as *Taxi Driver*'s Travis Bickle in hopes of winning the love of Jodie Foster. P then pulls out a gun. As the secret service agents leap for him he points the gun at himself before a blackout.

This is not the end of the play. There is a final scene, an epilogue, in which we learn that the stage did work its magic by separating P from his most terrible fantasy. He says, "I sat in my seat, and whispered: Mary, stop the play, and an old woman next to me said: shh."⁴⁸ He resisted the temptations of a devilish figure to leap onto the stage, not to turn stones into bread, to have angels break his fall or to worship him in return for all the kingdoms in the world as Jesus was tempted for forty days after his baptism, but to embody violence, striking out against a consummate actor who could spin seductive, destructive, politico-religious fantasies for his massive constituency. The play went on peacefully, as did the lives of the characters. He tells us where they are now: J is a soap opera actor, Mary receives part of his monthly disability checks, and Violet has become a painter with a favorite subject: birds. P meanwhile continues to drift, but he has found God again and some small measure if not of peace, at least of understanding: "I don't know if this country needs more religion or less of it. Seems to me everyone needs a good night's sleep. That way we'd all wake up for real in the morning. It's good to be awake. When you're awake you can fight for what you believe in, no matter what costume you're wearing."⁴⁹ P conducts the winds, bids a good night to the audience and to Violet, and sails off into the distance "on an enormous boat," through a chorus of boats, courtiers, and "big, beautiful fish puppets." In this closing image, P completes his performance not of Pontius Pilate but of Jesus. He crucified himself earlier in the play by driving the nail through his hand, and now he stages his own ascension.

Ruhl describes and evaluates some of P's famous ascensions:

> As for the boat that P gets on at the end of the play . . . at Arena Stage, P rigged himself into flying gear and ascended, with no boat. At the Goodman Theatre, where we had a fairly large budget, they constructed a massive boat that P got onto and sailed away. In Brooklyn, on our modest budget, we had a moving ladder (the large kind you hang lights with); P climbed it, a sail was attached to it, and the chorus moved him offstage. I was very fond of the "poor theatre" version in Brooklyn, as it allowed the audience to fill in the metaphor with their own imagination, and it used the simple tools of theater to create transformation: a little height, a little movement, a simple sail—and suddenly—an enormous boat.⁵⁰

Her preference for the staging that demands the audience's imaginative intervention is significant to her larger project not just in this final act but in the whole play. By play's end it has become clear that Ruhl has been playing with notions of eschatology, or the end of things, and wants her audience to join her actively in this thinking. The way P ascends is crucial to this project.

According to Valerie Karass, as feminist theologians have reconceived what eschatology might mean, locating it not merely in humanity but in a broader cosmology, they have shifted from a perception of eschatology as unrealized, or existing in some distant future, to eschatology as realized, or as part of the here and now. "Can we construct a human society which is radically different from the way human societies are currently structured? This is the essence of the distinction between realized and unrealized eschatology: the former answers yes to this question, the latter answers no."[51]

In the third act, as images and figures accumulate, we see time as not linear but circular. It becomes impossible that we might be moving toward an "end" historically or spiritually. We cannot hope for a better society later and we cannot wait for the kingdom of God to arrive at the dawning of some new epoch. P's lines are well worth repeating: " It's good to be awake. When you're awake you can fight for what you believe in, no matter what costume you're wearing." Ruhl urges her audience to wake up, to fight for what's right, regardless of the costume they've been wearing or the role in which they've been cast. In each act, characters recast themselves—sometimes for good and sometimes for ill. Ruhl shows us this is possible and potent. We have responsibility and we must use it wisely as we take our turns upon the stage.

Church

In an interview with the *Brooklyn Rail* prior to *Church*'s opening at PS 122 in the spring of 2007, Young Jean Lee told Eliza Bent, "With all the George W. Bush stuff . . . I was hearing more and more blanket beliefs that all Christians are evil morons . . . I have always been really hostile to Christianity. But then . . . my parents aren't evil morons . . . they're really smart, really good people. How crazy it is to say that an entire group of people is evil and that they're morons? Blanket mentality is really dangerous even when applied to someone who you think deserves it."[52] Though she colors her remarks with an edgier attitude, the sentiment undergirding Lee's comments is very similar to those Ruhl expressed in the quotation opening this chapter. Both writers are deeply concerned about the blanket mentality enveloping the country in 2007, but despite similar subject matter, they employ very different dramatic form.

Lee's form in *Church* is no doubt linked to her own experience with religion. Lee was raised in Washington State, where her parents, who were brought to the United States from Korea with the help of a missionary, were devout adherents to the Evangelical Free sect. She says, "As soon as I was born, they both directed all of their energy into making me a Christian. I converted when I was 5, but by the time I was 8, I sort of didn't believe anymore."[53] She attended church with them every Sunday despite the fact that "I would just sit there and look around at the people and hate them . . . just think how awful they were."[54] While she was in college at Berkeley she stopped attending church, became an atheist, and developed a circle of left-leaning peers who shared her distaste for devoutly religious people. She stayed at Berkeley after she finished her undergraduate degree in order to pursue a doctorate in English, but she dropped out in 2002 to move to New York and become a playwright.

In *The New York Times*, Lee was interviewed along with director Lear DeBessonet about how their experience with Christian fundamentalism has influenced in their work. Lee said, "The premise that all of my shows begin with is, I ask myself the question, 'What is the last show in the world that you would ever want to make?' Then I force myself to make that show. . . . For 'Church' the last show in the world I would ever want to do was an evangelical Christian service that's sincerely trying to convert the audience to Christianity, and that's not ironic or a joke or making fun of Christianity at all. That just seemed like a real nightmare and a challenge for me, and it has been."[55] Clearly religion has long made Lee uncomfortable, so in *Church* she tackles it head on, trying to find value in the very thing she had previously rejected. She said specifically of the play, "It's been an exercise in cutting away every audience defense. I had to come up with a system of morality that is something that I believe in but don't live by—any more than anyone I know lives by it."[56]

Her first strategy in cutting away the audience's defenses is the sincerity of performance that she demands from her four principals in the cast. She says in the note on performance that precedes the published text, "The performers are natural and sincere at all times. They should come across as real Christians who are doing an actual church service. They are unpretentious and appealing and never seem fake, pushy, or creepy . . . Everyone speaks with total conviction."[57]

Three of these speakers are women. Lee asks that these reverends be named after the women who are the playing them. She thus reinforces a sense of naturalness by collapsing performer and character—the character is at once a mask covering a real performer and a marker of that real performer as she operates outside the theater.

Reverend José is different. While the names of the female characters vary from production to production, the sole male stays the same. But even this is somewhat complicated—José was not played by a Latino at either PS 122 or the Public. He was in both cases played by a Caucasian Anglo. Writing on the plays collected in *Songs of the Dragons Flying to Heaven* (in which *Church* is anthologized) Jeffrey M. Jones says, "If there is an 'issue' that crops up throughout these plays, it's racism."[58] In some of her plays, Lee confronts racism explicitly and centrally, but in *Church*, this characteristic concern is more subtle and peripheral. Common cultural expectations of the way names and faces might match and which faces are most likely to be found at church are challenged. Jones quotes Lee on her attitude toward race in her plays: "I'm just trying to transplant the confused jumble of racial stuff in my head into the audience's head so that they're forced to think about it and be disturbed by it in a way that they wouldn't be if I were trying to preach some message at them. I want them to recognize contradictory aspects of themselves and explore their own reactions and motives. I just want them to think, and come to their own conclusions."[59]

Just as José may challenge audiences in terms of their racial assumptions, he may also challenge them in terms of their gendered assumptions about church leadership. José gets the first word, the last word, and the bulk of the nonchorally recited words in between. The three other reverends are clearly secondary presences. The place of women in worship is a significant issue within feminist theology. Outside of scholarly circles perhaps the best-known area of inquiry is advocacy for women's ordination, and within the play, clearly the women are named as reverends. They have the opportunity to give testimony to their particular experiences, so those stories of faith and temptation are not lost. But there are, as Susan A. Ross argues, other things to consider. She writes,

> Feminist explorations and critiques of worship extend, of course, beyond inclusion of women in traditional preaching and presiding roles. The choice of lectionary readings for the church year as well as the kinds of bodily postures worshippers are expected to take raise profound questions about the formative role of worship. The ancient formula lex orandi lex credenda, the law of praying is the law of believing—or, we believe what we worship—suggests that liturgy shapes the person, even in ways we may not be aware of. Thus the exclusion of women from the lectionary suggests that we inherit and transmit a tradition in which women's contributions . . . are absent. The forms of prayer that we use in asking for forgiveness, in standing (or kneeling) before God, suggest relationships of male dominance and female submission, relationships that are all too often imitated in daily life.[60]

So if viewers come to the theater expecting a male to be the leader of worship, they will be surprised to find three female reverends. But if they come expecting women to have a full and equal presence in worship, then they may be disappointed. Surely one of the questions Lee poses is what place should women have in the worship service.

In this regard and in a couple of other key ways, Lee seems set on clearing away the false gods that her viewers—believers and nonbelievers—may have about what church is and does. A passage from the groundbreaking *Beyond God the Father* by Mary Daly (feminist theology's most famous proponent) seems almost tailor-made for Lee:

> If it is true that human beings have projected "God" in their own image, it is also true that we can evolve beyond the projections of earlier stages of consciousness. It is the creative potential itself in human beings that is the image of God. As the essential victims of the archaic God-projections, women can bring this process of creativity into a new phase. This involves iconoclasm—the breaking of idols. Even—and perhaps especially—through the activity of most militantly atheistic and a-religious members, the movement is smashing images that obstruct the becoming of the image of God. The basic idol-breaking will be done on the level of internalized images of male superiority, on the plane of exorcising them from consciousness and from the cultural institutions that breed them.[61]

Daly urges the clearing away of three particularly harmful ideas about the nature of God: that God can be used as a stopgap for incompleteness of human knowledge (that things are unanswerable and should simply be understood as "God's will"); that he is characterized by otherworldliness, so that justice in this life might be deferred in hopes of some eternal recompense; and that he is a judge who instills "false guilt," making women feel guilty for seeking abortion rights, birth control, and nonsubmissive roles in family structures and at church.

Through the course of the play, Lee, who positions herself as "militantly atheistic" takes aim at most of these false idols. In regard to the image of God, after admitting that he doesn't know for a fact that God exists because "the world is a mystery," Reverend José says, "I keep referring to God as a 'he' because this is a patriarchal, sexist culture and many people find it more comforting to think of God as a father—but you can call God whatever you want."[62]

And though he says that "humans are filled with sin," he means the sin of complacency not the sin of rebellion: "Jesus didn't go around picking on people for having premarital sex or drinking too much or being homosexuals—he was not interested in condemning people for their personal lives. Jesus was interested in the things that we experience as clichéd abstractions: police brutality, illegal immigrants in prison, the child living in poverty trying to do his homework without electricity."[63]

Reverend Weena expands, "We must stand against racial discrimination, homophobia, anti-abortion, capital punishment, commercialism, war, and indifference . . . We believe that it is a sin to engage in masturbation-rage against the perpetrators of this evil without doing anything concrete to create change."[64] Thus Weena also makes clear that action in the here and now is essential. People are not allowed to sit by, turning the other cheek or waiting for a reward in heaven. They should fight social injustice actively and now.

While this portion of the rhetoric proceeds rationally, that is not the only mode Lee employs. Her reverends tell stories ripe with extravagant language and surreal imagery that pushes her auditors past logic. José says, "I have walked through the wilderness, and I have seen the cacti looming, bulbous as watermelons, their long quills extruding like hairs from a boil. And then their bobbing forms were upon me, piercing my heart like a grape and lifting me high into the air whilst my blood pooled at their feet."[65] José's message evokes nearly all the senses as he tells of this magical experience, which eventually leads to the devil appearing to tempt José, offering to rescue him from the pain of the cacti. The desert scene then turns icy, and more fantastical creatures appear:

> And then one day I was walking down an icy street I saw a beautiful pathway of stars stretched out before me leading up to the sky, and a unicorn came to me and said, "My dear son, I am coming to you in this vision because I knew that you would accept me in no other way. You are in the grips of a powerful fetishistic obsession with magic and fantasy, which are of the Devil and you can see nothing that is not filtered through that evil. I am here to tell you that I am a mummy, an evil mummy who wants to turn you away from the Lord and lure you into the valley of suffering and death."[66]

Jeffrey Jones interprets Lee's strategy thus: "*Church*, the least ironic of Lee's plays, turns out to be a surprisingly powerful demonstration of the thesis misattributed to Tertullian: credo quia absurdum ('I believe because it is absurd.') and raises for the first time the only possible alternative to the crazy confusion of the world—the crazy possibility of hope."[67]

Lee takes a second, complementary path to the metarational: she uses music and dance. She explains her choice: "Because I am my target audience the entire show was just to reach me and try to convert myself. It was definitely the most difficult thing I've ever—I really had to pull out all the stops and all of the dancing, all the singing all of the entertaining stuff in the show is basically for me so that I can handle, so that I can survive all of the stuff which just makes me feel terrible." And indeed she does pull out all the stops, using a variety of musical forms, some conveyed through recorded music and others performed live.

Lee includes three pieces of recorded music, giving her auditors expert renditions of famous songs. Stage directions indicate that "Sherburne" by the Alabama Sacred Harp Singers, Mahalia Jackson's version of "Joshua Fit the Battle of Jericho," and "Every Move I Make" by Passion should be part of the show. And the final piece of music in the show is performed live—a sixty-person gospel choir, call and response, "Ain't Got Time to Die." All four pieces of music have deep connections to Christian worship, but the fifth piece, performed by the three female reverends is an a cappella version of "Bread" by on!air!library!. As one review said of the now defunct independent band, "The trio play somewhere between pop and experimental music, but their songs mostly land on one side or the other . . . 'Bread' is a drinking song for shoegazers."[68] Lee's reinvention of this song for her religious service is significant. She gives her downtown audience the sort of lyrics with which they are likely familiar, but she radically recontextualizes them. She shows them how the soundtrack of their daily lives might be transformed into something sacred.

Analysis of the praise dance in the show is difficult, both because it does not exist on the page—though it has been captured on YouTube—and because scholarly attention has not yet been paid to this form. Academic search engines turn up only passing references to the phenomenon, but a Google search yields instructive choreography video, associations, and many opportunities to purchase dance wear. There are also many popular sites that discuss praise dance. I was particularly struck by this passage:

> The only true requirement to be a praise dancer is a willingness to be empty of self, so that you can become full of Him. Ability, training, talent, or gracefulness aren't requirements, just a heart that truly wants to worship the Lord. In fact, training, talent, and ability can get in the way, because they can be the tools that Satan uses to bring pride into our dance, instead of a heart of worship.
>
> That doesn't mean that training isn't helpful though. Just like singing, or playing an instrument in worship, it is necessary to learn it. When you sing, you are using the vocabulary of the language, and the notes to express your worship. If you play an instrument, you need to learn a vocabulary of notes for each instrument you learn to play. Otherwise, you won't sound a clear note . . . To praise the Lord in dance, you should learn the vocabulary of movement. This will give you the necessary "words" to use in expressing your love to Jesus.[69]

A new language—whether of praise or entertainment—seems to be what this kind of dance, at its best, is capable of providing. It reaches viewers in a different way so that a message, whether fundamentalist Christian or avant-garde theatrical, might land on an audience with force.

Ultimately Lee uses every tool in her considerable arsenal to effect change in her audience. She takes on her own fear and confusion, and turns them into a theatrically powerful verbal, musical, and physical meditation on how faith might look and resonate beyond its popularly assumed demographic.

100 Saints You Should Know

Kate Fodor's play on faith and religion differs markedly from Ruhl's and Lee's. Hers is, especially by comparison, a traditionally structured play. Three key relationships—between an ousted priest, Matthew, and his faith-seeking cleaning lady, Theresa; between Theresa and her teenage daughter, Abby; and between Matthew and his aging mother, Colleen—converge when Colleen's young neighbor, Garrett, falls to his death after a night of drinking with Abby. It also differs in terms of its path to the stage and the stage on which it first fully landed. While a part of Ruhl's play first saw production while she was a student and then went through years of full-production development at prestigious theaters around the country and abroad, and while Lee as the artistic director of her own company was able to mount her show as soon as she deemed it ready at the quintessential downtown New York space PS 122, Fodor's play—only her second after 2003's Blackburn Prize–nominated *Hannah and Martin*—had readings at Hartford Stage, Playwrights Horizons, Steppenwolf, and Chautauqua before it had its world premiere at Playwrights Horizons. But despite these differences in form and production history, Fodor expressed a similar sentiment to Ruhl and Lee about religion in America:

> I feel like it's easy at this particular historical moment if you are not a religious person to begin to feel like religious people are the enemy, and I'm sure it's also true in the opposite direction. What I have strong objections to is fanaticism in any form. One of the reasons I love theater is that it teaches people to respect how many voices and points of view there are in the world and the subtlety of things. So it was important to me to look at religion in a respectful—no, not even respectful—that's wrong—to look at religion in an empathic way, to try to feel what it feels like, to understand it.[70]

Before analyzing the play itself, it is useful to see how Fodor came to write this play in particular. Unlike Lee, and unlike Ruhl, who was raised Catholic, she was not raised in a religious home. She grew up in Connecticut and New York City, the child of a philosophy professor and a linguistics professor. Of her religious background Fodor has said, "It was so obvious that we weren't a religious household that we didn't even talk about it. We didn't even say, 'We're atheists and here's why.' I just didn't really know people who went to church; my family didn't go to church, my grandparents didn't go to church. It just was not part of the world I knew."[71] She was, however, "baptized, the whole thing, full immersion," when she was 12 and spending time with her Connecticut neighbors. She said in a *Los Angeles Times* interview, "It was a sort of lonely period of my childhood, and there was a family with a lot of kids who offered to pick me up and drive me to church and to the youth meetings. There was this incredible sense of community and bustle and joy that was completely missing from my life there otherwise."[72]

While her parents didn't encourage religious devotion, they did encourage the arts, taking her to plays and surrounding her with books—some of which they had written themselves. When it was time for high school, she attended St. Ann's in Brooklyn Heights, a school known for its arts programs. There she acted in plays and took creative writing classes. Then it was on to Oberlin where she majored in English and emphasized creative writing. Up to this point, her writing was exclusively in the fiction genre. After college, and after a two-year stint in Teach for America, she worked as a business journalist for Reuters, writing about pharmaceuticals.

When Adam Szymkowicz asked Fodor about her theatrical heroes, she told him, "Margaret Edson is one, because she came in, wrote a gorgeous, heart-stopping, fiercely funny, unbearably tragic play, and then went back to teaching kindergarten, because that's important, too."[73] Given the trajectory of her studies and career, the answer makes great sense, since she too came to playwriting from the outside. She had, however, long been friends with Melissa Friedman and Ron Russell of the Epic Theatre Company (the same company that would stage *Passion Play* in 2010), and they inspired and encouraged her writing of *Hannah and Martin*. Fodor tells of having lunch with Friedman and talking about Hannah Arendt's life. She remembers Friedman saying, "There's a part I'd love to play onstage." Fodor continues, "On the way home on the subway, I was thinking it would actually be a really interesting play and that maybe it was something I could do."[74] So she started writing on the weekends while maintaining her day job at Reuters, until she was laid off there. She used the severance package to complete the play, and her life as a playwright had begun.

Before long she decided to write another play—*100 Saints*. In a *New York Times* interview regarding her method in composing *Hannah and Martin*, she said, "I tried to think about it from each character's point of view and not align myself with one camp or another."[75] The same strategy would serve her well as she felt inspired to create something new, contemporary, and intimate. She was also struck by a news story she read about the pedophilia scandal in the Catholic Church that referenced the priest's cleaning lady. She says, "I knew I wasn't interested in writing about the sex scandal itself, but I got sort of fascinated by the idea of what it would be like to be a priest's housekeeper, since it seemed like it would be your job to cross the line into some sort of intimacy, you know washing his dishes and folding his socks, things most of us don't think of in connection with a priest."[76] It is this particular intimacy that launches the first scene of the play. As the lights come up, the audience sees Theresa on her knees—not lost in prayer, but scrubbing a toilet. Matthew enters, and is surprised to find her there because he's forgotten she's there to do the cleaning. They have only a brief and awkward exchange in which he eventually admits to the physical need that propelled him in there. Thus Fodor introduces one of her key themes with only a few lines of dialogue.

As the scenes of the play unfold, the audience begins to learn of the desires driving both Theresa and Matthew. Matthew has moved back in with his mother, Colleen, for at least three weeks. He was caught with artistic nude male photographs and has been relieved of his duties in his parish to contemplate his error. While Matthew seems to be straying from the path of religious devotion, Theresa, the single mother of a teenage daughter, is finding herself increasingly drawn to it. After she cleans Matthew's empty living quarters and finds his copy of *Dark Night of the Soul*, by the sixteenth-century mystic St. John of the Cross, she uses the book as an excuse to seek out Matthew. After she returns the book, she says to him, "I guess I have some questions about God and maybe prayer."[77]

Theresa isn't the only person seeking Matthew's spiritual guidance. Her daughter Abby rode along with her mother to return the book to Matthew, but she fails to stay in the car as her mother instructed. After she chooses to relieve herself behind a tree, she meets Garrett. Garrett also has a question for Matthew, which he first confesses to Abby. She summarizes and mocks, "You wanted to ask a priest whether it's okay for you to be looking at gay guys having sex on the internet? That was your big plan for coming here?"[78] And in addition to taking his confession, she offers him penance: "Take five shots, take off your clothes, stand on your head and say ten Hail Marys! Go!"[79]

Abby's idea for penance leads to disaster. Garrett follows the "ceremony" Abby prescribes, climbs a tree, and falls. The scene shifts from Colleen's house and yard to the hospital. There Abby, Theresa, and Matthew discuss communication with the divine—how one gets called by God, how one loses the path to God, and the meaning of prayer—as they tensely await news of Garrett's condition.

As Garrett was falling from the tree, Matthew was telling the audience first how he got called to service, and then how he feels he's fallen from grace: "He called me through beauty. In the church there was incense and quiet. Dark wood. Masses and requiems . . . But I know, also, now, that one can be called away from God by beauty . . . When I look at the pictures, I inhabit the bodies of the men; I don't look at them as objects of desire; I become them . . . I feel for the first time since I was child what it might mean to have a body. Maybe even what it might mean to have a body in relation to another person's body."[80] Though the images that attracted Garrett were pornographic rather than artistic, both men have been drawn by physicality and desire into a territory that discomfits them and others.

Feminist spirituality is an aspect of feminist theology that addresses the problems felt by Matthew and Garrett. Nicola Slee explains, "There is a strong emphasis on desire, eros, and passion in much contemporary feminist spirituality which may be seen as a reconceptualisation of the Spirit's work of inspiring, energising, and enlivening faith in ways which take seriously the human body, emotions, and drives. Matthew Fox suggests that 'a feminist spirituality as distinct from a patriarchal one will value the erotic and teach us disciplines of erotic celebrating, creating and justice making.'"[81] Rather than marking the desires of the body as sinful, feminist spirituality opens possibilities for embracing this part of life within faith.

Matthew and Theresa continue to explore issues of embodiment and moral conduct in the hospital as they wait for word on Garrett's condition. They consider whether thoughts and desires without actions can be wrong, and Matthew eventually explains, "There's not a lot of touching in this kind of life. I don't really touch anyone, and no one touches me, which is OK, because I'm not very comfortable with being touched."[82] Matthew and Theresa work to understand how a desiring body might be reconciled with a faith that seems to distrust sensuality and how the need for human connection might be satisfied if physicality has been prohibited. Their ideas resonate with those articulated by feminist theologian Sarah Coakley in her essay, "The Trinity, Prayer, and Sexuality."

Coakley's first thesis, as she calls it, reads thus: "the revival of a vibrant Trinitarian conceptuality of an 'earthed' sense of the meaningfulness and truth of the Christian doctrine of the Trinity, most naturally arises out of a simultaneous commitment to prayer, and especially prayer of a relatively wordless kind."[83] In discussing her quest to understand Saint Theresa, Theresa researches the saint on the Internet. Theresa discovers that "she said, 'For me, prayer is a surge of the heart, a cry of recognition and love.'"[84] This seems to be what transpires between Theresa and Matthew in the hospital waiting room. When he reveals his need for human connection, Theresa offers to touch him the way she sometimes touches Abby. He sits in front of her, and she touches him silently. In this delicate, intimate moment, which in the Playwrights Horizons production conjured an image of the Pieta, the audience has the sense of a silent form of prayer in which both Theresa's and Matthew's hearts are experiencing that surge of recognition and love.

Coakley finds that exploration of this kind of prayer will lead to a profound realization about the entwined desires of humans for God and for sex. She writes, "In any prayer in which we radically cede control to the Spirit there is an instant reminder of the close analogue between this ceding (to a Trinitarian God) and the *ekstasis* of human sexual passion. Thus it is not a coincidence that intimate relation is at the heart of both of these matters."[85] The kind of prayer that both Coakley and Fodor evoke—whether in word or stage image—has the potential to bring embodied experience back into the fold of faith without the kind of guilt and denigration that Coakley notes has historically cast "the non-celibate woman or homosexual . . . as the distractor from the divine goal."[86]

Coakley ultimately argues,

> We need to turn Freud on his head. Instead of thinking of "God" language as really being about sex (Freud's reductive ploy), we need to understand sex as really about God, and about the deep desire that we feel for God—the clue that

is woven into our existence about the final and ultimate union that we seek. And it matters in this regard—or so I submit—that the God we desire is, in Godself, a desiring Trinitarian God: the Spirit who longs for our response, who searches the hearts, and takes us to the divine source (the "Father"), transforming us Christically as we are so taken.[87]

The God Coakley describes echoes the desires of the characters in Fodor's play. Theresa's line about prayer as "a surge of the heart, a cry of recognition and love," is repeated by Theresa as she and Abby finally come to an understanding of each other and their needs and by Matthew as he and Colleen at last find a bond in their experience of loneliness.

In the penultimate scene in the play, the antagonism that has colored Abby and Theresa's relationship falls away. Garrett does, in fact, die from his injuries. At the hospital, before she is questioned by the police about the incident, Matthew suggests that Abby might pray for forgiveness when she tells him how she felt about Garrett's accident: "When he fell and he hit the ground really hard like that and bounced back up again? It was satisfying. I liked it. That's gotta make me a bad person, don't you think?"[88] She declines Matthew's offer because she doesn't believe there is a God to hear her and opts to go to the cafeteria instead. But by this late scene with her mother, Abby is able to say simply, "I feel really bad about that kid, Mom . . . I feel so bad."[89] She's also able to admit the part she played in what happened: "It happened because I'm so mean." Theresa aims to absolve her of the guilt, not by prescribing penance, but simply by explaining to her, "I want to be different too, you know."[90] In the Playwrights Horizons production, the two come together physically, this time with Abby holding Theresa in a Pieta-esque pose. Abby questions what her mother is looking for when she watches televangelists, but she also tries to understand what she is saying about faith:

> **ABBY:** Is that why you've been watching that God show on TV? . . . They're liars on those shows, Mom.
> **THERESA:** I know. But that doesn't mean there isn't something out there worth trying to find.
> **ABBY:** Like what?
> **THERESA:** A surge of the heart, a cry of recognition and love.
> **ABBY:** What does that mean?
> **THERESA:** I don't know. It has to do with God. Or maybe just some kind of spirit or—connectedness or something.[91]

The union of Abby and Theresa isn't sexual, but their connection is intimate and complete. They connect not just emotionally but spiritually, and in this their hearts surge and they recognize each other fully. This idea reverberates powerfully with feminist spirituality, which Nicola Slee argues has "an emphasis on relationality, connectedness, and community . . . which invites new ways of grasping the work of the Holy Spirit in forging bonds and creating koinonia."[92]

In the final scene, Colleen and Matthew also forge a new connection. Their path to this moment is as rocky as Theresa and Abby's was. When Matthew returns home from the hospital, he tells his mother that he was unable to administer last rites to the dying boy; he could only hold his hand as the doctor rushed about frantically and the machines whirred. This leads to the climax of their conflict over Matthew's crisis of faith. Matthew has explained neither the surface details nor the subtext of his hiatus from service to the church. He tells his mother, "I don't know if I love God properly anymore." Colleen thinks this has to do with Theresa and Matthew's desire for her, not even beginning to understand who or what her son might desire. Matthew tries again to explain what he longs for:

MATTHEW: A surge of the heart, a cry of recognition and love.
COLLEEN: What about God's love? What about the love God has for you?
MATTHEW: Sometimes I feel God like a gentle hand on my back, guiding me. I really do . . . But that's not much. A fatherly hand on one's back isn't much to serve as one's whole life's experience of intimacy is it?[93]

And though Matthew is here trying to explain his need for sexual, physical connection, as the argument continues, what he is really seeking is parental love from his mother. When Colleen asks, "What should I love you for," Matthew replies "For nothing, Ma! For nothing! That's what you're supposed to love me for!"[94] He wants not only the sexual love of a partner but the unearned and total love that only parents—human and divine—are supposed to be able to give. But his mother, at this point, can only repeat, "You should pray."[95]

This scene ends, and the Abby and Theresa scene plays out before Colleen and Matthew are reconciled. Colleen wakes from sleep and is overwhelmed with obsessive thoughts about what the loss of Garrett will mean to his parents. She wants to pray—with Matthew for Garrett. But first she says, as she's kneeling, "I didn't know you were so lonely . . . I know what lonely is, with my husband dead six years. I wouldn't wish it on my son."[96] At last they are able to pray together. Matthew is able to speak the prayer of commendation, sending Garrett and himself off to God. He and his mother have at last been able to recognize something that binds them together, their hearts surge, and Matthew finds his way back to spirituality and prayer.

As Fodor was explaining how as an atheist she had written this play, she said, "There are religious leaders and religious movements that I disapprove of, but I don't disapprove of a yearning for God, if that's what you have in your heart.

At the same time, I think part of the reason I liked these two characters sort of moving in opposite directions, is that there are also other ways of being loving and living fully in the world and fulfilling yearnings."[97] But at play's end, the two characters' opposite directions and distinct yearnings seem to have met at the same point on the circle of faith. Neither has abandoned the power of prayer, and both are working toward an understanding, not unlike Slee's and Coakley's, of how prayer and embodied life need not be at odds.

In her introduction to *Passion Play*, Ruhl acknowledges the scope of her text but still voices her hopes for how it might be produced:

> Ideally *Passion Play* (Parts One, Two, and Three) would be performed all together in one evening (it should run about three hours plus intermissions) or else in rotating repertory. Together, the three parts form a cycle play—alone they do something different, but they can technically stand alone. If done in repertory, I suggest doing Parts One and Two on one night, and Part Three on the next. If the resources of one theater are too limited to produce the entire cycle, I can imagine two theaters in one city collaborating to put up the cycle together. In the original guild productions of the Passion, the carpenters in the village would handle the crucifixion scene and the bakers would handle the Last Supper. Perhaps our theatrical communities could borrow from the primitive guild model.[98]

After reading the plays of Ruhl, Lee, and Fodor beside one another, I too yearn for our theatrical communities to borrow from the guild model, but not in order to collaborate on Ruhl's work alone. I revel in imagining theater companies across a city working instead to stage all three of these women's work, because, like the cycle plays that Ruhl emulated, the three stories together paint a profound picture. The cycles were often organized in order to show a repetition of figures or analogies within biblical history that served to tie all the books of the Bible together into a coherent whole. In the cycle that I imagine, we would see the variations on the repeated motifs of sanctification, grace, and transformed imagery that Ruhl, Lee, and Fodor created resonating powerfully as their messages and techniques would be amplified when fully realized together.

CHAPTER 5

Mobile Lines

In "Transporting the Subject: Technologies of Mobility and Location in an Era of Globalization," Caren Kaplan writes, "As technologies of transportation and communication become more and more disembodied, more and more displaced from corporeality, and more and more a practice of mind and of simulation, the unified subject of the European Enlightenment is less and less a requirement. Whether or not we believe such a creature exists ever existed, the shift in the paradigm of the subject is significant enough to warrant theorization."[1] It is also significant enough to warrant dramatization, and that is precisely what Sarah Ruhl, Bathsheba Doran, and Quiara Alegría Hudes do in the three plays I will analyze in this chapter.

In *Dead Man's Cell Phone*, *Kin*, and *Water by the Spoonful*, Ruhl and her contemporaries explore the terrain of intimacy when mobile technologies—of wireless communication, Internet chat rooms, social networking, and international travel—have redrawn the dramatic subject's spatial boundaries. As Kaplan notes, "The oscillation and tension between the liberating promise of mobility and the security of fixed location is one of modernity's most enduring and oppositional binaries."[2] She observes not only the long history of the oppositional pairing but its continued and pervasive presence in contemporary discourses on globalized culture. Ruhl, Doran, and Hudes transport the binary and its many related permutations into their plays: the lines demarcating the public and the private, the internal and the external, home and away, and the native and the foreign blur in global networked society and are in flux, in process, and in contention in these texts. When the female characters at or near the center of each play—Jean, Anna, Haikumom/Odessa, and Yaz—negotiate a sense of self and place, Ruhl, Doran, and Hudes ask, how and where can they ground the relationships that define them and how they might distinguish the moral from the immoral as they create the maps for shaping and maintaining these relationships? The characters traverse boundaries marked by technology, geography, class, language, and morality as they try to resituate themselves as efficacious subjects capable of mapping their own destinies and realizing their desires while they connect to others around them.

Dead Man's Cell Phone

As *Dead Man's Cell Phone* opens, Jean sits at a table in a café. She's finished her soup and is drinking coffee and writing a letter. There is but one other person in the café. According to the stage directions, he sits with his back to the audience, very still. When his cell phone starts ringing incessantly, shattering the lonely peace of her reverie, Jean eventually comes to understand—after thinking he was either asleep or deaf—that the man is in fact dead, and she chooses to answer his phone. Repeatedly. Jean makes the tenuous journey from her quiet, vintage space of isolated but nourished comfort to the loud, fast new dimension of global information and wireless communication. She leaves the tranquility of her own life and enters the turmoil of Gordon's. As she's waiting for the ambulance to come, she promises Gordon (twice) that she'll stay with him. The audience soon learns that she didn't mean only until the ambulance arrived. She prays in the next scene, "Help me to help the memory of Gordon live on in the minds and hearts of his loved ones."[3] In the following scenes it becomes clear that Jean wants to replace the actual Gordon with a better, more sensitive and moral version who reflects back to Jean her own desires as she travels through the intimate and networked spaces of his life.

Before we follow Jean on her journey, we should be mindful of the strange place in which the opening scene takes place, as this provides crucial orientation for the rest of the play. In the premiere New York production designed by G. W. Mercier, the café seemed abstracted and theatricalized—with considerable space between the spare tables and dramatic shafts of light evoking a sense of Edward Hopper's urban isolation, but place did not become absurd until Jean attempted to locate the café for the emergency operator on the other end of the cell phone. The text reads, "I'm at a café. I don't know. Hold on. *She exits with the cell phone to look at the name of the café and the address. We just see the dead man and an empty stage. She returns.* It's on the corner of Green and Goethe. *(Pronounced Go-thee)* . . . There seems to be no one working at this café." As Jean seeks help for Gordon, we realize she literally doesn't know where she is. Because of the pronunciation of Goethe, and our biographical knowledge of Ruhl herself who grew up in Illinois and still has strong connections to the Chicago theater scene, we get the vague sense of the famous Chicago street with the name that is frequently mispronounced by nonnatives. Jean's facility with the name tells us something about her roots. But it is nevertheless odd that Jean and Gordon are alone in a public place—there are no other customers and there are no employees. The strange isolation should warn us that place will not function in conventional ways in the play. The final stage direction in the scene calls for the sounds of sirens, rain, and church. The aural, the key sense engaged in early cell phone culture, rather than the visual, will propel us from the first place and scene to the next.

Jean begins her journey in a church—at a funeral mass for Gordon. As Mrs. Gottlieb, Gordon's mother, begins her eulogy, a cell phone interrupts her. Though she had just been expressing her thanks for the particular space of churches because grief requires "a sensation of height," her language swerves low when she hears the ring: "Could someone please turn their fucking cell phone off. There are only one or two sacred places left in the world today. Where there is no ringing. The theater, the church, and the toilet."[4]

Mrs. Gottlieb's barb points to what sociologists have called the domestication of public space. Krishan Kumar and Ekaterina Makarova explain the way technology is changing the ways the two interdependent realms are demarcated: "We take the private world of the home out into the public sphere. We privatize or 'domesticate' the public space. We carry our private lives and private emotions with us into the world of the public." A particular situation they analyze is behavior in public places designed for private contemplation: "Society has ordered its arrangements in such a way that it has allowed for the existence of these public places where certain kinds of private activities can occur without breaching any of the accepted understandings governing the relations between public and private . . . Their spatial and physical character as public sets certain limits on what can be said and done, if not thought and felt. In certain respects they shade off into those public spaces that are sites of sociability-another way, as we shall see, of conceiving being private in public."[5] Ruhl's scene complicates this description. If we are expected to be private in the public space of the church, what happens when we insist on continuing our usual mediated public behavior instead regardless of the special aspects of a space? The mourners, Jean included, do in fact break the conventions of the private-public place by allowing their phones to ring—again it is the aural, rather than the visual, that dismantles place.

Mrs. Gottlieb recomposes herself and begins to talk about Charles Dickens's *A Tale of Two Cities* and particularly the idea that "every human creature is constituted to be that profound secret and mystery to every other,"[6] but she doesn't get much further before the phone Jean has taken from Gordon starts to ring. Sandwiched between the signals for these calls, the audience senses that constant public communication challenges this antique notion of the mysterious human soul. Frustrated, Mrs. Gottlieb gives up on her eulogy and calls for a hymn. "You'll Never Walk Alone" begins to play, prompting Mrs. Gottlieb to declare, "You'll never walk alone. That's right. Because you'll always have a machine in your pants that might ring."[7] Though the line is likely to elicit laughter from the audience, Ruhl's message here is quite serious. Technology has radically re-placed human interaction and is dismantling what once was deemed sacred and private.

But however clear this message may be to the audience, it is not clear to Jean. She eagerly answers the phone and sets up meetings with the people in Gordon's life. Her first meeting is with "The Other Woman" who in addition to being the only character in the play named for her function in his life, dresses like Jean. "The Other Woman" is thus other to Gordon's wife, but she is also the Other Jean. The Other Woman talks about changing behavior in public places: "Women are responsible for enlivening dull places like train stations. There is hardly any pleasure in waiting for a train anymore. The women just—walk in. Horrible shoes. No confidence. Bad posture."[8] The Other Woman describes how a glamorous woman should make an entrance—doing so is a public act generated with her audience in mind. She self-constructs and she self-promotes. Instead the contemporary woman isn't interested in performing this version of femininity for public consumption. She is literally pedestrian. She is not concerned with her presence on the public stage, only getting where she needs to go. We also get our first intimation of the nowhere of transit—now that there is no pleasure in the waiting for a train. Later we will hear about the more contemporary spaces of subway cars and luggage claims counters in airports where place has been even more radically altered.

Despite her sexy and confident façade and despite the fact that she forswears the sentimental, The Other Woman is hungry to learn Gordon's last words. Jean claims that Gordon declared his love for her right before he died. The Other Woman doesn't express the joy Jean anticipates, however. She is frustrated that she hears the sentiment from Jean instead of Gordon himself and calls him "a shit."[9] Not content to let Gordon be Gordon, or to let him walk alone in the memories of others, Jean embellishes further, "He said that other women seemed like clocks compared to you—other women just—measured time—broke the day up—but that you—you stopped time. He said you—stopped time—just by walking into a room."[10] Jean quickly learns how to improvise off what her conversational partners give her as she aims to transform Gordon into the poetic soul he was not. She plays off the notion of how the desirable woman walks into a room and links this image to another aspect of the nowhere of transportation—the illusion of time suspended.

Jean's next encounter is with Mrs. Gottlieb in the private space of the Gottlieb home. Again, Jean rewrites the story of Gordon's interactions with those closest to him. When Mrs. Gottlieb reveals that she and her son were estranged Jean tells her that Gordon tried to call her the day he died. She claims that Mrs. Gottlieb's phone number was listed on the "out-going calls."[11] Her phrasing draws attention to the fact that calls are like travelers—incoming and outgoing—taking journeys loosed from the bodies that launch them. This small tale earns Jean an invitation to a family dinner with Gordon's wife and brother. Here Jean's "confabulations" as Ruhl refers to them in her notes for the director at the printed play's conclusion, shift from mere words to material objects: Jean delivers gifts from the café to each of Gordon's family members. As the scene begins, the family is playing a kind of musical chairs around the table. After Mrs. Gottlieb declares, "Place cards, there are place cards!"[12] the stage directions note that everyone moves about landing in the wrong spot. We get the sense from this moment that identity is mobile and arbitrary at least on the surface if not on a deeper level. An innocuous-seeming object like a place card can in fact dictate meaning and definition to those who feel they lack it. Jean's stories and their gifts only accentuate this notion. For Gordon's wife Hermia, Jean brings a salt shaker. Jean says, "He said you were the salt of the earth."[13] For his brother Dwight, Jean brings a cup—"Because you can hold things. Beautiful things. And they don't—pour out." With these two gifts, Jean is quite successful. The recipients are moved by these supposed tokens of remembrance, and at the same time we see Jean longing to ground the people she encounters and to endow them with stability. But when she gives Gordon's mother a spoon, "Because of your cooking,"[14] Jean's narrative success comes to an end. Mrs. Gottlieb shrieks, "He could not have meant that nicely!" and storms off stage. Though the objects were in themselves bereft of meaning until Jean reimagined them, when she repositioned them inside a fantasy of Gordon's final moments they accrued new significance for themselves and the recipients—sometimes exceeding Jean's intentions. Individuals' places in relationships are revisited and redefined through the gifts and Jean's stories.

Soon Jean and Dwight find themselves alone, and they discuss the value and meaning of remembrance. Jean tells Dwight that she works at the Holocaust Museum, a job that she says is sad but that allows her to practice the art of remembering: "I want to remember everything. Even other people's memories."[15] They also debate whether remembering requires something tangible. Dwight says, "These digital cameras—you know—and all the digital—stuff—the informational bits—flying through the air—no one wants to remember. People say I love you—on cell phones—and where does it go? No paper. Remembering requires paper."[16]

Dwight's view of the interference of digital screen culture with the act of remembering might be enhanced by considering Kirsty Best's ideas in "Interfacing the Environment":

> With traditional photography the visual interface comes into being as the photographic paper reacts with the film, requiring annexed conditions from the moment

of capture (the dark room, access to chemicals, etc.). Digital cameras incorporate the visual interface directly into the technology. The screen of a digital camera substitutes for the later processing of visual imagery, bringing the future into the present. This time-shifting bears directly on the actual process of recording, as operators of the camera readjust their choice of object and framing in relation to the visual textuality of what has already been registered–re-snapping photos, reworking images after consulting the constantly updated on-screen view.[17]

Best suggests several key points. First, digital cameras change the relationship of time to memory. The production of the image—the icon we will mentally retain and build upon to reinforce (or recreate) memory—occurs immediately. If we don't like what we see on our digital camera, we reshoot. We restructure the image and in so doing, we restructure the memory. The events of our lives do become digital bits flying through the air, available for instant editing, cropping, rotating, and red-eye reducing. At the same time, we might never print these images—they might remain as stored pixels, never making it onto paper. Hermia returns to the strange quality of digital images later in the play when she grabs for Gordon's phone looking for a picture he took of the Pope in Rome: "Those mobs at the Vatican waving their cell phones, stealing an image of the Pope's dead face, and Gordon among them. I can still hear him laughing, I have the Pope in my pocket. There it is. Dead Pope."[18]

Jean's desire for the tangible as a route to self-definition in an increasingly disembodied, immaterial world is brought vividly to light in the scene in the stationery store (pun no doubt intended) immediately after the dinner. Before Jean and Dwight head off to the store where Dwight works, Jean says, "I *love* stationery . . . When you touch the invitations, it feels so nice. Creamy and thick, and you can close your eyes and *feel* the words. I think heaven must be like an embossed invitation."[19] Once they arrive, Jean luxuriates in the feel of the paper, touching them carefully and naming the sensations they create for her. This experience helps her articulate her feelings about cell phones and Gordon's in particular:

> I never had a cell phone. I didn't want to always be there, you know. Like if your phone is on you're supposed to be there. Sometimes I like to disappear. But it's like—when everyone has their cell phone on, no one is there. It's like we're all disappearing the more we're there . . . But when Gordon's phone rang and rang, after he died, I thought his phone was beautiful, like it was the only thing keeping him alive, like as long as people called him he would be alive . . . All those molecules in the air, trying to talk to Gordon—and Gordon—he's in the air too—so maybe they would all meet up there, whizzing around—those bits of air—and voices.[20]

During her musings about the nature of presence in a technologically mediated world, and Dwight's own story about his brother, Dwight braids Jean's hair.

This intimacy becomes a kiss and soon much more as paper begins to fall magically all around them. When Gordon's phone rings and Dwight begs Jean not to answer, Gordon materializes onstage right before the lights fade for intermission. As objects flutter and bodies collide, the audience is forced to be present and grounded—aesthetically—in the very way Jean wishes she could be, if only she could ignore the caller at the other end of the line.

When the play resumes after intermission, the audience hears Gordon's voice for the first time, learning about his perspective on his marriage and of his searing desire for a bowl of lobster bisque the day he died. The audience also learns what Gordon did for a living, but first he recapitulates many of themes from the first act when he tells of his final day, a rainy one, that he faced without an umbrella: "You know when people are so crushed together in the rain, in the city, so many people, that no one person needs an umbrella, because one umbrella covers three bodies? And everyone's yelling into their cell phones, and I'm thinking, where have all the phone booths gone? The booths are all dead. People are yammering into their phones and I hear fragments of lost love and hepatitis and I'm thinking, is there no privacy? *Is there no dignity?*"[21] Gordon's words reinforce our sense of the ubiquity of mobile communication and how all manner of human relationships, and even the space we occupy, has changed. All the secrets of our hearts and bodies have become transparent; small, intimate physical spaces designed for privacy are now obsolete in the vast new global public. Distinctions between the public and the private have eroded.

Throughout the play's first act, the precise nature of Gordon's work was a mystery. The characters who knew him talked around the fact in guarded terms while Jean pretended to be his coworker—that she worked in "incoming" while he worked in "outgoing." The terms emphasized a kind of mobility and echoed the terms of the mobile phone call but otherwise kept the nature of the transit and the transaction concealed. At last he says, "I wouldn't really say that I sell organs for a living. I connect people."[22]

Gordon's work provides the most radical alteration of self and space in the play—and Jean's realization of what this means will catapult her out the realm of the quasi-realistic and into the domain of the emphatically surreal. Gordon continues, "A man in Iran needs money real bad but he doesn't need his own kidney. A woman in Sydney needs a new kidney but she doesn't need her own cash. I put these two together . . . There are parts enough to make everyone whole; it's just that the right parts are not yet in the right bodies."[23] Gordon doesn't just have a cell phone; he becomes one as he erases the distance between Sydney and Iran and merges bodies.

Jean does not hear Gordon's monologue. Instead she learns the truth about Gordon from Hermia—while drinking cosmopolitans in a bar. A bar is another kind of hybrid public-private space—where intimate relationships are often variously on display and under construction—so it is fitting that Jean sees a new side of Gordon here. Jean is suitably appalled and rather than considering any intervention by the justice system, she thinks she can delete Gordon's mistakes. Hermia tells her, "Too late, Jean. The kidneys, the corneas, the skin—they're the rings on my fingers and the fixtures in our bathrooms. What's done is done."[24] Hermia's casual statement encapsulates the crime and its spoils perfectly. Bodies are permeable and transformable—into commodities that travel and morph into expensive but meaningless baubles. Jean then gets a call telling her that a kidney from Brazil is waiting in South Africa, so off Jean goes, jetting across the world to right the wrongs done by Gordon.

The next two scenes are the most fantastical in the play, so according to the logic of the script, they are set in locales at once exotic and nowhere. The first is in the Johannesburg Airport. Jean is ready to confront Gordon's colleague—this time she's dressed in a red rain coat instead of the blue that matched Jean's early in the show and her accent has migrated from South America to Eastern Europe, according to the stage direction—armed not with the gun suggested by Hermia at the close of the previous scene, but with a kidney-shaped lamp. Jean has come to Johannesburg intent on donating her kidney so a stranger won't have to give hers up, but the stranger is in fact there, not to relieve Jean of a biological organ. She wants her technological appendage instead—the cell phone.

As she analyzes Mark Poster's concept of the "netizen," N. Katherine Hayles helps us appreciate the consequences of Jean's relationship to the cell phone and its value to her adversary. From Poster's distinction between the "citizen of the nation" and the netizen, or "the political subject constituted in cyberspace,"[25] Hayles goes a step farther to reveal a new understanding of what it means to be human in our technologically enhanced age. She writes, "Cognition in this view happens between human and environment rather than solely in the brain ... Intelligent machines are intrinsic to a human's 'extended mind' to use Andy Clark's phrase. Together with deterritorialization, this vision makes the human less an unchanging entity that grounds notions of human rights and human dignity than an evolving, historically contingent, and technologically enabled creature whose distinctive characteristic is continually and aggressively to enroll objects in its extended cognitive system."[26] Hayles's analysis helps us see the cell phone as an essential cognitive organ. It expands our knowledge, it enhances our memory, and it stores our relationships. These functions are vital to the networked self, so it is no wonder that the object in Jean's possession is a valuable commodity, as life sustaining in the new world order as a kidney.

While almost every detail of the scene seems bizarre—from the character details of Jean's adversary, to Jean's mission, to the prop she wields—it retains the logic of the space in which it is played and the effect that kind of space and getting to it has on human psychology. In *The Global Soul: Jet Lag, Shopping*

Malls, and the Search for Home, Pico Iyer writes of the overwhelming, discombobulating stimuli of the airport terminal. He says, "People take on strange identities in airports" and continues, "Not knowing whether I was facing east or west, not knowing whether it was night or day, I slipped into that peculiar state of mind—or no-mind—that belong to the no-time, no-place of the airport, that out-of body state in which one's not quite there, but certainly not elsewhere . . . I felt myself in a state of suspended animation, five miles above the sea—unsure of how much pressure to put on things. I had entered the stateless state of jet lag."[27] Jean does become stateless, taking leave of her usual identity to become a character loosed from noir-ish international thriller, wrestling her opponent for a gun. But soon the woman becomes more violent, hitting Jean over the head with the weapon. With a flash of light the lamp breaks and Jean is transported to a place more outlandish than the Johannesburg airport.

The next scene finds Jean in the "spiritual pipeline," a station in the afterlife, with Gordon. The locale looks like the café from the top of the play, and Ruhl suggests in her stage directions that gestures from the first scene echo through this one in order to convey the idea that Jean and Gordon are "doomed to repeat their first encounter over and over again for eternity."[28]

Gordon explains to Jean that when people die they return to the person they loved most and the moment they discovered that love.[29] While this may have been true for Jean at the top of the scene—she loved Gordon because she thought she could make him good—she realizes by the end of the scene that she doesn't want to love him most, nor does she want to be like him. Gordon tells her, "In-coming calls, out-going organs, we're all just floating receptacles waiting to be filled—with meaning—which you and I provide."[30]

Jean has an epiphany when Gordon makes the "cell phone ballet" perceptible to her. He says, "It's what they call the music of the spheres—listen—."[31] If there is one of element of the show likely to look radically different in each production, it is surely the cell phone ballet. Ruhl offers notes for the director at the conclusion of the script, and the first topic she addresses is the cell phone ballet. She tells future artists, "One thing I learned is that if the movement is complex, the music and voices should be simple; if the voices are complex, the movement should be simple. I wish I could tell you that there is one definitive way to crack this oyster but it's up to your collective imagination."[32]

However directors, choreographers, and sound designers choose to crack the oyster, the nowhere of mobile communication—its disembodied, displaced connection—is imaginatively redeemed when bodies become visible again and the polyphony of voices melds into pure sound. This sensual experience, which will eventually take Jean back into her body, prompts her to free Gordon and herself. She tells Gordon the truth—that his mother calls him even when he's gone and that she loves him dearly. This allows him to shoot through the pipeline to wait for her. Meanwhile Jean learns to love who Dwight actually is instead of her fantasy of Gordon. She reestablishes the values and orientation that she had lost since answering Gordon's phone. She imagines calling Dwight—since she can't make the phone actually work in the ether—she tells him of her fear and her mistake and calls out the letter Z, recalling Dwight's dream that the two of them formed the letter: "two lines—us—connected by a diagonal. Z."[33] Jean chooses to link their parallel lives, drawing the diagonal. She makes an active choice grounded in the values she's defined for herself, and as she connects to Dwight and the healthy love he represents through image and sound, she is transported back to the everyday world.

In the final scene, Dwight has rescued Jean from the airport, where he says she passed out, and has brought her home to his mother's house. Jean thinks only hours have passed, but according to Mrs. Gottlieb, it's been months, and much has changed. So while place has stabilized for Jean, her perception of time has not. She remains in a state of spiritual jet lag. Carlotta (the Other Woman has acquired a name and a distinct identity), with the help of the phone Jean lost in Johannesburg, has taken over Gordon's business; Hermia has resumed her professional ice skating career and is on tour—"Denmark, then San Jose"— and Dwight is on the government watch lists thanks to his letterpress publication of subversive political theory and poetry. Mrs. Gottlieb still mourns until Jean tells her where she's been and that Gordon waits for her. Mrs. Gottlieb responds by throwing herself on the barbeque pit and self-immolating.

Once the rest of the cast has exited, Jean and Dwight are free to spell out the terms of their love for each other. Jean suggests that they should "love each other absolutely." Dwight responds by referencing the worthies from John Donne's poem, "The Undertaking:" "Let's love each other better than the worthies did." He doesn't pull the poem up on his phone or otherwise recite it for her from either actual or virtual memory, and the production at Playwrights Horizons did not publish any part of the poem in the program as a refresher for those audience members several years away from their British Lit survey courses in college. But for those with sharp memories or curiosity after the curtain, the last stanzas of Donne's poem provide a last nudge toward the maintenance of privacy as a protection for love and virtue:

> If, as I have, you also do
> Virtue in woman see,
> And dare love that, and say so too,
> And forget the He and She;
>
> And if this love, though placèd so,
> From profane men you hide,

Which will no faith on this bestow,
Or, if they do, deride;

Then you have done a braver thing
Than all the Worthies did;
And a braver thence will spring,
Which is, to keep that hid.

In the play's final moments, Ruhl also makes a closing statement about place. After all the dislocations Jean has endured as she has struggled to find love and herself within it, at long last she finds herself truly placed. When Jean inquires if Dwight intends to show her the poem he replies, "Not right now. Now we kiss. And the lights go out."[34] For the first time Ruhl has her characters actively acknowledge their place on the stage. They have learned from what has transpired and they find themselves in the present moment, under the lights, in the theater. Place and time are real, local, and shared for characters, actors, and audience.

Kin

Bathsheba (Bash) Doran's *Kin* premiered at Playwrights Horizons March 21, 2011, on the same stage where *Dead Man's Cell Phone* had its New York premiere (after its world premiere at Washington, DC's Woolly Mammoth) a little more than three years earlier. Those three years were crucial for expanding the kinds of technologies and mobility a dramatist might choose to explore en route to crafting the contemporary female character. While Ruhl's text manifests a keen suspicion of how mobile technologies might redefine human interaction and the ways it can be placed, Doran's play projects an optimism about the ways technology might help the individual construct her own globe-spanning network of meaningful connection. She finds a dramatic analogue for the ideas of Manuel Castells: "Communication technologies materially allow the postpatriarchal family to survive as a network of bonded individuals, in need of both autonomy and support at the same time. As people rebuild and extend their lives along their networks, they bring with them into these networks, and into their networking devices, their values, perceptions, and fears."[35] Doran's play shows the ways that communication technologies can be active, beneficial partners as we create and expand the network of our kin and create value within it.

Doran has a unique perspective on mobility's forceful shaping of identity in the contemporary world: in February of 2011, she became an American citizen. Doran left her native England on a Fulbright Scholarship in 2000. After several years of graduate study in theater in the United States, first at Columbia and then Juilliard, and after staying in the country with a green card and artist visa, she earned citizenship.[36]

Like Doran, *Kin* spans countries (and time as well) as a whole constellation of characters choose who and where they want to be. While Doran identifies time and place as spanning the last seven years in America and Ireland, she also provides the following note on design:

> When I began writing, I thought of this play as taking place in what I found myself referring to as "the landscape of the mind." Many of my characters were based in what I only thought of as "the city." It could have been any Western capital—New York, Paris, London, or an imaginary city entirely. Other characters were simply placed "far away." I was attempting to conjure the globe. Eventually I found it helped the storytelling to be specific. So now there is a literal geography to the story, but I hope that the directors and design teams will help recapture my early sense that this play is taking place in a non-literal landscape.[37]

Ultimately both a literal and a metaphoric geography are important to the nomads in *Kin*. The first four scenes take place in various spots in New York City. In the first scene we meet Anna, the play's central figure and a graduate student in English, in her professor's office, en route to the dissolution of their romantic relationship. She sits nearly mute while he says a variety of hilarious, ridiculous things—that she must have been interested him as a father figure because of her childhood loss of a father (she interrupts that her father is in fact alive) and that in his poetry he had described vaginas as revolving doors and penises as office staple guns. That, he says, "is the fucking monotony of searching for your soul mate."[38] While the physical geography of the Ivy League campus office sets up some details of Anna's character, her departure from this narcissistic figure and the rocky emotional terrain he surely forced her to inhabit also launches her back into the world of dating and romance as she seeks her own soul mate.

The next scene finds Anna in Central Park, searching in the dark with her cell phone for her theatrically bereft friend, an underemployed actress named Helena. Castells is once again helpful. He writes, "Because mobile communication relentlessly changes the location reference, the space of interaction is defined entirely within the flows of communication. People are here and there, in multiple heres and theres, in a relentless combination of places. But places do not disappear. Thus, in the practice of rendezvousing, people walk or travel toward their destination, while they decide which destination it is going to be on the basis of the instant communication in which they are engaged. Thus, places do exist . . . but they exist as points of convergence in communication networks created and recreated by people's purposes."[39] Anna and Helena's communication, both before Anna's arrival and after, helps redefine the public space they eventually inhabit together. Helena's "soul," her dog Zoë, has just passed, and she is determined to bury her in the place she loved best. When Anna finds her, Helena says, "Keep watch. Fucking city regulations, I mean what the fuck, it's sick, it's Greek, it's . . . what happened to universal space? Isn't it my fucking planet? Wasn't it Zoë's fucking earth?"[40] As Helena succeeds in converting quite famous public space to her private use in a sort of mock performance of *Antigone*, the physical transformation spurs an emotional reaction in Anna. She recalls standing at her mother's grave when she was a child. She tells Helena—for whom it takes a while to realize that Anna's loss and her own are not equivalent—"My Dad was so crippled with grief at the graveside and all I could think was that the way he was crying made me want to fall in love."[41] Though Anna is in the renegotiated park/burial place with Helena, she is also back at her mother's graveside, propelled there by the emotion of her experience with Helena.

By the end of the play's first two scenes we already have a sense of the way Doran is setting up the central emotional relationship of the play through a dramatic version of negative space. In an interview with Helen Shaw in *Time Out New York*, Doran explained, "I had seen an art exhibition of conventional structures realized as negative space . . . Instead of building the walls, they solidified the space in the rooms. So I mapped out the central stages of what a journey towards the altar are, but I represent those beats through the other characters in the play."[42] The first two scenes, in addition to placing Anna squarely in New York, show the negative space at the foundation of her relationship. Rather than showing her meet her lover, we see the forces propelling Anna to wander and to seek him out.

In the third scene, we meet Sean—independently of Anna. He too is in New York, but we see him in the private space of his apartment, on the phone on a Saturday night with his mother in Ireland. While he is physically in New York, he is still emotionally bound to Linda—a woman unable to leave her house. They discuss his failed relationship—he tells her he's looking for "someone who doesn't freebase"—and he tells his increasingly soused mother that he's taking a break from dating. The call ends with Linda describing the color of the Donegal sky and musing on the variations in the New York one. Though an ocean separates Sean from his mother physically, clearly their connection is strong (for better and worse). As they talk on their phones, the colors from one night sky seem to bleed into the other as does their loneliness. In this scene, we get a dramatized picture of the ways Castells describes technology's force on place: "Wireless communication does not eliminate place, it redefines the meaning of place as anywhere from which the individual chooses or needs to communicate . . . Places are individualized and networked along the specific networks of individual practices . . . Ubiquitous connectivity rather than mobility is the fundamental process in the redefinition of space. Places are subsumed into the space of flows, thus losing their meaning in the space of places. In concrete terms, the places from which people communicate with their mobile devices become a backdrop of communication, rather than the locality of communication."[43] Sean and his mother aren't mobile during their exchange; unlike Anna and Helena in the first scene, their phones aren't leading them to a face-to-face rendezvous. Nevertheless, they cultivate a connection, and as the bond deepens, geographical distance is not literally eliminated, but through the emotional space of communication, place transforms.

In the next scene Anna and Helena discuss Anna's struggles with online dating, and the audience begins to see how technology will bring Anna and Sean together. Anna tells Helena she's changed her search criteria to avoid being paired with lawyers and bankers. Helena responds, "The hunt for the soul mate, that is a mysterious thing, and I don't care how much you pay this website, the big old American dollar is not going to short-cut that process. What if you're supposed to be with a coal miner or something? Or an acrobat? But the machine can't think out of the box." We never learn exactly how Anna changes her search criteria, but eventually she does so in order to meet Sean, a personal trainer from Ireland.[44] Though Anna's education and intellectual interests might suggest that the professor from the first scene is an ideal match for Anna, "the machine" accesses a different layer of Anna's identity and desires despite Helena's fears to the contrary.

"Who Visits Online Dating Sites? Exploring Some Characteristics Online Daters" shows that Doran's construction of Anna, Sean, and Helena is right in step with the characters' real-world counterparts. Patti M. Valkenburg and Jochen Peter write, "The growing popularity of online dating sites is hardly surprising. First, on the Internet, spatial proximity is irrelevant, and meeting similar people is easier than in real-life dating." This is true for Anna and Sean, whose geographic backgrounds do not stand in the way of their meeting. Valkenburg and Peter continue, "Second, online dating can occur without help from friends." Given Helena's neediness, not to mention her judgment of Anna's methods for seeking companionship, one might reasonably assume that Helena could hinder rather than help a nonvirtual search for romantic connection. Valkenburg and Peter conclude with what is the strongest point in regard to Anna and Sean: "Third, the reduced visual and auditory cues that characterize online communication facilitate self-disclosure. This may apply even more to online dating because, contrary to many other types of computer-mediated communication, online dating participants often anticipate future interaction. The anticipation of future interaction increases the depth of communication and may thereby encourage relationship formation."[45] Whatever Anna and Sean's search criteria might have been, they communicated something vital to each other away from the visual and auditory miscues of face-to-face communication that might have kept them apart.

Anna and Sean's interaction through a dating website also enacts Steve Woolgar's third and fourth "rules of virtuality." In *Virtual Society? Technology, Cyperbole, Reality* he names rule three, that "virtual technologies supplement rather than substitute for real activities," and rule four is "The more virtual the more real."[46] These two interrelated rules highlight the fact that online dating, real-world and fictionalized, augments rather than substitutes for in-person interaction. Furthermore, it was through virtual contact, and the kind of filtered sharing it promoted, that Anna and Sean were eventually able to have more productive "real" contact.

In addition to cell phones and Internet dating, Facebook also plays a part in the play's action, collapsing time and space. Much later in the play, when Sean is having doubts about making his relationship with Anna permanent, he sets up a Facebook page so he can reconnect with the freebasing girlfriend of his past, Rachel. Rachel has cleaned up, found work as a hairdresser in Maine, and married a man from India. Though he has discovered most of this virtually, he still needs to see her physically, so he travels to Acadia National Park in Maine. When he sees her he tells her, "Facebook. Tells you everything, really. So much stuff. I had no idea. Ten minutes after I joined three ex-girlfriends in Ireland wanted to know what I was up to. Sending me quizzes to find out which golden girl I'm most like. (beat) Rose by the way."[47]

Sean's Facebook experience rings true with José van Dijck's analysis in "Facebook as Tool for Producing Sociality and Connectivity." Van Dijck writes, "In consciously deploying the tactic of disclosing private information to boost one's public persona and build relationships, Facebook users do not fundamentally change the relation between the private and public sphere in setting the norms for sociality. What does challenge these norms, though, is the fact that Facebook triggers the disclosure of personal information in exchange for participation . . . Facebook, perhaps more than any other social network site, has stretched the boundaries of the private sphere by pressing its user to divulge intimate details to a general audience."[48] In order to participate in Facebook, in order to learn about where Rachel's journey had taken her and who she had become, Sean had disclosed information about himself, which only prompted further disclosure—of his Golden Girl–esque characteristics. Details about his private self (that in this rather humorous example had no doubt even eluded him) became public knowledge to his "friends."

But while Facebook discloses much, it also fails to plumb some depths for the medium's electronic audience. Facebook didn't tell Sean that Rachel sees a therapist. The therapist provided the following prescient advice. Rachel says, "She said when I think of you, and I do think of you, it's just a fantasy of escape.

The Sean I think of doesn't exist anymore. He's gone. And I don't exist to you either. Not really."[49] The truth Rachel tells him when they connect in person frees him from his memories of the past and the fantasies he's used to people it—his internal "profile," to borrow Facebook terminology. This allows him to commit to the physical and emotional reality of his current, offline relationship with Anna.

Sean's journey to see Rachel is but one of several instances of travel in *Kin*. While Jean is the primary traveler in *Dead Man's Cell Phone*, all the major characters in *Kin*—with one key exception—are highly mobile. Furthermore, while travel in Ruhl's text seems to emphasize the no-places of the journey, in Doran's the specificity of the destination is far more important. Adam, Anna's father and a military man, wanted to move his family to Japan when Anna was young. Though he chose not to do so, he now flies in and out of New York regularly in hopes of bridging the emotional distance he feels with his daughter. When he's not there, he doesn't stay put in his home in Texas. His longtime lover, Kay, lives in Washington, DC, so he goes there regularly too. But Kay is considering giving up on conventional cancer treatment and plans to head to India for alternative medicine. When Anna's dissertation becomes a book and she builds a professional name for herself, she is sought after as a speaker at international conferences. Helena's movement is propelled by a less positive force. After she suffers a nervous breakdown, Helena decides to leave New York and acting. She moves to the woods of North Carolina to attend massage therapy school.

Sean has left his native Ireland, but when he is ready to propose to Anna, he takes her back there. In Ireland Anna can meet his mother—the character who does not travel. And not only does she not travel; she cannot leave her house. Linda was raped when Sean was a boy, and the trauma has morphed into agoraphobia. It is a monumental step for her when she manages to sit on the threshold of her doorway talking with Anna. When it is time for the wedding, even more will be required of Linda. She tells Adam the secret that she has kept from her son: that the beautiful heather-covered cliffs of Donegal, the place where Sean proposed to and now intends to marry Anna, is the site of her rape decades before. She tells Adam of the things her rapist took from her, such as her marriage, her ability to mother well, and her church but says, "But I would not let this man destroy my son's favorite place in all the world. And now I'm going back to watch my son marry there. And perhaps now *I* win."[50]

For some twenty years, Linda has lived without justice: her assailant was never identified. In this regard too, *Kin* joins *Dead Man's Cell Phone*. Criminal acts ranging from the corporate to the violently physical go unpunished by any formal system of justice. But in Ruhl's play and in Doran's, women find ways of redressing wrong for themselves—even if Linda must wait decades to do so.

In *Kin* Doran, a lesbian, seeks to redress another kind of wrong—not precisely criminal, but certainly social, and for her deeply personal. She told *Time Out*'s Helen Shaw, "A lot of 2008 had been spent thinking about the point of getting married when it's not, for us, legal. I realized that it's impossible to tell me that I can't get married: You can't legislate language, you can't legislate ritual. And I started to think about it as a more ancient and powerful thing than was being talked about politically. That thinking informs the play." While *Kin* dramatizes the movement toward marriage for heterosexual rather than homosexual characters, Doran's excavation of the essential human impulses at the heart of the institution—those that led to her own sacred union with Katie Hefel and her family in 2009—demonstrate why the formalization of these bonds should be open to all people. Helena's speech as she officiates Anna and Sean's ceremony makes this clear: "I am here not to marry them but to witness with all of you as they choose to marry each other. And what we are witnessing is the birth of a new family."[51] The audience gains a powerful sense of this as the entire cast reassembles onstage. And in the play's premiere production at Playwrights Horizons, the audience was included in the family too. Great waves of mist not only set the scene onstage but also rolled out and over the audience. The sense of witnessing an elemental power extended throughout the house.

In her essay "Playwright's Perspective," preceding the first published version of the play, Doran explained that she had two quotations taped to her wall. They were more than just inspiration. She writes, "The words of these writers were like compass points. If I followed them I'd get where I was trying to go,"[52] thus reinforcing the idea that like her characters, Doran too is a kind of nomad. The first of the quotations is from Rumi's *Spiritual Couplets*: "I saw a crow running about with a stork. I marveled long and investigated their case in order that I might find the clue as to what it was that they had in common. When amazed and bewildered I approached them then indeed I saw that both were lame."[53] The passage clearly applies to Sean and Anna who are indeed two very different birds. Over the course of the play, Doran allows us to seek their common bond as we get to know the major players in their lives and stories.

Doran's other quotation, her other compass point, was from Chinua Achebe's *Things Fall Apart*. It reads, "A man who calls his kinsmen to a feast does not do so to save them from starving. They all have food in their own homes. When we gather together in the moonlit village ground it is not because of the moon. Every man can see it in his own compound. We come together because it is good for kinsmen to do so."[54] By play's end we have a sense of kinship despite time and space, geography and age, culture and life path. Throughout the play, characters far apart—in New York and Ireland and North Carolina—have looked out at the sky or the stars on their own. These ancient guideposts have directed their wandering—physical and emotional. Mobility has at long last brought them to a place of connection and a new (old) kind of network. At last as they are enveloped in the mist together, they feel the good of that communion in a shared time and place. As do we. Doran demonstrates for us quite beautifully the power of technologically facilitated kinship networks and the power of theater.

Water by the Spoonful

Only 18 months separate the premiere of Doran's *Kin* from Quiara Alegría Hudes's *Water by the Spoonful*, which premiered at the Hartford Stage in October of 2011, but once again the changes in the way a writer imagines using mobile and Internet technologies is profound. While Hudes shares Doran's optimism about technology, she exceeds both Ruhl and Doran in theatricalizing mediated connectivity as she reconceptualizes the ways her female characters can create both family and home.

In "Fugue, Hip Hop and Soap Opera: Transcultural Connections and Theatrical Experimentation in Twenty-First Century US Latina Playwriting," Anne Garcia-Romero writes, "A tension can exist between theatrical experimentation and commercial viability. If a playwright writes a play which challenges traditional notions of structure, character and language, will her play get produced?"[55] Garcia-Romero goes on to argue that Quiara Alegría Hudes's *Elliot, A Soldier's Fugue*, a finalist for the 2007 Pulitzer Prize, a formally adventurous text that interweaves the story of three generations of Puerto Rican veterans into a fugue structure, is also commercially viable.

Though she is analyzing the text that first brought Hudes widespread critical attention, she could just as easily be discussing *Water by the Spoonful*, the winner of the 2012 Pulitzer Prize. After a second designation as Pulitzer finalist (in 2009 for the book of the hit musical *In the Heights* that made her name familiar to her broadest audience to date), Hudes took home what is arguably the highest prize in American drama only nine years after receiving her MFA in Playwriting from Brown in 2003.[56]

Of Hudes's several plays, *Elliot, A Soldier's Fugue* is, in fact, most pertinent to the discussion of *Water by the Spoonful*, because they are the first two pieces of a trilogy Hudes is in the midst of creating at the time of this writing.[57] Like all her plays, however, *Elliot* is deeply rooted in her family's experience.[58] The title character shares the name of her cousin, who enlisted in the Marines when he was 17. And like the title character, Hudes's cousin was injured in Iraq. When Hudes saw her cousin after his return, she found that he had the same charming veneer and "cheeseburger smile" he'd always had, "but after Iraq there was something different."[59] This difference motivated her to interview Elliot about his war experience and his father about his experience in Viet Nam. Of the interview with her uncle, Hudes said, "I didn't ask a single question . . . He spoke for three or four hours straight . . . [The next week] . . . I called to thank him, and he said he felt lighter than he had in years."[60] Meanwhile Hudes's Aunt Eugenia, or Ginny, who raised Elliot, provides the lone female perspective in *Elliot*. As Liz Jones and Asher Richelli explain, "Quiara is as much of a theatrical 'chronicler' as she is a playwright. Through Quiara, the stories of her family, friends and acquaintances become available and relevant to the larger culture. But Quiara does not merely take their words and experiences verbatim; rather these stories serve as the inspiration around which she carefully crafts her unique theatrical worlds."[61]

The very first reviewer of *Water by the Spoonful* immediately spotted something unique in Hudes's latest theatrical world. Writing of the script's premiere production at the Hartford Stage, Frank Rizzo declared in the *Hartford Courant*, "This is one of the best new plays I've seen in years,"[62] and he opined for *Variety*'s regional reviews, "The play is a combination poem, prayer and app on how to cope in an age of uncertainty, speed and chaos."[63] It is the reference to the play as an app that I find most striking, particularly when the play is put into conversation with Ruhl's and Doran's work on the topic of mobile technology.

An app is a smartphone application—a recent yet pervasive cultural and technological phenomenon.[64] Gerard Goggin explains, "An app can make it possible to imagine and do things with a mobile phone that were previously never associated with the technology."[65] He goes on to cite examples of apps that can turn a phone into everything from a "virtual stethoscope" to a bowling ball. Apps are everywhere and everything—as Apple's early marketing declared, "There's an app for that"—and in addition to their ubiquity, "with the various new classes of apps aspects of everyday life, bodies, effects and identities are rendered much more visible, calculable and governable."[66]

The app as Goggin describes it thus provides an interesting lens for viewing *Water by the Spoonful*, a play that in ways structural and thematic succeeds in doing revolutionary dramatic things. Hudes's innovation begins with her conception of stage space. She describes her setting's two worlds thus: the "real world" is filled with chairs of various styles hailing from different locations and facing different directions; the "online world" is an empty space that connects the chairs.[67] Hudes's doubled vision is provocative. The real world is a collection of place fragments—disconnected shards of locales. While the online world is empty, it also forges connection among the disparate real elements. Like Goggin's description of the app, this vision of the online world makes connections more visible. Hudes also asks that characters do not mime typing when they are online. Instead they should give the sense that they are having a regular conversation while they are in the midst of everyday tasks. Hudes's ideas about stage business also suggest the permeability of the two worlds, and the ways activity and communication in one space will have measurable effect, if not governance, in the other.

The play's action shifts back and forth between these two worlds over the course of its 15 scenes. For the first 6 scenes, those leading up to the intermission break, there is a very regular pattern: first we witness a scene in the "real world," and then we witness a scene in the virtual world. It is likely to take the audience several scenes to put together the narrative clues that link some of the characters in each scene type into one biological family.

The play opens in the real world. Elliot, an injured vet looking to find his way now that he's back at home and physically healed, and Yaz, Elliot's cousin and an adjunct professor of music at Swarthmore, are on campus eating breakfast together, discussing food, the health of Elliot's "mom" Ginny, and Yaz's impending divorce. They are waiting for the arrival of a colleague of Yaz's, a professor of Arabic, named Aman. Elliot has been haunted by a phrase and he's looking for a translation. Aman is hoping for quid pro quo—that Elliot might agree to serve as consultant for a gritty documentary about Marines in Iraq that his friend is producing in Hollywood. Though Elliot doesn't accept the offer until play's end, Aman translates the phrase that's been tormenting him: "Can I please have my passport back?" We learn immediately that travel and identity will figure prominently in the play.

The next offline scene, scene 3, is more complicated than the first because it finds Yaz and Elliot in different locations though eventually they unite by cell phone. Elliot is at work at a Subway sandwich shop, a dead-end job at a restaurant with a name that carries ironic weight in a play interested in travel. This mundane situation is troubled by the presence and voice of the ghost, who repeats the line Professor Aman had translated three times. Yaz is also at work—at Swarthmore lecturing early in the term to students about the importance of dissonance. It is well worth interjecting here that dissonance explains the relationship (and the power) of the play's early scenes. Yaz tells her students of her experience of her first music lesson during which she played Mr. Rappaport one of her own compositions: "He said, 'It's pretty, everything goes together. It's like an outfit where your socks are blue and your pants, shirt, hat are all blue.' Then he said, 'Play an F-sharp major in your left hand.' Then he said, "Play a C-major in your right hand. Now play them together." He asked me, 'Does it go together?' I told him, 'No sir.' He said, 'Now go home and write.' My first music lesson was seven minutes long. I had never really heard dissonance before."[68] The pairing of the F-sharp major and C-major is analogous to Hudes's pairing of the real and virtual worlds in the play. For the first act, it seems as though they do not go together, but the beauty of their difficult, dissonant relationship will eventually become perceptible to the audience.

Like the young Yaz, the audience has probably never imagined the relationship between the real and virtual worlds in quite the way Hudes helps them to hear and see it.

Yaz and Elliot's worlds become one when they speak on the phone during a class break, and the class chasm of their work lives closes. Elliot's been calling Yaz repeatedly—to tell her Ginny has been hospitalized and put on a breathing machine. He's angry with his father, who conveyed the news electronically. He says, "Who texts that? Who texts that and then doesn't pick up the phone."[69] Before we have time to ponder the etiquette of mobile communication fully, Yaz hears the ding of a text on her phone. She converts the message back into spoken words reporting that Ginny's life support will be turned off as soon as Elliot arrives. The scene demonstrates that even in the "real world," mobile communication technologies shape the narratives of the characters' lives.

Scene 5 makes it instantly clear that what seemed inevitable at the end of scene 3 happened. Ginny has died, and Yaz and Elliot must select the floral arrangements for her funeral. They can't afford the "Orchid Paradise" that would create a virtual version of Ginny's lush garden for the service, but the frustrating shopping expedition leads the characters to ponder identity and rootedness. Ultimately Ginny's death is radically altering the landscape of the family. When Elliot and Yaz debate who will deliver the eulogy, Elliot tells her it is her job and her place: "You're the elder now."[70] Yaz may only be 29, but it nevertheless has become her job to lead the family, though this is a definition of self she is not yet ready to embrace.

Physical places are essential to determining identity and belonging in the offline world, and this is something that Ginny, a master gardener who expressed and healed herself through her plantings,[71] understood well. Elliot says Mami Ginny "had to have her ashes thrown at a waterfall in El Yunque, just to be the most Puerto Rican motherfucker around."[72] Even in death, Ginny was fighting to establish who she was, and she was linking that identity to a very particular place and its natural formations. No doubt Ginny was also wise enough to know that her wish would require the next generation to travel to Puerto Rico with her. They might need to traverse a long distance, but they would bring her "home," which in turn would have an indelible effect on their definition of home.

Shortly thereafter, Yaz recalls how identity-defining distance is measured not only in miles but also in cultural difference: "William told me every time I went to North Philly, I'd come back different. His family had Quaker Oats for DNA. They play Pictionary on New Years. I'd sit there wishing I could scoop the blood out of my veins like you scoop the seeds out of a pumpkin and he'd be like, 'Whatchu thinking about, honey?' and I'd be like, 'Nothing. Let's play some Pictionary.'"[73] When Yaz visited her family, the experience changed her in some way that was perceptible to her husband, or perhaps that threatened her husband's image of her; when she visited her husband's family, she wanted to change herself at a genetic level so that the cultural distance between them wouldn't seem so vast.

Hudes has spoken of her own experience with Philly neighborhoods: "Going from West Philly, or from Center City to North Philly . . . you would see these nice houses, with nice paint on the window ledges and all that stuff. Then block by block you'd see it transform. Alongside the nice house would be a vacant lot filled up with tires. Then there'd be three vacant lots, and one house that's boarded up, and one that has burned down. I learned to be aware of that class dichotomy, even within my own family."[74] Hudes's personal experience colors Yaz's monologue.

Whatever ambivalence Yaz feels to the place that has been home doesn't keep her from bristling at the thought of its disappearance when Elliot tells her that his dad plans to sell Ginny's house. Yaz says, "Our family may be fucked up but we had somewhere to go. A kitchen that connected us. Plastic covered sofas where we could park our communal asses . . . I mean, once that living room is gone, I may never step foot in North Philly again."[75] The drive to claim a home space and cultivate roots will only intensify in the second act, but the action in the virtual world is essential to that action.

Communication in scenes 2, 4, and 6 happens in the virtual world. Though Odessa is making coffee, we see her screen name, Haikumom, and avatar, a beach scene, projected on a screen. She posts to her chat room by speaking her lines, which end "your Thursday morning haiku: if you get restless/ buy a hydrangea or rose/ water it, wait, bloom."[76] Not only does the Haiku begin to explain Odessa's screen name, but it also continues Hudes's image thread of gardens and cultivation that echoed so powerfully in scene 5.

Haikumom is not just a participant in the chat room; she is the site administrator. When characters resort to profanity, Haikumom says, "Censored." She also intervenes when exchanges become too intense. The role that Hudes imagines for Haikumom revises typical online divisions of labor. As Bowker and Liu explain, "Although the internet has been touted as a place for significant social, cultural, and political change, results from this research suggest this may not necessarily be the case. While statistics suggest women are flocking to the Net in increasing numbers, with women representing half the new users, those women venturing into positions of power within popular online communities such as IRC [another term for chat rooms]are far fewer. Further, the demographic make-up of an average male or female operator reinforces the cultural inequities of access to the online medium."[77] Among the reasons Bowker and Liu found for women's tendency not to hold power positions were their lack of programming experience and "socialization" against technological sophistication and differences in communication style—their disinterest in dealing with hostile and rude user behavior. When women do assume power roles, they tend be "of North American descent," college students, or from the managerial or professional classes, and have a mean age of 27. According to Hudes's opening character description, Haikumom is "39 . . . works odd janitorial jobs, lives one notch above squalor."[78]

This is a significant place where the dramatic interpretation of online culture clashes with its offstage counterpart. Given Hudes's penchant for research, this cannot simply be an oversight. Instead, she is making the kind of feminist intervention into online culture that Bowker and Liu urge their readers to consider: "Feminists are concerned that rather than developing new stories and adventures, some of which may empower women, the familiar old gender stereotypes fueled by the interests of the powerful are being used within the arena of virtual imaginations. Marketers, designers, and producers of software programs are dictating to the stereotyped desires of boys and men. These stereotypes limit what women think, and want to do online . . . We need to be . . . constructing a much wider pool of expectations for men and women in Cyberspace."[79]

Soon we meet Orangutan. Haikumom and the next person to log on, Chutes and Ladders, are relieved to hear from her. Her first post to the group is "ninety-one days. Smiley face."[80] This alerts the audience that the chat room is for addicts; later in the scene we learn the precise type of addiction: crack cocaine.

The kinds of exchange that Haikumom, Orangutan, and Chutes and Ladders have is in keeping with what Sarah Nettleton (et al.) has described as virtual esteem support. In "The Reality of Virtual Social Support," she reports, "In our research . . . we can observe that people found 'virtual contacts' to be particularly valuable for esteem support. Users [of these particular kinds of chat rooms] described how their virtual friends provided them with much emotional support. Furthermore, giving emotional support to others was often perceived to be a source of esteem."[81]

Orangutan has been out of contact with the group not because she's fallen off the wagon, nor because she no longer requires their support, but because she's in Japan, at the Mango Internet Café on the Hokkaido waterfront. She's decided to go to Japan, which she calls her "homeland," to teach English.

Orangutan's reference to Japan as home comes as a surprise to the others—they've only known her by her screen icon, a wide-eyed orangutan, and they knew she lived in Maine. When Haikumom asks if she's Japanese, Orangutan answers, "I was, for the first eight days of my life. Yoshiko Sakai. Then on day nine I was adopted and moved to Cape Lewiston, Maine, where I became Ma—M.M., and where in all my days I have witnessed one other Asian. In the Superfresh. Deli counter."[82]

This exchange begins the virtual world's variation on the theme of home. Like Yaz, Orangutan's understanding of home is complicated by the different worlds she's traveled through—her native Japan and her adoptive Maine, where she felt as different from those around her as Yaz did from her ex-husband's family. Second, we witness the power of naming and identity construction. Orangutan has no trouble revealing her birth name, but she stops herself from revealing the name she uses in the offline world, divulging only her initials. We also reflect further on the fact that her screen name and icon also conceal more about her—at least in terms of race—than they reveal.

In "Virtual Speakers, Virtual Audiences: Agency, Audience, and Constraint in an Online Chat Community," Gazi Islam argues, "The web name, just like any other pseudonym, does not only separate the real world identity of the individual from their virtual identity, but it serves the important psychological function of 'liberating' the individual, enabling he/she to construct an identity of choice . . . In other words, maintaining a distinct identity in the chat room promotes the maintenance of two distinct and oppositional 'worlds,' thereby promoting the integrity of the chat room as an autonomous sphere of action."[83] Islam's analysis of web names only partially describes the way they function in Hudes's play. The chosen name does provide the character freedom to remake herself in a new way. But throughout the play, the freedom that characters find in the virtual world has an effect on what they desire in the real world. For Hudes these worlds resonate—first with sounds of discord, but by play's end, far more harmoniously.

Coupled with Haikumom's avatar (and the waterfall near which Ginny wants her ashes scattered), it is already becoming clear that water imagery will be important to the play. In fact, it is an element of Hudes's dramaturgy that helps us differentiate the two worlds. On the one hand, we have Castells's famous appellation of the space of flows: "Simply put, the space of flows is the material organization of simultaneous social interaction at a distance by networking communication, with the technological support of telecommunications, interactive communication systems, and fast transportation technologies."[84] Virtual information is channeled physically, so like a body of water, it can flow and transport those who use it. And on the other we have the physical element that sustains and threatens all life that is referenced in both worlds. In the play's second act, actual water will flow onstage in ways that facilitate and culminate in the play's final action.

Another water reference appears with the screen name of the fourth online character—Fountainhead—whom we meet in scene 4. When he enters the chat room, he gushes, spouting forth about himself (his Wharton MBA, his 300 K salary, his yellow Porsche), his family (gorgeous wife of seven years, gifted and talented sons), and his addiction to crack for a full two pages of manuscript-formatted text.

Like the other somewhat more succinct monologues that punctuate the play, Fountainhead's self-analysis shows Hudes's reinvention of the monologue. When Eric Grode argued that a good play can be read as well as seen in an article of that title for *The New York Times* ArtsBeat, he'd been inspired by *Water by the Spoonful*, and the play's monologues in particular. He wrote, "The innovation comes in those chat room sessions: Ms. Hudes stresses in her stage directions that they should be delivered while the characters mill about living their lives, not sitting and miming typing with their fluttering fingers. As a result, reading these scenes approximates the act of reading posts in a chat room far more than watching actors recite them ever could."[85] And while reading the monologues is an extraordinary experience thanks to Hudes's imaginative merging of cultural modes, the monologues, at least in Frank Rizzo's experience, are just as powerful when performed. He wrote, "Hudes ('In the Heights') brilliantly taps into both the family ties that bind as well as the alternative cyber universe, exploring the latter's use of language, attitude and freedoms of expression. Confessional monologues here make more sense here than they do in O'Neill plays."[86] Hudes reanimates a standard dramaturgical device, repurposing and reenergizing it for twenty-first-century audiences.

The characters in the chat room are also interested in critiquing the performance of Fountainhead's monologue. Neither Orangutan nor Chutes and Ladders find his a welcome presence. Orangutan wants to shut him out of the discussion by starting a new thread, while Chutes and Ladders declares, "Some purebred poodle comes pissing on my tree trunk? Damn straight I'll chase his ass out of my forest."[87]

The other characters' various forms of posturing forces Haikumom into some posturing of her own. She refutes the claim that Fountainhead is manufacturing an identity, because in her role as site administrator she can see his log-in history and lack of other aliases. She also repeatedly censors Orangutan's and Chutes and Ladders's posts for language and for engaging in personal attacks, reminding them, "This is my forest." Finally she shuts the thread down, offering to email with Fountainhead directly. Islam observed that in a chat room, "identity negotiations are particularly powerful in the presence of an audience,"[88] and that proves to be true not just for Fountainhead as the star performer but for the other characters who are forced into performances of their own in response. In this scene, we see Haikumom as a forceful parent, setting limits on her unruly children who want to keep their web family a closed unit and living up to the second half of her web name.

Scene 6 lays the groundwork for the strange offline pairings of the second act. Orangutan is in the chat room first, there because she's feeling lonely in

Japan: "I flew halfway around the world and guess what? It was still me who got off the plane ... Everything in this country makes sense but me. The noodles in the soup make sense. The woodpecker outside my window every evening? Completely logical. The girls getting out of school in their miniskirts and shy smiles? Perfectly natural. I'm floating. I'm a cloud. My existence is one sustained out of body experience ... I'm a baby in a basket on an endless river. Wherever I go I don't make sense there."[89] Orangutan has learned that leaving a country doesn't equate with leaving an identity. The freedom she had for redrawing her virtual boundaries didn't translate offline. In this world she feels formless and watery. She longs to find her way to the "land of the living," where in her description people watch DVDs, take walks, eat popcorn and ice cream, and gossip about celebrities. She reaches out to Chutes and Ladders, asking him to fly to Japan and make this real for her by being her friend. This is something he can't yet do, even with Haikumom's straight-typing maternal encouragement.

Because of the stress of these exchanges, when Fountainhead logs on, Chutes and Ladders goads him repeatedly. Ultimately this leads Fountainhead to a breakthrough and an honest presentation of self about the job he lost and his struggles. This prompts Haikumom to reach out to him since like him, she lives in Philly. She tells him, "Stop being a highly functioning isolator and start being a highly dysfunctional person."[90] This prompts a litany of slogans from the group, including Haikumom's own favorite, "nothing changes if nothing changes," which brings a light up on Elliot, boxing with a punching bag while the ghost whispers to him. This, along with Haikumom's discovery by reading the obituary in the paper that Ginny has died, maps where the play will go in the second act.

After intermission, characters from the virtual world meet face to face, characters from the real world go online, and scenes intercut in ways that show in Hudes's play as well as Doran's the wisdom of Woolgar's fourth rule of virtuality, "the more virtual the more real," and its reversal, the more real, the more virtual.

Scene 7 brings meetings, confrontation, and explanation. The scene takes place at a diner in Philadelphia where Odessa and John have shed their online personae, Haikumom and Fountainhead, to meet over coffee. Their conversation is interrupted by the arrival of Elliot and Yaz, who are there to demand help paying for Ginny's funeral flowers. Elliot quickly becomes hostile toward Odessa—who, he reveals to John, is his birth mother—and in the real world there is no site administrator to close the thread. Instead Elliot does his best to unravel the narrative Odessa has woven for herself—"I looked at that chat room once. The woman I saw there? She's literally not the same person I know,"[91] and in the process, he explains the play's title.

When he was a child, Elliot and his two-year-old sister Mary Lou had severe stomach flu. Emergency room doctors had given the instruction that the children, who had been unable to keep liquid down for three days, were to receive a teaspoon of water every five minutes. Elliot recalls, "Five minutes. Spoon. Five minutes. Spoon. I remember thinking, wow, this is it. Family time. Quality time. Just the three of us . . . And then I watched you do the same thing with my sister. And I remember being like, 'Wow, I love you, mom. My moms is alright.' Five minutes. Spoon. Five minutes. Spoon. But you couldn't stick to something simple like that. You couldn't sit still like that. You had to have your thing. That's where I stop remembering."[92] Elliot then says the human services report replaces his memory—bearing witness to the dehydration and death of his little sister. In so doing, Elliot destroys his mother. She gives him a key to her apartment and tells him to pawn her computer to pay for the flowers. The audience knows that the computer has been her lifeline, keeping her tethered to safety in the sea of her addiction, and she has just let it go.

The next scene is the first of the split scenes where we see the convergence of the online and real worlds. In the online world, Orangutan has been trying to convince Chutes and Ladders to call the son he's been estranged from for a decade. (He does call, but he hangs up when he hears his son's voice.) Elliot and Yaz go to Odessa's apartment, where instead of just leaving with the computer, Elliot logs on as Haikumom. Yaz immediately understands his transgression saying, "I think legally that might be like breaking and entering,"[93] indicating that Elliot is trespassing in Haikumom's private space. Orangutan has no trouble sensing that someone else is using Haikumom's account, so Elliot's plot to destroy Haikumom's online relationships—the surrogate family she's nurtured—quickly fails. What he doesn't anticipate is that he will be the one to leave the chat room stripped of a piece of his own manufactured identity. When Orangutan realizes that Elliot is in his mother's account, she reveals all that she knows about him. Haikumom has bragged about him, telling of his war service and his recent success starring in a toothpaste ad, but she's also told the group that he's addicted to prescription pain medication. When Orangutan offers a link to a chat room on the topic, this aspect of Elliot is revealed to Yaz, who had no idea about his addiction. Unlike Odessa, Elliot has tried to face his demons alone—and though he's sober he hasn't been able to contain them. He says, "The only thing I got left from those days is the nightmares. That's when he came, and some days I swear he ain't never gonna leave."[94] At that point, the stage directions indicate, the ghost blocks Elliot's path as he tries to walk away from Yaz. Much like Orangutan who can't escape herself no matter how far she travels, Elliot can't continue on his life path without encountering the ghost of the war.

Hudes does not let her audience linger on a single melancholy note for long—instead she offers us a new tone. Scene 9 finds Orangutan and Chutes and Ladders chatting. She's telling him about several Japanese projects to straighten rivers, bringing us yet another water reference. As we ponder the force necessary to make such a massive physical change, the two argue over whether Orangutan should seek out her birth parents as she's planning to do. She is in fact waiting at a train station to board a train to Kushiro, her birth city. They both log off angry, but at scene's end Chutes and Ladders open the care package that Haikumom has sent him—a single water wing, to help him float until he is able to swim.

Scene 10 brings the female characters in the play together at a crossroads that will determine the action for the rest of the play. Yaz is delivering Ginny's eulogy counting the things in her life (godchildren, restored houses, arrests for civil disobedience) that can be calculated to tally a life in concert with Elliot until he is overcome and she must finish alone—this is her first performance as family elder; Orangutan is on the train platform, paralyzed as the final boarding call for Kushiro is broadcast in Japanese; and Odessa pours water by the spoonful onto the stage floor, forming a "slow ribbon" until her cup is empty. In this scene Hudes asks how to take the measure of a life, whether a river can be unbent either as a child seeks to go back to the home from which she was set adrift in a basket or as a mother looks to administer the care she was unable to give a quarter of a century ago. As the ribbon unfurls across the stage floor things virtual—numbers, ideas, memories—become real in the elemental flow.

After Chutes and Ladders makes the massive personal move of selling his Tercel to finance a trip to Japan (with the water wing around his wrist, empowered and encouraged by his virtual mother), we find Orangutan asleep on the train platform in Sapporo, having never boarded her train. Odessa meanwhile is motionless on the floor of the apartment. After years of sobriety, she's used crack. Elliot and Yaz break open the door of her apartment, and they come very close to losing her. Odessa watches the scene while the actors playing Elliot and Yaz mime carrying her to the sofa. Odessa's only lines in the scene are these: "I've been to the airport, one time. My dad flew here from Puerto Rico. First time I met him. We stood by the baggage claim, his flight was late, we waited forever. There was one single, lone suitcase, spinning around a carousel . . . Everyone had cleared away from the carousel. Everyone had their bags. But this one was unclaimed. It could still be there for all I know. Spiraling. Spinning. Looking for an owner. Abandoned."[95] This real-world post (or is it from a spiritual and physical purgatory?) from Odessa is heartbreaking. We feel her loneliness and her disappointment, for physical trips not taken and the drug trips she couldn't stop taking. Yaz sees a beautiful light that Elliot cannot, and she encourages Odessa to take this final trip. After Yaz makes her peace, she tells Elliot he needs to forgive his mother; Odessa has taken her place on the couch returning to the real world of her damaged body and her offline life.

As we near the play's end, the characters must make difficult journeys. Odessa will need to start over, at day one of sobriety (she had fallen down the chute that another character's name predicted), but she will require the help of Fountainhead. He is her emergency contact, and though he doubts whether he will be able to rise to the task of helping her, when Chutes and Ladders tells him, "Your lifeboat has just arrived. Get on board or get out of the way,"[96] he climbs aboard. In the play's final scene, he bathes Odessa, cleansing her and himself as he helps her return to the water. A new family is taking seed.

Chutes and Ladders fights his every instinct, not to mention motion sickness, and makes his way to Japan to meet Orangutan. It is no small thing for her to wait for him—he's chickened out, rebooked, and managed to be the last one off the plane, but she waits for him at the baggage carousel, changing the flow of the image that Odessa had during her overdose. At last they reveal their real names to each other, and Hudes suggests in her stage directions, they hug, making the connection physical.

Elliot and Yaz fly to Puerto Rico, to scatter Ginny's ashes per her wish. But while they're there, Yaz logs on to the chat room, having assumed her own name "Freedom and Noise," while she's chosen the image of a keyboard. She's going to take over as site administrator and thus she goes to another space. As she introduces herself and claims the authority of the job she says, "A few days ago I met a new woman: Haikumom. A woman who created a living, breathing ecosystem, and since I've never sown a single seed let alone planted a garden, the least I can do is censor you, fix glitches, and one other thing . . . Formulating first line. Did Haikumom really do these on the fly? Five-seven-five, right?"[97] Yaz truly understands the ways that Odessa was good in her chosen life—no matter her failures as a mother to Elliot and his sister. She will take on the role of elder in the virtual world.

In Puerto Rico, Elliot and Yaz both chart the courses for the next phases of their lives. Elliot has a final confrontation with his ghost, who tries to grab something from his pockets—it's not the passport he's been asking for; it's the pills Elliot's been carrying around. At last he is able to empty them out into his hand and bring them out in the open—we are left to hope he will throw them out.

When they visit El Yunque, Yaz gathers bulbs of spiral ginger to plant in Ginny's garden. She eventually reveals to Elliot—after he gets a text from his father that someone bought Ginny's house—that she's sold her baby grand and purchased the property. After Elliot confesses that he wanted Odessa to relapse, that he set the process in motion because of his anger at the loss of Ginny, and that he fears he too will become completely lost to addiction, Yaz urges him to take the movie offer in California. She says, "Go and don't you ever, ever look back. But if you do, there will be a plastic-covered sofa waiting for you. I'm the elder now. I stay home. I hold down the fort."⁹⁸ With that they count to three and scatter the ashes as the lights go out.

The play's ending, and Yaz's mapped future, are bittersweet from a feminist perspective. In the play's penultimate scene, Yaz tells Elliot of a list she composed of all she'd hoped to accomplish by the time she was thirty—two kids, a marriage defined by equality, tenure, and Carnegie Hall debut of her Oratorio for Electric Guitar and Children's Choir—that she'd buried in the ground in Fairmount Park. She admits, "I promise you I'll never have the courage to go to that spot with a shovel and face my list full of crumbs, decoys, and bandaids."⁹⁹ Yaz had big dreams for herself, and she berates herself for the ways she came up short. A few lines later she says, "We're in PR and I'm gonna dig a new hole and I'm not putting a wish or a list in there, I'm putting a scream in there. And I'm gonna sow it like the ugliest foulest and most necessary seed in the world and it's going to bloom! This time it's going to fucking bloom!"¹⁰⁰ This inspires Elliot to say that when Yaz was telling him this, it was as though Ginny were standing in front of him—Ginny who was able to make whatever she put in the ground burst into glorious bloom. With this Yaz excuses herself to make a call, the call we later figure out was to purchase Ginny's house and truly take her place in the neighborhood and the family.

This choice is complex. On the one hand, Yaz connects with a woman she admires, and she aims to live her own life following that example. She defines a meaningful life and how family can be structured on her own terms, and she puts a plan into action to realize her goals. But on the other, Yaz gives up much. She sells the piano that might have helped her realize her musical dreams—though she says she can be content with an upright. And while Elliot goes off to chase his fortune, to follow his star to Hollywood, Yaz chooses to sacrifice, to hold the family together, and to give up her physical mobility, even if she maintains virtual mobility maintaining Odessa's site under her other identity, Freedom and Noise. Yaz maps her destiny, but it is one that rings dissonant notes for the feminist viewer.

In May of 2012, after years of anticipation, stocks of Facebook were available for purchase by the public. Investors large and small leapt into the fray, but at the end of five days of trading, *Bloomberg Businessweek* called the IPO "the biggest flop of the decade."¹⁰¹ At the end of the week of trading, Ross Douthat opined in *The New York Times*, "Of all the major hubs of Internet-era excitement, Mark Zuckerberg's social networking site has always struck me as one of the most noxious, dependent for its success on the darker aspects of online life: the zeal for constant self-fashioning and self-promotion, the pursuit of virtual forms of 'community' and 'friendship' that bear only a passing resemblance to the genuine article, and the relentless diminution of the private sphere in the quest for advertising dollars."¹⁰² While *Dead Man's Cell Phone* does not address Facebook, it is not hard to guess, given Ruhl's 2008 sentiment toward the cell phone and other mobile technologies, how she probably felt about the burgeoning phenomenon at that time. Her play strongly cautions against the substitution of virtual relationships for nontechnologically enhanced ones (not to mention the contemporary penchant for eschewing privacy) and celebrates moments when we connect on the most human of levels. Doran and Hudes, on the other hand, question the privileging of one sphere over the other, see ways that one space might enhance the other, and look for any means available to allow their characters (and through them their audiences) to reimagine connection and place. The three plays together mark a continuum of reaction to the cultural revolution wrought by mobile technologies, offering audiences the opportunity to weigh the new pleasures and challenges they promise—while variously venerating and expanding the ancient power of theater.

CHAPTER 6

Natural Forces

In the Next Room or the Vibrator Play, a tale set in the late nineteenth century, chronicles the changing relationship of Dr. Givings and his wife Catherine. Dr. Givings is experimenting with a new technology—the electric vibrator—to treat hysteria in the operating theater adjacent to the drawing room in their home. When the Daldrys come to the doctor seeking help for Mrs. Daldry's symptoms, they also connect the Givings to a wet nurse to help nourish the Givingses' infant daughter. Later, another patient, Leo Irving, enters the Givings home. After the Givingses confront the challenges provided by their guests and learn to appreciate the wonders of their own bodies, a beautiful thing happens onstage. Ruhl's stage directions suggest, "Although the domestic space seemed terribly permanent—a settee, a statuette—suddenly it disappears and we are in a sweet small winter garden."[1] In the 2009 Broadway production the detailed, realistic interiors of operating theater and drawing room broke apart, and this natural, outdoor scene was revealed in a flourish of pure theatrical magic. Before the final curtains falls, Catherine and her husband achieve a transformative intimacy as she sees his body as she never has before. She revels in the beauty of his body—a body she had never actually seen—and at her instruction, they lie down and make a snow angel as the snow falls around them. As Catherine claims emotion, intimacy, and physicality in way she has never been able to do before, she does so in a (more) natural setting.

Ruhl's placing of a woman's sexual freedom outdoors in the midst of the natural if cultivated snowy beauty of a winter garden has resonance with the concerns of ecofeminist philosophy. Karen Warren explains succinctly, "Ecological feminists ('ecofeminists') claim that there are important connections between the unjustified dominations of women, people of color, children, and the poor and the unjustified domination of nature."[2] A corollary to this idea is that there are important connections between women's liberation and a just relationship with and respect for the natural world and its forces.

But this is the end of the play. To understand the beautiful moment in the garden fully and to appreciate what it meant to arrive there, one must first journey with the Givingses through the other events in the play. After viewing the references to natural forces in the play through an ecofeminist lens and analyzing the relationship between Mrs. Givings and her African American wet nurse, Elizabeth, the significance of the Givingses' snow angels in the garden will be all the more striking.

In addition, I will put the ideas, images, and events of Ruhl's play into conversation with other plays by women that benefit from a similar sort of analysis. The chapter will chart plays that ran or debuted in New York within a single season[3] that move from the least obviously ecofeminist in their concerns (Ruhl's) to the most blatantly ecofeminist in outlook. After I discuss *In the Next Room*, Sarah Ruhl's Broadway debut, I will explore the most honored play of 2009—Lynn Nottage's Pulitzer Prize–winning *Ruined*. I will also examine Kia Corthron's *A Cool Dip in the Barren Saharan Crick*. Corthron's play is not just the most forthright of the three in its ecofeminism; it also offers the most forceful engagement with notions of spirituality that are sometimes linked to ecofeminism.

Before moving into the plays, let me first provide a brief overview of ecofeminism. It is a movement that acquired a name in 1974—from Francoise d'Eaubonne, who used the term *ecofeminisme* to "call attention to women's potential for bringing about an ecological revolution"[4]—and a landmark event in the burgeoning movement's history took place that same year—the Chipko movement. Twenty-seven women from northern India protested the felling of trees in the Himalayan forests by threatening to hug, or in Hindi, *chipko*, the trees that lumberjacks sought to cut down. Their action saved "12,000 square kilometers of sensitive watershed."[5] As the next decade unfolded, Colleen Mack-Canty explains,

> in the West, an ecofeminist focus in activism emerged during the second wave of the women's movement and was predicated on seeing the relations between militarism, sexism, racism, classism, and environmental damage. By the middle 1980s, many women, committed to direct action against militarism, started naming themselves ecofeminists to depict the interdependencies of their political concerns (Sturgeon 1997, 27). As ecofeminism evolved, it took up additional issues such as toxic waste, deforestation, military and nuclear weapons policies, reproductive rights and technologies, animal liberation, and domestic and international agricultural development (Sturgeon 1997, 25), in its efforts to reweave the nature/culture dualism.[6]

In terms of ideas, the nature/culture dualism that Mack-Canty names is crucial. Throughout the work of the major ecofeminist thinkers of the past decade—Chris Cuomo, Greta Gaard, Val Plumwood, Catherine Roach, and Karen Warren stand out on this list—there is a desire to examine the effects that multiple kinds of dualistic thinking have had on both women and the environment.

Val Plumwood lays out the working of dualistic thinking first in regard to nature: "What is taken to be authentically and characteristically human, defining of the human, as well as the ideal for which humans should strive is not to be in what is shared with the natural and animal (e.g., the body, sexuality, reproduction, emotionality, the senses, agency) but in what is thought to separate and distinguish them—especially reason and its offshoots. Hence humanity is defined not as part of nature (perhaps a special part) but as separate from and in opposition to it. Thus the relation of humans to nature is treated as an oppositional and value dualism."[7] The terms that Plumwood identifies as building the inferior or dominated side of the humanity/nature dualism are the same terms that have long been associated with women. So the terms that permit domination of the natural by "man" are the same terms that sanction the domination of women. The natural/animal/nonhuman and feminine are linked so that domination of one is implicated in the domination of the other. Thus many ecofeminists—like feminism more generally, the movement is large enough to encompass many differences of opinion—would like to dismantle, or in Catherine Roach's phrasing, "biodegrade," such dualistic thinking as they advocate the ethical treatment of the natural world and all its inhabitants, regardless of species, genus, or gender.

This ethical treatment sometimes has a spiritual inflection. Karen Warren summarizes what ecofeminist spirituality—a key component of what some kinds of ecofeminists value—entails:

> First ecofeminist spiritualities are feminist: They express a commitment to the elimination of male-gender privilege and power over women in their myths, rituals, symbols, language, and value systems. Second ecofeminist spiritualities are spiritualities: They express faith in a life-affirming (rather than life-denying) power or presence (energy, force, being, deity or deities, God or Goddess) other than and in addition to one's individual ego. They affirm that this power or presence is "greater than the individual ego, greater than their name, their family, their special attributes as individuals" . . . Third ecofeminist spiritualities are ecofeminist: They express a twofold commitment to challenge harmful women-other human Others-nature interconnections and to develop earth-respectful, care-sensitive practices toward humans and earth others.[8]

As ecofeminism emerges in the texts of Ruhl, Nottage, and Corthron, so too does ecofeminist spirituality in sometimes subtle, sometimes striking ways.

In the Next Room

Throughout *In the Next Room*, nature imagery abounds. Near the top of the play, the Daldrys arrive at the home and adjacent office of Dr. Givings and his wife so that Mrs. Daldry might begin treatment for hysteria. Mr. Daldry describes his wife as being very sensitive to both light and cold, thus immediately establishing a connection between his wife's physicality and the natural world. He also complains of the way she weeps at things he finds nonsensical, like their green curtains. Mrs. Daldry explains herself by recalling her mother's weekly cleaning: "When the curtains were cleaned you could see right through to the grapes, you could almost watch them growing, they got so plump in the autumn. My mother would make loads of jam—my mother was not a nervous or excitable woman. It was jam, it was laughing, it was long walks out of doors. We haven't a grape arbor here—I am full of digressions these days, Dr. Givings—but the point is I haven't the strength to wash the curtains every week and beat the ghosts out of them."[9] While Mr. Daldry is rather dismissive of the effect that the natural world might have on a person, Mrs. Daldry is appreciative of plants, views, and simply being outside. In her description of her mother we see a picture of happy, sensually engaged person, so it makes sense that Mrs. Daldry is frustrated by the fact that she is unable to achieve this situation for herself within her own domestic environment.

While Mrs. Daldry is in session with Dr. Givings, after which Mr. Givings has promised he will soon have his "blooming wife"[10] back, thereby further associating Mrs. Daldry and her physicality with the natural world, Mr. Daldry has been dispatched to walk the grounds of the Givings home. Mrs. Givings is curious about how Mr. Daldry will feel about the rain that's falling. She tells him that there are three kinds of people: those who use umbrellas when it isn't raining; those who do not use umbrellas even when it is raining; and those who use umbrellas only in the rain. Mr. Daldry, it turns out is of the kind who uses an umbrella while it is raining, not the romantic kind happy to stride through the rain all wet, like his wife (a facet of her personality he calls "damned annoying"), or the kind with a "scientific" bent, like Dr. Givings who opens his umbrella when the sky threatens rain and keeps it up even when the promise is not kept. Mr. Daldry surprises Mrs. Givings by asking what kind of person she is. She replies, "My husband has always held the umbrella. Isn't that funny. I don't know at all what kind of person I am . . . I'll show you the grounds and we can use this very large umbrella and perhaps *I* will hold it and we shall see what kind of person I am."[11] Here Mrs. Givings recognizes that people are knowable by the way they relate to the natural force of rain. She was immediately drawn to Mrs. Daldry, so it comes as no surprise to her that she would revel in getting wet, and it already comes as no surprise to the audience that Mr. Daldry would be annoyed by his wife's pleasure. But it has never occurred to Mrs. Givings that she might know herself in this simple, physical, natural way—and demonstrate agency in the act of knowing. Within the world of the play, taking an umbrella in hand is a forceful, defining act. Meanwhile contemporary audiences with a greater understanding of women's sexual response than the characters onstage possess will appreciate Ruhl's play with the word "wet."

The natural forces given the greatest attention throughout the play are light and electricity. At the very top of the play, Mrs. Givings is turning the light on, telling her baby that light came "straight from man's imagination into our living room."[12] One of the key arcs of the play is a movement in understanding about what relationship man's imagination plays to light and electricity.

Near the midpoint of the play, Mrs. Givings begs Mrs. Daldry to explain the mysterious treatment she's been receiving. Though the operating theater is in her home—just in the next room—Mrs. Givings is not privy to what happens in there beyond hearing the patients' cries and seeing the electric lights flicker when her husband's humming invention draws too great an electrical charge. First Mrs. Daldry tries to explain what happens in the terms that Dr. Givings has used in explaining it to her, but a medical description of the procedure alone does not satisfy Mrs. Givings. She wants to learn of the sensation. Mrs. Daldry describes it as "Pleasure, and pain all at once—electrical current runs through my entire body—I see light—patterns of light, under my eye-lids—and kind of white-hot coal on my feet—and I shudder violently, as though struck by a terrible lightning—and then a darkness descends, and I want to sleep."[13] Here Mrs. Daldry uses light and electricity to try to explain what she feels in her body. The women continue talking, and they ponder what electricity will mean to people over time: they imagine voice recordings, prosthetic limbs, electric pianos and fireflies, and the elimination of candles. Mrs. Givings muses, "Do you think our children's children will be less solemn? A flick of the finger, and all is dark! On, off, on off! We could change our minds a dozen times a second! . . . We shall be like gods!"[14]

At this point, they continue to regard electricity as unnatural. The women try to fathom how electricity might change their lives—their senses of their bodies, of time, and their relationships to others. Eventually they become bold enough—perhaps because of Mrs. Givings's first steps in reaching for the umbrella—to take electricity into their own hands in the form of the vibrator. They conduct their own experiments on themselves as the first act closes and we get the sense that they are acquiring godlike agency as they come to know their own bodies and their capacity for pleasure.

At the top of the second act, Ruhl introduces a new character—Leo Irving, a painter and "male hysteric," who also requires the doctor's stimulating treatment. Mrs. Givings, no doubt like many in the audience, is surprised by his presence, but including a male patient has great reverberations with ecofeminist thought. As Richard T. Twine explains, "Reminding men of their embodiment potentially subverts the gendered mind/body dualism," and furthermore "this allows us to glimpse an important method by which bodies have been historically marked, namely by dualistic associations. It is only by moving beyond this thought cage that ecofeminism can make *all* aware of their closeness to nature and embodiment."[15]

When Mrs. Givings takes her turn at expressing how the vibrator made her feel, she tells Leo, for whom the experience has also been perception shattering that "we surround ourselves with plants, with teapots, with little statuettes to give ourselves a feeling of home, of permanency, as if with enough heavy objects, perhaps the world won't shatter into a million pieces, perhaps the house will not fly away, but I experienced something the other day, Mr. Irving, something to shatter a statuette, to shatter an elephant. Here is my riddle: what is a thing that can put a man to death and also bring him back to life."[16] Leo guesses love, but she gives her answer a few lines later: electricity. For Mrs. Givings, electricity threatens to burst apart life as she knows it. She sees its danger but also its possibility.

Through much of the play electricity seems to be juxtaposed with nature, positioned as its opposite, but it is Dr. Givings who is eventually able to articulate what is wrong with this false duality. In so doing, he continues to lead us to question what other dualities that we take for granted might also be false. After much persuasion, Mrs. Givings convinces her husband to try the treatment on her—to experiment with her healthy, nonhysterical body. As he's just beginning to touch the vibrator to her body, he tells her not to be afraid of electricity's natural force and of his own surprise at generating sparks in his cat's fur as a child: "My father said this is nothing but electricity, the same thing you see on the trees in a storm. My mother seemed alarmed. Stop stroking the cat. You might start a fire. I kept on stroking the cat. I thought: is nature a cat? If so, who strokes its back?"[17] As Mrs. Givings reaches orgasm, she asks her husband to kiss her. Though he had seemed able to see that the electrical and the natural could be one and the same, when she wants to introduce this kind of intimacy into his experiment, his courage falters. He says, "Men of science should never mix their family lives and their medical lives"[18] and urges her to forget their mutual mistake.

Mrs. Givings disagrees stridently and tries to use nature to remind him that such dichotomous thinking—intimacy and science, nature and culture, men and women—keeps people from seeing what's around them clearly. She recalls that during their courtship she used to write her name in the snow outside his window and wonders if he ever saw it before it melted. She laments, "If you saw my name in the snow all you'd see was a natural substance."[19]

The episode in the operating theater pushes their relationship to the brink of collapse. Mrs. Givings was almost immediately attracted to Leo—he is definitely not the sort of man to be encumbered by an umbrella—and she tries flirting with him in front of her husband to provoke a reaction. Her strategy fails. Dr. Givings says calmly that the fault is his due to the treatment, and "a hand on the cheek, these are muscles, skin, facts."[20] This only frustrates Mrs. Givings the more. She eventually declares her love to Leo, and when he rebuffs her advance, she breaks down and must confront the loneliness she feels in her marriage. At the crucial moment, however, Dr. Givings is at last able to express his love for his wife. As he kisses her tenderly on her face he names and blesses her joints, arteries and nerves by their Latin names, concluding, "I bless thee, Catherine."[21]

It is this moment that precipitates the shattering of the domestic space. Catherine asks her husband to "Open me . . . Away from the machine. In the garden."[22] In these last moments, as the body becomes holy in the act of blessing, and a couple is able to enter a garden, we see nature, freedom, and electricity of a particular sort come together in a moment of grace.

While the main plot of *In the Next Room* is complex in and of itself in the way it resonates with ecofeminist concerns, that effect is heightened by the play's subplot, which concerns the Givingses' hiring of Elizabeth, an African American wet nurse. At the same time, the religious undertones of the main plot are amplified emphatically in the exploration of wet-nursing.

We hear about Elizabeth before we meet her. She is the Daldrys' housekeeper, and Mr. Daldry recommends her to the Givingses when he learns they are in need of a wet nurse. In addition to explaining that she recently lost her baby, he speaks of her education and manners but suspects she might reject the idea because, "you know what they say about wet-nurses, nine parts devil, one part cow—but that's what you want, isn't it? A nice young woman who never intended to be a wet nurse but who has milk, milk to spare."[23] While Mr. Daldry respects Elizabeth, clearly he doesn't hold wet-nursing as a practice in high regard. This is not because he worries about the way that wet-nursing exploited financially desperate women, their bodies, and their children[24] but because he suspects that women who engage in the practice are both immoral and animal. Meanwhile he lays no blame at the feet of those who pay for the services of the wet nurse. Again the kind of prejudicial dichotomous thinking that ecofeminism seeks to dismantle is present here.

Delores S. Williams provides further nuance. In "Sin, Nature, and Black Women's Bodies," she argues,

> Because, in the nineteenth century, slave owner consciousness imaged black people as belonging to a lower order of nature than white people, black people were to be controlled and tamed like the rest of the natural environment. Black

women (and black men) were "viewed as beasts, as cattle, as articles for sale" (Nichols 1963, 12). The taming of these "lower orders of nature" would assure the well-being of both master and slave—so slave owner consciousness imagined. Put simply, the assault upon the natural environment today is but an extension of the assault upon black women's bodies in the nineteenth century.[25]

Ruhl is careful to show that men were not alone this kind of thinking. Mrs. Givings balks at the idea of hiring an African American wet nurse. She says, "It is only that they say morality goes right through the milk. Mrs. Evans said just the other day, oh I wouldn't use a darkie, the morality goes right through the milk."[26] Mrs. Givings's association of the body's functions with morality is underscored as her husband tries to ameliorate her feelings about the help he feels she needs with nursing. He tells her, "The body is blameless. Milk is without intention," but she replies, "A good mother has a fat child. And everyone knows it."[27] The script does not answer whether the baby truly was failing to thrive due to Mrs. Givings's milk supply. Mrs. Givings seems less convinced than her husband. When she notices how attached her daughter, Lotty, is getting to Elizabeth, she begins to cry and declares her need to feed her own child. Dr. Givings dismisses her desires saying, "But you can't, love. Your milk isn't adequate."[28]

Since her husband has made clear that the wet-nursing will continue despite her wishes for control of her own body, Mrs. Givings must come to terms with the situation. So she asks Elizabeth if she feels love for Lotty while they are nursing, and when Elizabeth responds that tries not to think of love, specifically for her own dead son, Henry, Mrs. Givings launches into a long monologue about the birth of Lotty that establishes the subplot's striking religious imagery:

> And then she came out and clambered right onto my breast and tried to eat me, she was so hungry, so hungry it terrified me—her hunger. And I thought: is that the first emotion? Hunger? And not hunger for *food* but wanting to eat other *people*? Specifically one's mother? And then I thought—isn't it strange, isn't it strange about Jesus? That is to say about Jesus being a man? For it is women who are eaten—who turn their bodies into food—I gave up my blood—there was so much blood—and I gave up my body—but I couldn't feed her, couldn't turn my body into food, and she was *so hungry*. I suppose that makes me an inferior kind of woman and a very inferior kind of Jesus.[29]

While the main plot also employs Christian symbolism in terms of light and gardens, the wet-nursing discussion does so more boldly. Here we find, much as we did in Ruhl's *Passion Play*, that traditional Christian imagery fails to amplify women's experience of the world and their bodies and how this can be reconciled with their spiritual life. For Mrs. Givings, the act of giving birth radically challenged her beliefs about self, motherhood, and spirituality. It becomes impossible for her to reconcile labor, nursing, and caregiving with the central narrative of Christianity.

Through much of the play, she aims, despite increasing challenges, to preserve the system of thought and belief that is familiar to her. When Leo, who is much enamored of Elizabeth, offers to pay her handsomely to pose for him while nursing Lotty, he anticipates shocking the art world with a portrait of a realistically nursing Madonna. Mrs. Givings attributes the paucity of such images to the following: "We are to think of Him feeding us, I suppose. Not the other way around."[30] Mrs. Givings tries, somewhat half-heartedly, to perpetuate the ideas that religious and social convention have taught her. But as she's confronted by the image of Elizabeth nursing and the effect it has on Leo, the ideas aren't enough to quell her jealousy. Ruhl's final critique of the image of Christ's sacrifice as sustenance as ample to convey women's experiences of both physicality and spirituality comes when Elizabeth is about to take her final leave of the Givingses' household. Elizabeth tells Mrs. Givings that her husband saw Leo walk her home with the painting of his wife as Madonna in hand; he will no longer accept his wife working for the Givingses.[31] Before Mrs. Givings lets Elizabeth take her final exit, she prods her to explain how she has lived with the sorrow of the loss of her son. Elizabeth reveals, "The more healthy your baby got, the more dead my baby became . . . Sometimes I hated her for it. But she would look at me, she would give me this look—I do not know what to call it if it is not called love. I hope every day you keep her—you keep her close to you—and you remember the blood that her milk was made from. The blood of my son, my Henry."[32] The ambivalence that lurked behind the image that circumstance and artifice created is deeply instructive. What Mrs. Givings says to Leo a few moments later also applies here: "Oh—I see nothing, I understand nothing—".[33] In her jealousy and self-concern, Mrs. Givings had been blind to the physical and spiritual sacrifice Elizabeth and her son have made for baby Lotty. By play's end, when Ruhl shows her audience the powerful, transformative beauty of Mrs. Givings's liberation in the garden, when the desires of both the body and the spirit are met, she asks us to see clearly the price paid by those whose liberation is at the end of the nineteenth century (if not still in the early twenty-first century) far more difficult to stage.[34]

Ruined

Ruined won the 2009 Pulitzer Prize. It played Off-Broadway at the Manhattan Theatre Club beginning January 21, 2009, and extended eight times (with a total of 22 preview performances and 238 regular performances), and there was talk of moving what became the most acclaimed play of the 2008–9 season to Broadway. Its final performance was September 6, 2009. But *Ruined* was not Lynn Nottage's first theatrical triumph. *Intimate Apparel* had already changed her status in the theater. Though she had been admired in cognoscenti circles for early plays like *Crumbs from the Table of Joy* and *Mud, River, Stone*, she became widely acclaimed thanks to *Intimate Apparel*, an elegant tale of an African American seamstress in turn-of-the-century New York. She garnered several awards, and the play went on to be the most produced play in American regional theater in the 2005–6 season. *Fabulation*, which opened in New York the night *Intimate Apparel* closed, was another critical victory for Nottage.

Intimate Apparel is significant to the history of *Ruined* because it began the productive working relationship between Nottage and director Kate Whoriskey.[35] Though Whoriskey, who had directed the world premiere of *Intimate Apparel* at the South Coast Repertory in Costa Mesa, California, was replaced by Daniel Sullivan for the New York premiere of *Intimate Apparel*, she was back at the helm of *Fabulation*, which led indirectly to *Ruined*.

Whoriskey recounts the tale of the genesis of *Ruined* in the introduction to the first published version of the play: "Five years ago, Lynn and I were preparing for our second collaboration, *Fabulation*. On a break, we got into a conversation about Brecht and found that both of us admire *Mother Courage* . . . Lynn wanted to do a version of *Mother Courage* set in the Congo. A violent war over natural resources had been raging there for years, causing one of the highest death tolls of any war, and, yet, the violence generated very little media attention . . . She thought that doing an adaptation might call attention to the crisis."[36] The day after their collaboration on *Fabulation* opened in June 2004, Nottage, Whoriskey, and Nottage's husband, filmmaker Tony Gerber, flew to Uganda, a country bordering the warring Congo. An Amnesty International office became the base from which the trio could interview refugee women who had survived the violence of the war and document their stories. In her travelogue of the journey in *American Theatre*, Nottage wrote, "The stories of the refugee women—all victims of rape and torture at the hands of armed forces—are heart-wrenching, horrifying, and poignant. They are told with dignity and conviction, and we feel honored to be entrusted with their personal narratives. Their stories literally take my breath away. The long afternoon proves to be one of the most emotionally taxing experiences of my life."[37] She returned in 2005 with her husband, her daughter, and her father, touring all over East Africa.

The more Nottage got to know the stories of African women and the complex context in which they played out, the less she felt interested in doing the adaptation of *Mother Courage*, Bertolt Brecht's 1939 masterpiece about the impossibility of goodness and virtue surviving when one attempts to do business during a war. Though the initial impulse had been productive—"we wanted to figure out a way to discuss war, since we're in the midst of a war, but to look at it from a woman's point of view"—³⁸ the specific situation in the Congo required a dramaturgical strategy different from Brecht's.

So Nottage let go of many vestiges of her original inspiration. A gentle nod to that starting point is, however, still discernible in the central character's name, Mama Nadi, and the fact that she, like Mother Courage, is a business woman. Mama Nadi owns a bar and brothel. She both shelters and profits from the young women who have been cast out of their villages and families after being raped by soldiers. As she says, it was the landscape of war that shaped her occupation and her identity: "I didn't come here as Mama Nadi, I found her the same way miners find their wealth in the muck."³⁹

As *Ruined* was opening in New York, Nottage told *The New York Times'* Celia McGee that beyond moving past most specifics of Brecht's narrative, she had also eschewed some of Brecht's dramaturgical techniques. McGee reports, "One of the first things Ms. Nottage was able to jettison by developing her own conception rather than staging a version of Brecht's was the 'kind of distancing Brecht strove for from his audience so he could engage it intellectually,' she said. 'I believe in engaging people emotionally, because I think they react more out of emotion,' than when they are 'preached to, told how to feel. It was important that this not become a documentary or agitprop.'"⁴⁰

From the play's first moments in the public eye, Nottage thus aimed to distance herself and her writing from Brecht's most famous theory and technique, alienation or Verfremdung—which has as a goal disrupting the emotional identification of the audience with a play's characters and action. Instead Brecht wanted cool, rational spectators who would judge the characters and action of the play and then apply these lessons to events outside the theater. *Ruined* almost immediately began receiving considerable scholarly attention—at the 2010 Association for Theatre in Higher Education Conference, for example, five scholars delivered papers on the topic. Academic reviewers have focused on the first part of the play's development and have been unwilling or unable to see how Nottage's conversation with Brecht's ideas, especially those concerned with emotion in the theater, have evolved.

So In the October 2010 issue of *American Theatre*, Nottage tried again. She told interviewer Randy Gener, "People always enter from the thing that is familiar to them . . . I am probably to blame for saying, 'Oh it was inspired by *Mother Courage*'—which it was. But *Ruined* is a huge departure."⁴¹ I would like to embrace Nottage's view of her own play rather than fight it with an interpretation that privileges Brecht's ideas instead of hers. I'm interested in the ways Nottage used Brechtian ideas as point of departure. What she does with the play is unique rather than incomplete as some of the first studies of the plays have suggested.⁴² I find that Nottage has radically transformed Brechtian theory for her twenty-first-century ecofeminist project, finding a way to reclaim strong emotional reaction in the theater and turn it to specific political ends. She takes a central ecofeminist idea and renders it with rich emotion in dramatic form: the forces that exploit women are the same forces that exploit nature. In so doing she suggests that finding a morality in the midst of this domination requires substantial negotiation on the parts of the individuals in its wake.

Since Nottage aimed to tell the stories of Congolese women's experience of war, it makes sense that some aspects of Brecht's alienation might require reimagination. Silvija Jestrovic summarizes *Verfremdung* as follows: "The core of Brecht's *Verfremdung* resides in fictionalizing the real, demonstrating that fixed relations between the individual and social reality are fabrications as well."[43] In some regards, Nottage, too, wanted to fictionalize the real. As she said, she was not aiming to create a documentary. Elsewhere she said of her interview process, "I was not looking specifically for details and facts of human rights abuse. I was much more interested in personal narratives and stories of individuals and not just the trauma. The kinds of questions I asked were very different than if I were going to be writing a human rights article or a newspaper report."[44] Nottage clearly intended to make a theatrical, dramatic version of the personal and all-too-real physical and emotional experiences that women shared with her. A problem with Verfremdung—that may explain some of Nottage's discomfort with the concept—comes in the second half of Jestrovic's summary. In the case of women who had been raped repeatedly for months, the relation between the individual and the social reality was not a fabrication. Power was exerted on women's bodies in literal, actual ways. As Whoriskey phrased her realization of what she saw, "the human body becomes the weapon, the teenage boy the terror, and a woman's womb 'the battleground.'"[45] This kind of social relation has physical—not to mention psychological—consequences that cannot be described as fabrications.

The kind of social relations that form the backdrop to the play's action also have real ecological consequences. In the printed version of the play, both Nottage's setting statement and the opening stage directions emphasize that the action will take place in a small mining town. She also indicated that there are "the sounds of the tropical Ituri rain forest."[46] In the original New York production, the environment was a strong physical presence. Surrounding the bar were numerous large tree trunks. The bar seemed to have sprung up right in the middle of the forest, and there was no clear material demarcation between indoor and outdoor space. And before the end of the play's first scene, Christian, a traveling a salesman who does business with Mama Nadi and who hopes to find a roof for his "ruined" niece, tries to convince her of the changes that are coming: "Things are gonna get busy, Mama. All along the road people are talking about how this red dirt is rich with coltan. Suddenly everyone has a shovel, and wants to stake a claim since that boastful pygmy dug up his fortune in the reserve. I guarantee there'll be twice as many miners here by September."[47] Nottage based Christian's claim in reality. As the Western world's attention was first turning to the problems caused by mining for coltan, *The New York Times* reported, "All a miner has to do is chop down great swaths of the forest, gouge S.U.V.-size holes in streambeds with pick and shovel and spend days up to his crotch in muck while sloshing water around in a plastic washtub until coltan settles to the bottom. (Coltan is three times heavier than iron, slightly lighter than gold.) If he is strong and relentless and the digging is good, a miner can produce a kilogram a day. Earlier this year, that was worth $80—a remarkable bounty in a region where most people live on 20 cents a day."[48] By 2010 coltan, which when processed is called tantalum, a highly effective, heat-resistant conductor of electricity that is used to control the flow of current in miniature circuit boards, was even more valuable. As the Canadian *Globe and Mail* reported, "The global tantalum-capacitor market is worth about $2-billion (U.S.) annually. You'll find the capacitors in computers, cell phones, home appliances and myriad other electronic goods."[49] With this in mind, Christian's later report of his experience at a local mine should come as no surprise: "I don't know about the miners, but it's scaring me. I was just by Yaka-Yaka. When I was there six months ago it was forest filled with noisy birds, now it looks like God spooned out heaping mouthfuls of earth, and every stupid bastard is trying to get a taste of it. It's been ugly, chérie, but never like this."[50]

While the general theoretical grounding of Brecht's ideas might fail to accommodate the exploitation of women and the environment in the twenty-first-century Congo, the residue of his some of his specific theatrical techniques still leaves Nottage with much to work—and transform. When Nottage describes her use of music in the play there are strong similarities to Brechtian musical conventions: "The nature of the subject matter and the intensity of the situation made me interested in using music to ease the audience into the story and to give them a brief break from the reality of the world. But if you listen to the lyrics very carefully, they also serve as exposition and work in counterpoint to the music, which in many instances is very upbeat, inviting, and enticing. Whereas the lyrics that the young women [sic] is singing are quite serious and dark."[51]

Sophie, a beautiful, young new arrival at Mama Nadi's bar and brothel, sings for the soldiers and miners who frequent the establishment. Because her physical wounds are too fresh and too severe—Mama Nadi says to Sophie soon after she first meets her, "I know it hurts, because it smells like the rot of meat,"[52] her vocal talents must compensate for what she is unable to offer her boss's clientele. In act 2 she sings accompanied by guitar and drums that in the New York production were visible stage right. The sound of the music accented the festive atmosphere in the bar that was adorned with Christmas lights, painted in mismatched bright colors, and inhabited by a parrot. But the lyrics of the song, as Nottage explains, offer a different perspective:

> A rare bird on a limb
> Sings a song heard by a few,
> ....
> A cry that tells a story, harmonious,
> But time forgotten.
> To be seen, is to be doomed
> It must evade, evade capture,
> And yet the bird
> Still cries out to be heard.[53]

The dissonance between the music and setting and the lyrics bears a striking resemblance to the way Jestrovic describes Lotte Lenya's performance of Kurt Weill and Brecht's songs in a cabaret setting—nostalgia and romance in the music and atmosphere bumped up against lyrics that conveyed cruelty and violence. The things seen and heard contrasted. This is a kind of musical *Verfremdung* capable of "unmasking manipulative patterns [as] it reinforces an alternative ideological and political attitude."[54]

So too in *Ruined*, Nottage juxtaposes the music and lyrics for ideological effect. She mentions easing her audience into the story and giving them a break from the reality of the fictive world—and the tempo and the rhythms do that, working on the audience as they work on the bar patrons. They too are soothed and seduced. At the same time the lyrics are dark—referencing the danger of possessing a beauty that will be noticed and that will lead to doom and capture. In an echo of Brechtian technique, Nottage's music works on the audience on two levels at once.

But this song also has a specifically ecofeminist component. In the scene before Sophie sings her song, Salima likens her to a sunbird able to fly away from hands seeking to touch, but Sophie tells her what lies beneath this image: "While I'm singing, I'm praying the pain will be gone, but what those men did to me lives inside of my body. Every step I take I feel them in me. Punishing me. And it will be that way for the rest of my life."[55] When Salima imagines Sophie as a bird—a creature who is other to her—she is unable to connect with her empathically. Though they have both suffered similar grievous injury—both have been gang-raped repeatedly, though Sophie's more intense physical injuries have resulted in fistula, or holes between the vagina and the bladder or rectum that cause incontinence, infertility, and odor—Salima is unable to see her suffering. She imagines her happy and free instead of in the constant pain that Sophie describes. As Salima separates Sophie into a category of the natural as opposed to the human, it becomes impossible for her to remain cognizant of the injustice she continues to suffer. Dichotomous thinking, by the empowered and unempowered alike, stands in the way of liberation.

Salima describes her own trauma to Sophie later in the play. Though her husband, ironically named Fortune, shunned and beat her when she was first released by her captors, he has since felt remorse and has hunted for, and found, Salima at Mama Nadi's. Sophie, who devours romance books when she has the opportunity, thinks Salima should offer Fortune forgiveness, but Salima, who is now pregnant, knows that reconciliation is impossible. She recounts how a beautiful morning picking tomatoes alone[56]—because she sent her husband out to buy her a pot—changed her life forever: "The sun was about to crest . . . It was such a clear and open sky. This splendid bird, a peacock, had come into the garden to taunt me, and was showing off its feathers. I stooped down and called to the bird: 'Wssht, Wssht.' And I felt a shadow cut across my back, and when I stood four men were there over me, smiling, wicked schoolboy smiles."[57] What follows, as one man holds her down by pressing his boot into her chest, is rape by the rest of the men, the death of her baby (one man stomps on her head), and months of captivity and torture. She says, "They tied me to a tree by my foot . . . I lay there as they tore me to pieces, until I was raw . . . five months. Five months. Chained like a goat."[58] Salima's monologue plays in counterpoint to Sophie's song. It contains moments of stunning beauty—as the words conjure the fragrance of the garden, the heat of the sun, the majesty of creatures with which Salima shares the land—mixed with horror at the injury she endures as the men turn her into a chained beast who must serve them. Dichotomous thinking reaches its horrible zenith in this tale.

But Nottage also believes that if audiences bear witness to the consequences of such thinking together, they might also progress beyond it. She says,

> Our role as playwrights is to interpret the national narrative and to explore what the mythology of today *is* . . . I think to do that, as is the case with *Ruined*, people can interface with newspaper articles or human rights periodicals and have one sort of clinical response. What I can do as a playwright is paint a portrait of people in three dimensions that allows people to have a very visceral reaction and that moves people in a way that a newspaper article won't. People after seeing *Ruined* would say, "I've read these articles before and I know what's happening, but now I feel moved to act." They feel as though they've spent two hours with a living, breathing human being with a story that can't be ignored.[59]

Nottage and Salima are not done with us, however. When Mama Nadi refuses to turn Salima over to Fortune, he retaliates by telling Commander Osembenga, leader of the current government who frequents Mama Nadi's bar, that she has been harboring the rebel leader, Jerome Kisembe. Osembenga comes back to the bar to find Kisembe (who does sometimes drink there) and to punish Mama Nadi. Just as he and his soldiers are about to rape Josephine, Salima enters, and as the stage directions indicate, blood seeps through the middle of her dress and drips down her legs, and she gives what is perhaps the script's most powerful and significant line: "You will not fight your battles on my body anymore."[60] She has killed the fetus she was carrying and herself as well.

The best way to describe this climactic moment is with the Brechtian term *gestic*, which suggests the simultaneous visibility of many layers of meaning in a single physical stage image. All at once the audience sees the exploitation, pain, and the mastery of those things by both the actor and the character as she commits a rebellious act and owns the stage and the audience's attention. Elin Diamond clarifies the gestic moment thus: "The gestic moment in a sense explains the play, but it also exceeds the play, opening it to the social and discursive ideologies that inform its production. Brecht writes that the scene of the social gest 'should be played as a piece of history' . . . If we read feminist concerns back into this discussion, the social gest signifies a moment of theoretical insight into sex-gender complexities, not only in the play's 'fable,' but in the culture which the play, at the moment of reception is dialogically reflecting and shaping."[61] And if we read specifically ecofeminist concerns back into Salima's final statement, we see a powerful, indelible image of the cost of promoting ideologies and business practices that justify the interlocked domination of women and natural resources. As a reporter for the Canadian *Globe and Mail* succinctly put it, "numerous government and human-rights groups have drawn a direct line between coltan-mining profits and the ongoing atrocities in the region, including dismemberment and gang rape."[62] The exploitation and destruction of the land is not separate from the exploitation and destruction of its inhabitants.

Ann Fox has aimed to read *Ruined* through a disability studies lens. She writes, "The land is also implicitly referenced through disability metaphor, 'ruined' by being pillaged for coltan and gold. The earth, like the mothers, sisters, and daughters of the Congo, has been invaded, wounded, and forever altered. While the parallel is a problematic one from feminist and Disability Studies perspectives (reifying the ideas of nature-as-conquerable-feminine and disability-as-lack), these bodies, juxtaposed, do call attention to their fragmentation."[63] While most of Fox's analysis is highly insightful, she misses the mark in her reading of the relationship of the land to the female body in the play. When Salima declares that her body will not be a battlefield, she is not reifying "naturist" ideas. Instead she is demanding respect and care for these two distinct, yet symbiotic, forms of existence from cultures (American as well as African) that have historically failed to do so.

Though I do not agree with Fox's reading of how Nottage's juxtaposition of the land and the female body works, I do heartily support her desire to reread the play's ending from disability studies perspective. And if we pair Fox's insights with an ecofeminist perspective, we can amplify the play's complicated ending further. The play's final scene finds Christian returning to Mama Nadi's after an absence of several months. In the interim he has heard about Salima's death and magically regained the sobriety that he lost earlier in the play when Mama convince him to take the drink that Osembenga was forcing upon him. He has returned seeking a romantic relationship with Mama and tells her he loves her. She reveals the secret she has hidden throughout the play—"I'm ruined"—and though she resists, saying, "Love. It is a poisonous word. It will change us. It will cost us more than it returns . . . It'll be an unnecessary burden for people like us,"[64] eventually her resistance melts, and the play ends with Mama and Christian in each other's arms as Sophie and Josephine look on.

The first major scholarly response to the play came from Jill Dolan. On her blog, *The Feminist Spectator*, Dolan wrote, "Would that Nottage had maintained her singular, Brechtian vision of the consequences of war for women to a more bitter end, instead of capitulating to realism's mandate that narratives resolve with heterosexual marriage that solves everything. The gender politics of the Congo that *Ruined* describes with such force are compromised by this conservative happy ending."[65] But as Fox noted after synthesizing the many newspaper reviews of the New York production, this was not the only response. She writes, "The final dance is a moment of profound tension; is this ending a palliative that allows audiences to escape their discomfort with the play's weighty subject, or one that allows them to broach a topic they might have otherwise avoided?"[66] When she looks at the ending through the lens of disability studies, paying special attention to Sophie's presence—there was hope earlier in the play that Mama's savings might pay for reconstructive surgery for Sophie, but Mr. Harari, whom Mama entrusted with a raw diamond, never returned to the bar, thus dashing those hopes—and her continued physical condition, she finds that "the conservatism of the heteronormative and ableist ending is subverted by the presence of Sophie's uncontained, unhealed body, its disability at once visible and invisible. The dance of Mama Nadi and Christian may have solicited the approving gaze of the audience, but it is Sophie's disabled body we are also compelled to recognize in its multiple significations."[67]

An even richer understanding of the play's ending can be gained by reading the several natural images layered into the play's final moments in concert with Fox's interpretation. When Sophie enters and catches Mama and Christian in a kiss, Mama says, "Why are you standing there looking like a lost elephant?"[68] Her insult helps environmental concerns resurface and trouble the romance. As Chris McGreal of the *London Guardian* reported, "environmentalists believe coltan is a threat to wildlife, claiming that thousands of elephants have been killed for food by miners and that gorillas are disturbed and targeted.

It is estimated that there are only two elephants left in the Kahuzi-Biega, from a population of 350 a few years ago."[69] A lost elephant is a rare and endangered being in this terrain. We might wonder, therefore, precisely what the union of Christian and Mama Nadi will mean to this lost elephant. Though Christian surprised Sophie with a letter from her mother when he entered, he said, "Don't expect too much."[70] Without Mama's brothel, Sophie, despite her unhealed body will, most likely be released back into the wild.

When Christian proposes to Mama, thus drawing her into the dance, he does so with a poem full of natural imagery:

> A branch lists to and fro,
> An answer to the insurgent wind,
> A circle dance,
> Grace nearly broken,
> But it ends peacefully,
> Stillness welcome.[71]

In the play's first scene, Christian also offered Mama Nadi a poem that referenced the wind. This one read,

> What, is this love?
> An unexpected wind,
> A fluctuation,
> Fronting the coming of a storm.
> Resolve, a thorny bush
> Blown asunder and swept away.[72]

Christian's poems—parables that help reinforce the allegorical quality of his name—chart the movement of the play. A storm came—that battered all in its wake—but the branch survived and a kind of peace has come in the stillness. And yet in counterpoint to Christian's poetry is the music of the women. If he claims the territory of language, the women claim the equally powerful regions of rhythm and melody. Sophie's voice was the one we hear most often, but Mama also sings with Sophie at the top of act 2. As Mama and Christian dance, the music playing is a guitar solo of "Rare Bird." And while the lyrics are now unspoken, their meaning hovers around, animating the notes—

> To be seen, is to be doomed
> It must evade, evade capture,
> And yet the bird
> Still cries out to be heard.

We get the sense that Sophie is not the only bird fighting for freedom—Mama Nadi is now linked with the bird too.

And it is a bird that has the last line of the play. When Josephine calls out (the stage directions indicate "joyfully"), "Go, Mama," the parrot that Mama has been keeping in the bar chirps, "Mama! Primus! Mama! Primus!"[73] The parrot is significant for a couple of reasons. First, like Christian's poetry, it takes us back to the beginning of the play and one of Mama and Christian's first conversations. They discussed how Mama acquired the vocal, complaint-prone bird after the death Old Papa Batunga, the last of a tribe that still spoke Pygmy. Mama said Papa Batunga "believed as long as the words of the forest people were spoken, the spirits would stay alive . . . When that bird dies this is place is gonna lose part of its story."[74] By play's end, the bird no longer speaks Pygmy. Though the bird is alive, it has lost its connection to the forest people, their language, and their stories. The language of the bird is a last reminder of the cost of the mining and the war it partially spawned to the land and its inhabitants. But the content of the bird's line is also significant. Primus is one of the Congo's most popular beers—though it is brewed by Bralima, which is owned by the Dutch company Heineken. The marks of colonialism and multinational capitalism are certainly legible on Primus. Further, as blogger Kim Gjerstad, an expatriate living in the Congo, explained, in addition to considering beer a form of currency, Congolese men are expected to bring cases of beer when they propose. Furthermore, "Beer is in fact so important, that the breweries were never touched during the two big pillages of the nineties. I've heard more than once that Rwandans only had to bring beer and music to invade Congo."[75] So what is the parrot calling for as the play ends? A celebratory drink—which would pose a danger to Christian as a recovering alcoholic? Payment—is the arrangement that seems romantic just another deal for a woman's flesh? Or is Primus a weapon of invasion? Will Mama wield the weapon against Christian again as she did with Osembenga? Through the bird, as a symbol of the natural landscape and its people's memory, we once again can read a deep ambivalence into the play's closing moments. Is the heteronormative salvation offered by Christian at all efficacious in this deeply troubled environment?

Whether one finds a missed opportunity or a powerful critique in the play's ending, most audiences will surely find much value in the play as a whole. Writing in 2002, Victoria Brittain said, "However long it takes, the women of eastern DRC will one day have to be given a chance to express publicly what they have lived through. The Women's International War Crimes Tribunal for the Trial of Japan's Military Sexual Slavery took half a century to be organised, but has been key to a new understanding of one part of World War Two. The women of DRC deserve no less."[76] Lynn Nottage harnessed the emotional power of the women's stories she heard in the Congo and reframed them publicly and dramatically—sooner rather than later. Even though the tales told recount the depths of human brutality, they also bear witness to an equally human capacity to survive. Like Bertolt Brecht, the author of the play that originally inspired her but from which she quite forcefully departed, Nottage believes theater can lead audiences to action. But while Brecht looked to disarm emotion in the audience, Nottage reclaims it as a powerful tool. She believes that if audiences can first feel someone else's pain, not dismissing it because it belongs to another kind of being or is happening across a different sort of landscape, they may act to ease it. The power of Nottage's hope fueled one of the most powerful stories told on the American stage in several seasons. While the curtain was up, the women of the DRC got some small piece of what they deserve.

A Cool Dip in the Barren Saharan Crick

When the reviews started rolling in for Kia Corthron's 2010 play, *A Cool Dip in the Barren Saharan Crick*, she must surely have been frustrated, because the critics were sounding the same refrain they had long been singing. In his 2001 *New York Times* article on Corthron, "A Playwright Who's Unafraid to Admit She's Political," Don Shewey wrote, "Virtually every review she has received talks about The Trouble With Kia Corthron. 'She tries to cover too much ground.'"[77] In *African American Dramatists* Deborah Gleason-Rielly summarizes the critical response to Corthron's work in a similar way: "Kia Corthron has been hailed as one of the brightest contemporary playwrights and, at the same time, as a playwright who is too political and too subjective, who tries to bundles too many issues into one play."[78]

The reviewers of her 2010 play say essentially the same thing. Charles Isherwood wrote, "'A Cool Dip' wanders without focus through so many different dramatic byways that it never generates any dramatic pulse."[79] Erik Haagensen concurred: "her play is positively overflowing with themes, styles, stories, and politics. Corthron's arresting voice and restless mind aren't sufficient compensation, and the overabundance ends up drowning whatever it is that she wants to say in this maddening, disjointed, overly elliptical work."[80]

At the start of a new decade, and with some twenty plays and a successful television series under her belt,[81] Corthron was still writing big, multifaceted plays. Lisa M. Anderson has said Corthron's plays "are issue plays; while they explicitly take on social and political issues, they do not lack story or character. They ask us to consider questions of justice, especially in a U.S. context of racial oppression."[82] *A Cool Dip* is likewise an issue play, rich with character, but it puts US racial oppression in context with global racial and environmental oppression. The play tells the story of Abebe, a young Ethiopian man, who comes to the United States to go to college where he studies ecology and theology. His hosts are Pickle, a middle-aged African American woman, and her teenage daughter, H. J. Pickle has recently lost her father, husband, and son in Hurricane Katrina. Her mental health is shaky at best—she sees and converses with the ghostly heads of her dead family. In the economically depressed and drought-ravaged Maryland town in which they stay, a bottled water plant is, in act 1, in the offing. In addition to studying, Abebe protests the building of the plant, aims to save souls, and befriends a boy, Tay, whose whole family died when his father killed them and himself. In act 2, which takes place seven years after act 1, the landscapes of Abebe's native land and Maryland have changed. A megadam literally washes away his village (and in despair his best friend, Seyoum, drowns himself where his home used to be), while the bottling plant, and its kin around the Southeast, are drying up springs, adding pollution, and causing health problems for the area's residents. (Pickle now suffers from migraines caused by truck exhaust). Meanwhile H. J. has found Christianity—but has been waiting for baptism until Abebe can return to do it—had a marriage to a man who works at the bottling plant, Tich, annulled, and given a baby up for adoption. Tay has gone to prison for killing one of his several foster fathers.

The critics who disliked *A Cool Dip*—Michael Feingold said emphatically, "I hate this play; I love her work"—aren't wrong that Corthron takes on many issues in this play. Where they err is in not seeing or acknowledging how the parts are directly related, and if the play sprawls, it sprawls for very particular ecofeminist reasons. In *Feminism and Ecological Communities: An Ethic of Flourishing*, Chris Cuomo writes,

> When nature gets harmed, women and other Others (the poor, people of color, indigenous communities, laborers, and members of other categorically disempowered social groups) are inevitably harmed, or harmed more than the socially and economically privileged. The devaluation of women and other oppressed groups justifies
>
> a) Devaluing, and consequently harming, other "feminine" things;
> b) Disregarding their interests by plundering or neglecting land that they own, control, or rely upon;
> c) Ignoring or minimizing their assertions that land, water, or animals be treated more carefully (even when women or agricultural workers, for example, may have more intimate knowledge of the objects in question);
> d) Preventing them from ownership and decision-making that might result in less destructive practices.[83]

Corthron illustrates these very issues in dramatic form. She shows how when water is mistreated—in Maryland, on the Gulf Coast, and in Ethiopia—the economically disenfranchised suffer greatly. Abebe argues tirelessly, at home and in his host country, that the long-term consequences of water usage be considered, but in both places, his advice is eventually discounted. And in both places, ruin, environmental and spiritual, ensues. As Abebe says, "there is sin in godlessness and sin in waste. Waste *is* godlessness. I do not separate."[84]

As the play begins, drought is striking Pickle's Maryland community, but Abebe, newly arrived from Africa, is fascinated by the luxury of running water in their home and flushes the toilet repeatedly. Pickle and H. J. both try to get him to stop. Their lines of dialogue overlap, and while H. J. yells, "Don't think just because you're in America waste is a privilege, we have bills! And limitations, the dang reservoir's dry, boy," Pickle declares, "Water is a finite commodity, we have to be aware!"[85] From the play's first scene, multiple characters are articulating one of the play's key messages—and that message is falling on deaf ears. Corthron is also trying to show that drought doesn't just affect the world's arid locales. Even in the usually verdant mid-Atlantic and Southeast, water shortages are increasingly becoming a problem.

In a recent interview, Corthron discussed how her inspiration for the play came from her experience of two distinct landscapes. In 2007 she attended the World Social Forum in Nairobi, Kenya, with various artists from around the world. There she attended several sessions on global water issues and met Kennedy Odede, a young Kenyan who runs a community center and youth theater in one of Nairobi's slums where there is no running water or electricity. Odede visited the hotel where Corthron and the other Western guests were staying and Corthron reports, "Kennedy spent the night in one of our rooms, marveling that turning a spigot in the shower would, dependably, produce a stream of clean water. This was the beginning of *A Cool Dip* before I knew there would be *A Cool Dip*."[86]

But this wasn't the only location that provided Corthron with inspiration. When she returned from Africa, she headed to her native Southeast—she grew up in rural Maryland near the West Virginia border. As she was starting her first draft, she was in Sewanee, Tennessee, where, she discovered, the neighboring town of Monteagle's reservoir had run dry. Monteagle was buying water from Sewanee. She expressed her surprise: "Such scarcity is expected in cities erected in deserts: Phoenix, Las Vegas, Los Angeles—not to mention Dubai—but the moist, humid South*east*?"[87]

Throughout the play, Corthron juxtaposes the conditions in Africa regarding water with the conditions in the United States. Her goal is to show that in both places, the wealthy dominate the landscape, its resources, and the poor people who inhabit it. The problem is global. In the play's first act, Pickle and Abebe compare notes on the water-related news regarding their hometowns. Abebe reports that a World Bank–funded megadam is coming to his village. Pickle thinks this is good news, but Abebe anticipates catastrophe. Pickle, meanwhile, is excited about the jobs that her town's new water-bottling plant will bring, but Abebe says, "Terrible news! . . . Tons of plastic waste! Tons of fuel to deliver! Minimal health testing!"[88]

As the play progresses, we see the situations in both places get worse. Though Abebe had great faith in those at home in his community and their ability to become stronger as they opposed the megadam, while he was away studying in the United States the megadam came, and the village disappeared. While he was abroad, his activism was focused on his current locale—he protested the water plant, making placards and forming picket lines, and for a time he was able to delay the plant's construction. When he argued with H. J., he said convincingly, "I respect water, I do not take water for granted, how many gallons does one person in Ethiopia use per day? Three! . . . One person in the United States? One hundred fifty-one! Americans talk about conservation but you do not really think it will run out, only one percent of all the world's water is useable, when it is gone, gone, look at this drought!"[89] While his assertions in both places that water be respected or else the results would be cataclysmic were heard when he made them, no one took up the call after him. The interests of the powerful trumped the interests of those most concerned for and knowledgeable about the environment.

In both places, Corthron shows what the locals got in exchange for their resources. At the top of the second act, Abebe dreams of the conversation he might have with the now-dead Seyoum. Seyoum gives his own eulogy, tallying all that he lost when the megadam was built: his productive farmland, his cattle, and his wife and three youngest children to malarial infection. He continues, "And this on a loan of three hundred million dollars from an Italian corporation, right after the Italian government forgave our debt of three hundred million dollars, now ninety-four percent Ethiopia dependent on hydro power, what happen the next drought? Fools."[90] Corthron shows what the inhabitants of Pickle's community have reaped from the water-bottling plant in small, personal ways. When Abebe returns after his eight-year absence to help celebrate Pickle's fiftieth birthday, the sound of the water trucks interrupt Pickle and Abebe's reunion scene. By scene's end Pickle admits to the debilitating headaches she's been suffering as a result of the truck exhaust.

But Corthron also shows the larger impact of the bottling plant on the region. While Abebe was away, H. J. found God, but she has waited to get baptized until he returned. First she thought she'd be baptized where her mother was, but the Nestlé bottling plant had already taken over Glendale Springs. But she also remembered the story of the beautiful place where Abebe took two men for baptism when he was in college. H. J. says, "God has provided this splendid, pristine place for Abebe to come back and lay his hands on me."[91] When they get to the spot in Tennessee that had once been so beautiful, where they had been able to stand waist-deep in the water, the creek is simply no more. H. J. declares the spot "barren as the Saharan."[92] Ultimately Abebe is still able to baptize H. J., but instead of full immersion in either the place that had been important to her mother or the place that had been special for Abebe, the stage directions indicate that Abebe should let a little water trickle down to H. J.'s scalp through his fingers.[93]

A more forceful baptism occurs in the play's penultimate scene. In this scene the two sides of water issues come into direct conflict and merge with the spiritual. When Abebe described his thesis he said he would write on "public versus private water . . . water as a commons versus water as a commodity."[94] The two sides of this argument are presented from the point of view of Abebe, who does not regard water as a commodity, and Tich, who sees nothing wrong with viewing water as a commodity. Tich is the man who was briefly married to H. J. and probably fathered her child. He works at the bottling plant and believes what the company tells him about the good they claim to be doing. Abebe invites him to Pickle's and H. J.'s for dinner for two reasons: he hopes that H. J. and Tich might reunite, and he erroneously believes that Tich has significant authority at the plant and thinks that opening his eyes about the various problems the plant is causing will lead to change. Tich seems to believe genuinely that the company is bringing safe drinking water to the people (and Pickle continues to emphasize the jobs that have come to the area), but Abebe argues strenuously against this and urges them "to demand the purity of tap."[95] The argument escalates to its highest pitch when Abebe admits his personal reason for animosity toward Nestlé, the owner of the bottling company. He reveals that Nestlé advised his village's women that it was healthier to feed their babies with formula than breast milk. Many women, including his mother, took the advice, but they mixed the formula with contaminated water, which killed many infants, including his sisters.[96] Eventually Abebe grabs a pitcher of water and holds it over his head. He declares, "It is a RIGHT! Water is not a commodity Water is a RIGHT!" Tich wrestles him for the pitcher and eventually its contents cascade down upon Abebe. He says, "I understand now, Pickle. What you said: You cannot cross the same river twice. The first time I crossed, there was a wide crick, waist deep. And I baptized them, two new converts receiving Christ, a miracle! But when I returned to the crick to baptize H.J., when I returned to the miracle . . . Gone."[97]

While the meaning of baptism varies among Christian sects, common understandings of the rite include the washing away of sin, consecration, giving public testimony to one's belief, and showing one's obedience to God. The fact that Abebe begins his speech immediately after his "baptism" with "I understand" is significant. His vision, both political and spiritual, has been washed clean. He has come to a new understanding—about the world's impermanence, about loss and the scale of change he can affect. He cannot cross the river twice, and he cannot save the world's water by himself. He is not God, and he finds humility in this moment. He articulates his understanding to Pickle in the final scene: "When I introduced that little dam to my village, it was as if we saw God! God working through me, I felt I could do great things! But takes only one megadam to wash out all the little dams everything, I just want to . . . help I wanted to— . . . I tried!"[98] And here lies one of Corthron's other key messages. While no individual should mistake himself for God, it is everyone's responsibility to find inspiration and to try as Abebe did to make things better. Abebe repeats, "I tried" three times in quick succession, and clearly this is what Corthron hopes her audience will do when they leave the theater.

Corthron's tactics as she works toward getting her audience to see that they too must try to affect positive change in the world are multifaceted. Though the majority of the play operates in a realistic mode, Corthron also intersperses highly theatrical elements to emphasize that there is no single of way of knowing the world or seeing all its problems. We must look from multiple perspectives— political and spiritual, realistic and theatrical—as we seek answers. Corthron herself has written of the intermingling of styles in *A Cool Dip*: "And in joining the concrete/political with the ethereal, the structure of *A Cool Dip* is an amalgam of realistic and fantastical scenes, and the movement from one to the other should not be jarring to the audience but rather a natural flow, as both elements are organically part of the same world. The truth lies in both."[99]

At the end of the play's first act, when H. J. and Abebe are forcing Pickle to confront her grief at the loss of her father, husband, and son in Katrina, Pickle sees and communicates with the ghosts of her loved ones. In the Playwrights Horizons production the ghosts were visible to the audience but not to Abebe and H. J. Masklike faces emerged from the white cabinetry in Pickle's kitchen cabinets and seemed to be straining for release. Corthron has said, "There are often dead people that walk on stage in my plays. That is pretty typical with my work."[100] Here the dead don't walk, but they talk, sing, and demand that the living come to terms with the depth of their loss. Since loss moves the griever beyond logic—Pickle has been buying her son's favorite candy and showing up at soccer games confused about why he's not in the lineup—it makes sense that Corthron would dramatize that grief in extralogical ways.

So too when Abebe dreams of the dead Seyoum, his entrance onto the stage is quite spectacular. The stage directions indicate, "suddenly like a dolphin popping its face out of the water, Seyoum's head surfaces."[101] At Playwrights Horizons, there was a veritable ocean of cobalt blue fabric from which Seyoum emerged. The idea and its rendering were hardly realistic, but they moved the viewer into a different realm.

The play's final scene also contains this kind of vibrant theatricality. Earlier in the play, Pickle described the effect of her headache pills: "I think hey—this must be what morphine's like: morphing. Cuz suddenly here I am, some peaceful desert island, or swimming in calm seas with H.J.'s daddy and Carve."[102] And at the end, Pickle "morphs" again, this time with Abebe and Tay in tow. The stage directions describe the scene: "the room changes so it appears the bed is an island, water all around . . . sound of the tropics."[103] The stage picture was quite beautiful at Playwrights Horizons. Pickle and Abebe sat atop a bed dressed in natural tans while the scrim and the floor shone in the intense cobalt hues that colored Abebe's dream of Seyoum. And the trunk and limbs of large leafless tree glowed white and gave the impression of a rough, natural cross.

Earlier in the play, Abebe had told Pickle of the annual flooding of the Tonle Sap in Cambodia, which causes the Mekong river to reverse: "In America floods are bad, but in Cambodia it is the good flood! . . . A million people gather for the annual celebration of the reversal."[104] This is what Pickle imagines as she morphs—that she is witness to the reversal of the good flood.

It is important that Tay is also part of this final striking moment. If the joining of American and African water issues, theatrical styles, and the political with the spiritual can all be smoothly integrated into an ecofeminist analysis of *A Cool Dip*, the remaining strand that is not so easily woven into the whole is the storyline involving Tay. Abebe tells the audience about his first meeting with Tay early in the play. While working at a shoe store in the mall, Abebe helps the boy select some tennis shoes. This is not an easy task since the boy has not spoken since the night his father killed his mother, brothers, sister, and himself. But when the boy takes Abebe's shoehorn, they immediately form a bond. His foster parents notice the unusual attachment, and they in concert with Tay's teacher encourage Abebe to serve as Tay's big brother. They begin spending time together, though they are quite an odd couple. Tay has kept his father's collection of small confederate flags, and Abebe, who has no idea what these represent, joins Tay in a playground march with the flags.

Corthron has discussed her own struggle to integrate Tay into the play as a whole after writing the first scene with him: "I wanted to see him, see who he was. I don't know if I even knew I was going to keep him, but then I suddenly embraced that character, and that emotional connection between this small White-Is-Right community and this young African man."[105] She also mentioned that in audience talk-backs she'd received questions about the connection between Tay and water. Chay Yew, the director, verbalized the link in a way that Corthron found illuminating: "the play has to do with loss, and it's loss that ties them together."[106]

In the span of time covered in the gap between the play's two acts, Tay's loss increases. Just as the environments in Africa and America suffered without

Abebe's direct attention, so too did Tay. Though his foster family in Maryland had been kind and good, and he'd found a second family in Pickle, H. J., and Abebe (despite what he'd been taught about race by his father), a relative in California comes to claim him. But that situation did not last long, and Tay reenters the foster system within a year. Routinely abused, Tay finally strikes back, stabbing his foster father through the heart with a steak knife. According to Pickle, "Tay be middle-age before he up for parole."[107]

What we see in Tay is the most vulnerable segment of the human population. Young, parentless, and the victim of violence, Tay is entirely at the mercy of a broken social system. He is no better positioned to defend himself than the Maryland springs and creeks, and at play's end we see that he has been no better protected. And yet in a letter to Abebe that Pickle and the audience hear just as she begins her morphing, we see that the essence of the goodness Abebe saw there remains. After explaining that he stole his foster mother's credit cards to order a flag for Abebe, he writes of his experience in prison watching a knife fight but remembering what had once made him smile: "You and Pickle and H.J., Cindy and Pete [my Maryland foster parents], he died last spring when a diesel truck slammed his car. All these people for me never last long, but they was real. Two parts gratitude, right?"[108] Enclosed in the letter is the flag he ordered. It is not a Confederate flag as Pickle fears when she hears the letter. It is instead the flag of Ethiopia. His gift makes clear that the best part of Tay thrived in Abebe's care.

As Pickle morphs and dreams of reversing loss, she dreams Tay back into boyhood at the same time that she dreams of an abundance of water and the life it supports. She wishes for conservation of the environment and of the human potential of Tay that has also been squandered. Tay appears and joins Abebe and Pickle on their island of possibility. Together they remember the magical moment when Abebe saw his first snowfall. Abebe closes the show saying, "So soft! We stand on the edge, a tree limb overhead. Temperature rise, and now the miracle: three states of matter! Solid ice, and its gas mist hovering above it, and liquid: a sparkling icicle from the tree branch melts. Drip. Drip. Drip. Drip."[109]

What Corthron offers us at the end of *A Cool Dip* is a fantasy, but it is a fantasy that we should, like the ever-optimistic Abebe, try to realize. She has spoken several times over the years of her debt to Augusto Boal's *Theatre of the Oppressed*, a book she discovered in graduate school. She recalls that Boal "says if you leave an audience in despair, it's hard for them to then act. They're left feeling that there's nothing they can do. I always try to leave off with some remnant of hope."[110]

This characteristic vision of Corthron's is also one in keeping with Warren's definition of ecofeminist spirituality. It is at once free of gender privilege in its symbology and values; it is life affirming; and it models respect and care for humans, nature, and human-nature interconnections. If Ruhl showed her audience their sometimes-limited vision in appreciating whose liberation is possible within a given environment, and if Nottage hinted at spirituality through her complicated ending with the allegorically named Christian and Mama, Corthron envisions an unabashed moment of ecofeminist spiritual grace and optimism. It is a shame that the reviewers of the play's first production were dismissive of her high, multifaceted ambitions, because it is now unlikely that this play will ever reach a fraction of the audiences of the differently powerful *In the Next Room* and *Ruined*. Corthron's mighty voice should be heard, too.

EPILOGUE

"The Curtain Goes Up"

When a story isn't over, it's hard to write a conclusion. So instead I'll close by recounting the next chapters in the stories of Sarah Ruhl and her contemporaries. I will also dream of theater seasons to come from the vantage point of the summer of 2012.

Some of the writers in the study have spent significant time working outside theater in recent years. Television has been home to the talents of Diana Son and Bathsheba Doran lately. After spending several years writing and producing for *Law and Order: Criminal Intent*, Son worked on the police and crime dramas *Southland* and *Blue Bloods*. While Son has been working in television, her earlier play *Stop Kiss* continues to see production at a variety of venues around the country. As artists and audiences (re)discover her theatrical insights in *Stop Kiss*, perhaps they will be motivated to produce *Satellites* in subsequent seasons. Bathsheba Doran wrote for the second season of the Martin Scorsese/HBO Series *Boardwalk Empire*. She has also adapted *The No. 1 Ladies' Detective Agency* for HBO Films. Meanwhile *Kin*'s Chicago premiere in late spring 2012 garnered favorable reviews, and in an article just prior to the 2012 Tony Awards Charles Isherwood named a group of playwrights—Annie Baker, Stephen Karam, Amy Herzog, Will Eno, and Doran—that "shares a sensibility that has renewed my confidence in the fertility of theater as an art form that can speak to new generations."[1] I hope this critical attention will motivate more regional productions of *Kin* and generate more commissions for new work—in addition to those Doran already has from Atlantic Theatre, Playwrights Horizons, and London's Schtanhaus. Kia Corthron, who wrote for the acclaimed series *The Wire* earlier in the decade, has recently devoted her talents to an entirely new medium. She's most recently written a novel, *The Castle Cross the Magnet Carter*.[2] Clearly television, film, and fiction offer writers new opportunities and new audiences, but it is my hope that the American theater will benefit from these writers' evolving talents in future seasons as well.

Meanwhile some of Ruhl's contemporaries have continued (or are in the midst of continuing) the work represented by the plays studied here. In November 2011, Joan Didion released *Blue Nights*, a kind of sequel to *The Year of Magical Thinking* in which she focuses on the death of her daughter. Given the recent success of *The Year of Magical Thinking* at theaters around the country—clearly the script can shine even without Vanessa Redgrave's stellar presence as productions in Westport, Connecticut; Naples, Florida; Chicago, Illinois; Baltimore, Maryland; Kansas City, Missouri; and Houston, Texas, have shown[3]—perhaps Didion will soon adapt *Blue Nights* for the stage as well.

Quiara Alegría Hudes wrote *Water by the Spoonful* as part of a trilogy, and the final of the three plays, *The Happiest Song Plays Last*, will premiere during the Goodman's 2012–13 season. Since New York audiences will be seeing *Water* for the first time at Second Stage in the 2012–13 season, it seems reasonable to expect the *Happiest Song* will arrive in a season or two. It is also likely that theaters around the country will stage *Elliot, A Soldier's Fugue*, a 2007 Pulitzer finalist and first play in the trilogy, as well as these two newer plays in future seasons, since Hudes's Pulitzer win for *Water* will increase her marquee appeal considerably. It would be a uniquely fulfilling theatrical experience to see the three plays staged together.

Lynn Nottage often writes plays in pairs—one dark and one light. She used this strategy with *Intimate Apparel* and *Fabulation*,[4] and she's continued it with *Ruined* and *By the Way, Meet Vera Stark*. Nottage explains, "I wrote *Ruined* and *Vera Stark* at the same time . . . That's just how my brain functions—when I'm dwelling someplace very heavy, I need a release."[5] After dwelling with the stories of rape survivors in the Congo, she went some place very different in *Vera Stark*, first produced at Second Stage in 2011 and scheduled for a Chicago premiere at the Goodman Theater in the 2012–13 season. In the play's first act, Vera Stark, who has been working as a maid for a white film star, gets the opportunity to play opposite her in *The Belle of New Orleans*.[6] After seeing Vera play her career-changing role in a long clip from the film, the audience is transported quickly through time, seeing an out-of-vogue (and soused) Vera reuniting with her costar and former employer on a 1970s talk show and getting to see a panel of twenty-first century academics debate her film legacy. When Hilton Als reviewed the premiere production for *The New Yorker*, he found that *Vera Stark* might have been more closely kin to *Intimate Apparel* and *Fabulation* than *Ruined*. He suggested *Vera Stark* "could be the final piece in a trilogy about black women trying to have a professional life in America in the last century."[7] Though reviews were somewhat mixed for the New York premiere, as critics questioned the shift in writing and production style—from more realistically wrought characterization in the opening scenes to increasing levels of caricature in the play's later scenes—perhaps future critics will see meaningful critique in these choices rather than a dramatic shortcoming and Nottage will expand her trilogy into an epic cycle.

Several writers in the study are charting new dramatic territory. Jenny Schwartz's *Somewhere Fun* will have its world premiere at the Vineyard Theatre in 2013, bringing her back to New York audiences for the first time since the highly acclaimed *God's Ear*. The play involves two women, old friends who have lost touch but reconnect. *Playbill* reports, "With their children grown and the world changing rapidly around them, each [woman] finds herself coming face to face with the terrors, joys and surprises of life and time." I hope that *Somewhere Fun* will repeat the success of *God's Ear* and that New York will be the start of the play's journey and not its final destination.

Lisa Loomer has been prolific lately—and national audiences will be the richer if that trend continues and if her new works moves beyond the sites of their premiere productions. In the winter of 2012, the Denver Theatre Center produced Loomer's new comedy, set at a Passover seder, *Two Things You Don't Talk About at Dinner*. While critics did not warm to the premiere production,[8] perhaps the script might be retooled and remounted. Her *Homefree* was also read at the Denver Center's Colorado New Play Summit in February 2012. Farther west and just a few months later, Los Angeles's Cornerstone Theatre (in collaborations with Homegirl Café and Homeboy Industries) staged Loomer's contribution to The Hunger Cycle, *Café Vida*. In Loomer's play, two young rivals, Chabela and Luz, get a second chance at Café Vida "as they learn to compost, tend a garden, julienne an onion, and rock your lunch order with a smile and a heaping side of transformation." The *Los Angeles Times* called the play "a lyrical, gut-wrenching tale of love, violence, regret and redemption."[9]

Young Jean Lee has also been very busy in the past few theater seasons. She followed the stellar critical success of 2010's *Lear* with another highly praised show, *We're Gonna Die*, at Joe's Pub in 2011. Though Lee does not usually perform in her own work, she did in this cabaret-style pop-existentialist meditation on mortality that *The Huffington Post* called "an offbeat treat,"[10] *Backstage* called an "unusual, humble, and brave show,"[11] and *The New York Times* called "bracing, funny and, yes, consoling."[12] Lincoln Center was scheduled to bring the show back in September 2012 at its new third stage. In addition, her *Untitled Feminist Show*, which had a world premiere at the Walker Center in Minneapolis in January 2012, was scheduled to tour to the Warhol Museum in Pittsburgh and On the Boards in Seattle in early 2013. Audiences coast to coast will have opportunities to witness Lee's work in the 2012–13 season, and surely the number and variety of her fans will grow as her work travels.

Kate Fodor's *Rx* played at the 59E59 Theatres in a Primary Stages Production in early 2012. Charles Isherwood called the play, "A winning combination of light satire and romance . . . [; it] pokes gentle fun at our overprescribed culture . . . while it deftly charts the waxing and waning of love between a doctor working for a drug company and a patient enrolled in one of its trials."[13] The positive New York notices and topical subject matter suggest that the play might have a solid run in regional theaters across the country in future seasons. Her next new play to reach production, *Fifty Ways*, played in July 2012 in the Bratton Theater on the grounds of the Chautauqua Institution. Anthony Bannon, guest reviewer for *The Chautauquan Daily*, wrote, "*Fifty Ways* is fine work that hurts and hurts, and then finds enough hope to continue. *Fifty Ways* is a good play, but still rehearsing its metaphoric music. Its score will come when it becomes even more atonal."[14] Perhaps Fodor will continue to polish the script, and its next production will be even stronger.

Sarah Ruhl's canon is growing (and travelling) just as fast as those of her contemporaries. Her *Stage Kiss* was produced at the Goodman Theatre in 2011, within weeks of the Berkeley Rep's West Coast premiere of her version of *Three Sisters*.[15] And like some of those contemporaries discussed here, in *Stage Kiss*, Ruhl returned to ideas and motifs that she's been drawn to in other work. In the play, He and She were lovers some twenty years ago. They reunite when they are cast in the revival of 1930s melodrama. And though He now lives with a girlfriend, and She has a husband and daughter, the strange circumstance of playing lovers onstage rekindles dormant passions as the actors share a stage kiss. The characters they play onstage influence the roles they play offstage, a variation on one of themes in *Passion Play*. When Tanya Palmer asked Ruhl how this tale relates to the rest of her work, Ruhl replied, "I'm always interested in that great lie, the lie of the theater, of pretending to be something you're not in front of other people who are watching. If reality itself is something of an illusion . . . then plays are definitely an illusion."[16]

After helping the playwrights' collective of which she has been a part for a decade, 13 P, "implode" in the summer of 2012 with the revised chamber version of her earlier work *Melancholy Play*,[17] Ruhl will have yet another premiere in 2012 and another chance to test the limits of theater's illusion with *Dear Elizabeth*. Since the play is scheduled to open at the Yale Rep in November 2012 and then again at the Berkeley Rep in May 2013, it remains to be seen at the time of this writing exactly which of Ruhl's themes will resonate most strongly here, but the power of long-lasting emotional bonds and female creativity are likely to be among them given the subject matter, while she will return to the letter device she used so well in *Eurydice* and the richness of dramatized historical figures that she used in *Orlando* and *Passion Play*. The Yale Rep publicity materials for the upcoming play promise the script will chart the "thirty-year friendship between two of the most celebrated and honored American poets of the 20th century: Elizabeth Bishop and Robert Lowell. With postmarks from

Maine to Key West, and as far away as London and South America, *Dear Elizabeth* is a lyrical and moving portrait of two lives that unfold in letters."[18]

At the end of his article on Sarah Ruhl, "The Surreal Life," John Lahr recounted Ruhl's opening night ritual. As she sits in a darkening theater, she holds tight to a small Ganesh amulet and whispers words from her favorite childhood book series, the Betsy-Tacy stories: "The curtain goes up! The curtain goes up!"[19] As I dream of what the next theater seasons across the country will hold for Sarah Ruhl and her talented contemporaries, this is my wish for them all: that they will experience this magical moment of possibility as the curtain goes up many, many more times.

Notes

Introduction

1. Susan Jonas and Suzanne Bennett, "Report on the Status of Women: A Limited Engagement?" http://www.womenarts.org/advocacy/WomenCountNYSCAREport.htm (accessed 23 April 2008).
2. Jason Zinoman, "Theatre: The Season of the Female Playwright," *The New York Times*, December 21, 2003.
3. Alexis Greene, "What Women Want," *American Theatre*, February 2008, 63.
4. *The Good Negro* by Tracey Scott Wilson was the one play by a woman produced by the Public that season.
5. Patricia Cohen, "Rethinking Gender Bias in Theater," *The New York Times*, June 23, 2009.
6. Emily Glasberg Sands, "Opening the Curtain on Playwright Gender: An Integrated Economic Analysis of Discrimination in American Theater," The New York Times, June 23, 2009, http://graphics8.nytimes.com/packages/pdf/theater/speech_slides2x.pdf.
7. Marsha Norman, "Not There Yet," *American Theatre*, November 2009, 79.
8. For *Enron* and *Everyday Rapture*, respectively.
9. The examples are several but include Winnie Holzer's *Wicked*, Marsha Norman's book for *The Color Purple*, and Quiara Alegría Hudes's book for *In the Heights*.
10. See Patrick Healy, "Pulitzer Board members Saw 'Normal' Night Before Vote," April 12, 2010, http://artsbeat.blogs.nytimes.com/2010/04/13/pultizer-board-members-saw-normal-night-before-vote.
11. Yasmina Reza's *God of Carnage* closed in the first week of the season.
12. Please see the Broadway Internet Database for listings of the plays on Broadway in each season: http://www.ibdb.com/season.php?id=1281.
13. Theatre Communications Group, "Top Ten Most Produced Plays," accessed December 18, 2012, http://www.tcg.org/publications/at/attopten.cfm.

14. Ruhl's plays weren't just frequently produced; they were routinely honored at the dawn of the new century. Among the accolades she accumulated during the past decade are a MacArthur Genius Grant, the Susan Smith Blackburn Prize, the Helen Hayes Award, the Helen Merrill Award, the Pen Award, the Whiting Writers' Award, an NAACP Image Award nomination, two designations as a finalist for the Pulitzer Prize, and a Tony Award nomination.
15. James Al-Shamma, *Sarah Ruhl: A Critical Study of the Plays* (Jefferson, NC: McFarland, 2011). See particularly the second chapter of the book in which Al-Shamma discusses Ruhl's "whimsical realism" in her early work in relation to magical realism. Al-Shamma writes near the conclusion of his final chapter on *In the Next Room*, "The grief and whimsy so prominent in earlier Ruhl works, such as *Eurydice* and *The Clean House*, are here integrated as two elements amongst many . . . Whimsy is confined mostly to Catherine's personality . . . Ruhl's trademark magic is, without a doubt, powerfully demonstrated, although she withholds it until the final minutes" (176).
16. John Lahr, "Surreal Life: The Plays of Sarah Ruhl," *The New Yorker*, March 17, 2008.
17. Jill Dolan, "Feminist Performance Criticism and the Popular: Reviewing Wendy Wasserstein," *Theatre Journal* 60, no. 3 (October 2008): 433–57.
18. Dorothy Chansky's article, "Usable Performance Feminism for Our Time: Reconsidering Betty Friedan"(*Theatre Journal* 60, no. 3 [October 2008]: 341–64) was central in helping me critique and search for a place within third-wave feminism.
19. Sara Ahmed, *The Cultural Politics of Emotion* (New York: Routledge, 2004), 170.
20. Ibid., 176.
21. Ibid., 180.
22. Among the writers I wish were also included in this study are Annie Baker, Sheila Callaghan, Julia Cho, Melissa James Gibson, Rebecca Gilman, Gina Gionfriddo, Rinne Groff, Ann-Marie Healy, Lisa Kron, Suzan-Lori Parks, Theresa Rebeck, Lucy Thurber, and Anne Washburn.
23. Ahmed 184.
24. Catherine A. Schuler, "Editorial Comment," *Theatre Journal* 60, no. 3 (2008).
25. See Maya Roth, "Revealing and Renewing Feminist Theatrical Engagement: The Jane Chambers Contest for Women Playwrights," *Theatre Topics* 20, no. 2 (2010): 157–69.
26. Angela McRobbie, *The Aftermath of Feminism: Gender, Culture, and Social Change* (London: Sage Publications, 2009), 2.

27. Gayle Austin, *Feminist Theories for Dramatic Criticism* (Ann Arbor: University of Michigan Press, 1990), 5.
28. Austin 6.
29. See Rosemarie Tong's discussion and critique of liberal feminism in *Feminist Thought: A More Comprehensive Introduction*, 3rd ed. (Boulder: Westview Press, 2009), 11–47.
30. Sarah Schulman, "Supremacy Ideology Masquerading as Reality: The Obstacle Facing Women Playwrights in America," *Theatre Journal* 62 (2010): 567–70.
31. Ibid.
32. Astrid Henry, *Not My Mother's Sister: Generational Conflict and Third Wave Feminism* (Bloomington: Indiana University Press, 2004), 34.
33. Ibid., 34–35.
34. Eve Kosofsky Sedgwick, *Touching Feeling: Affect, Pedagogy, Performativity* (Durham: Duke University Press, 2003), 8.
35. Ibid., 35.
36. See Leslie Heywood and Jennifer Drake, *Third Wave Agenda: Being Feminist, Doing Feminism* (Minneapolis: University of Minnesota Press, 1997), 8.
37. Ibid., 3.
38. Sarah Ruhl, "Re-runs and Repetitions," *Contemporary Theatre Review* 16, no. 3 (2006): 283–90.

Chapter 1

1. Sarah Ruhl, "Re-runs and Repetitions," *Contemporary Theatre Review* 16, no. 3 (2006): 90.
2. Thomas Peter, "Playbill.com's Brief Encounter with Sarah Ruhl," October 9, 2010, http://www.playbill.com/news/article/143787-PLAYBILL COMS-BRIEF-ENCOUNTER-With-Sarah-Ruhl (accessed 28 February 2012).
3. Adam Greenfield, "Artist Interview: Adam Greenfield Discusses the Origins of *Cool Dip*…with Playwright Kia Corthron," Playwrights Horizons, last modified 2010, accessed February 28, http://playwrightshorizons.org.wehostwebsites.com/showfeature.asp?eventid=30&featureid=3.
4. Peter Gianopulos, "The Passion of Sarah Ruhl," *Northshore Magazine*, September 2007, http://www.northshoremag.com.
5. Ibid.
6. Sarah Ruhl, *Three Sisters* (unpublished manuscript, July 2009), 3. Word document. Ms. Ruhl's agent sent the manuscript to me electronically.
7. Ibid.

8. As she concluded her introduction to *The Three Sisters*, Ruhl wrote of this period in her life, "The year after my father died, when I was on the strange boundary between childhood and adulthood, I lived in a house with my sister, in a province, you might say, of Chicago, longing to move to New York. I don't mean to say that I can fully understand what it was to live in provincial Russia; all I know is, at the time, I dreamed of birch trees." Ibid., 5.
9. Greenfield, "Artist Interview."
10. See Chris Jones, "Snubbed for Years, Playwright Ruhl Finds Hometown Success." May 7, 2006, *Chicago Tribune*, http://articles.chicagotribune.com/2006-05-07/news/0605060225_1_sarah-ruhl-piven-theatre-workshop-prize-winning-playwright-paula-vogel (accessed 28 February 2012).
11. When she first got back to Brown, Vogel was off campus due to the success of *How I Learned to Drive*. At this point, early in her graduate career, she studied with Mac Wellman and Nilo Cruz.
12. Ruhl revised the text for the 2010 production. That version is not yet available, so I worked from the version available through New Dramatists with a 2004 date stamp. Ruhl comments on her process with the script overall reveal something about the differences among the two versions: "Well, I wrote it about 12 years ago for a theatre in Chicago called the Piven Theater Workshop. They commissioned the piece, and I worked on it for about a year with them, evolving it with a group of actors, and then we did it at The Actors Gang in L.A., with the same director, Joyce Piven, so there was a huge amount of playing around with actors and with a group. And then when I did rewrites in New York, I tried to take away things that were specific to those productions and pare it away a little bit more, and we experimented a lot with the choreographer. I mean, Annie-B Parsons I just adore—we didn't want there to be redundancy between the language and the movement, so I worked on that a little bit here, too. But at the end of the day, I had to go away and write the thing. I mean, I worked on it with a group, but I think ultimately, I did write the thing in isolation." See Peter, "Playbill.com's Brief Encounter."
13. Charles Isherwood, "Who's Afraid of Fluid Gender and Time?" review of *Orlando*, by Sarah Ruhl, *The New York Times*, September 23, 2010, http://theater.nytimes.com/2010/09/24/theater/reviews/24orlando.html?pagewanted=all (accessed 28 February 2012).
14. Peter, "Playbill.com's Brief Encounter."
15. Victoria L. Smith, "'Ransacking the Language': Finding the Missing Goods in Virginia Woolf's 'Orlando,'" *Journal of Modern Literature* 29, no. 4 (Summer 2006): 57–75.
16. Virginia Woolf, *Orlando* (New York: Harcourt Brace, 1928).

17. Ibid., 158.
18. Piven has said of Ruhl, "She's an old soul . . . She doesn't seem typical of this century. She just writes because she has to write," quoted in Jones "Snubbed for Years."
19. Laura Marcus, "Woolf's Feminism and Feminism's Woolf," in *The Cambridge Companion to Virginia Woolf*, ed. Sue Roe and Susan Sellers (Cambridge: Cambridge University Press, 2000), 209–44.
20. Christy L. Burns, "Re-Dressing Feminist Identities: Tensions between Essential and Constructed Selves in Virginia Woolf's Orlando," *Twentieth Century Literature* 40, no. 3 (Autumn 1994): 342–64.
21. Woolf 153.
22. Ruhl refers to Woolf as "incandescent" in this YouTube piece: http://www.youtube.com/watch?v=1RRPbWNUnb8.
23. Ibid.
24. Woolf 41; Ruhl, *Orlando*, 23.
25. Ruhl 23.
26. Sarah Ruhl, *Clean House and Other Plays* (New York: Theatre Communication Group, 2006), 9.
27. Alexis Greene, "Joking Aside: A Conversation about Comedy with Christopher Durang, Gina Gionfriddo, Sarah Ruhl, and Wendy Wasserstein" in *Women Writing Plays: Three Decades of the Susan Smith Blackburn Prize* (Austin: University of Texas Press, 2006), 181–90.
28. Woolf 57.
29. Ibid.; Ruhl 37.
30. Beth C. Schwartz, "Thinking Back Through our Mothers: Virginia Woolf Reads Shakespeare," *ELH* 58, no. 3 (Autumn 1991): 721–46.
31. Greenfield.
32. Sarah Ruhl, *The American Theatre Wing Presents America's Foremost Playwrights on the Plays That Influenced Them*, ed. Ben Hodges (New York: Applause Books, 2009): 123.
33. Ruhl 75; Woolf 239.
34. Ruhl 76; Woolf 244.
35. Ruhl 77; Woolf 241.
36. Ruhl 77.
37. Helen Wussow, "Virginia Woolf and the Problematic Nature of the Photographic Image." *Twentieth Century Literature* 40, no. 1 (Spring 1994): 13.
38. Viktor Shklovsky, "Art as Technique," in *Russian Formalist Criticism: Four Essays*, ed. Lee T. Lemon and Marion J. Reiss (Lincoln: University of Nebraska Press, 1965), 12.

39. Silvija Jestrovic, *Theatre of Estrangement: Theatre, Practice, Ideology* (Toronto: University of Toronto Press, 2006), 126–27.
40. Woolf 328.
41. Ruhl 98.
42. Woolf 264; Ruhl 99.
43. Woolf 264, 265, 271; Ruhl 100–101.
44. Greenfield.
45. Paula Vogel, "Interview with Sarah Ruhl," *BOMB* Magazine, http://www.bombsite.com/issues/99/articles/2902 (accessed 28 February 2011).
46. Ruhl 102.
47. Ibid., 285.
48. Ibid., 286.
49. Ibid., 287–88.
50. Ibid., 322; Ruhl 102.
51. Peter Gianopulos, "The Passion of Sarah Ruhl," *Northshore Magazine*, September 2007, http://www.northshoremag.com.
52. Lyudmila Parts, "Down the Intertextual Lane: Petrushevskaia, Chekhov, Tolstoy," *Russian Review* 64, no. 1 (January 2005): 80.
53. Anton Chekhov, "The Lady with the Dog," in *Later Short Stories: 1888–1893*, ed. Shelby Foote (New York: The Modern Library, 1999), 572.
54. Sarah Ruhl, "Lady with the Lap Dog," New Dramatists (unpublished manuscript, March 2000), 18.
55. Parts, "Down the Intertextual Lane," 83.
56. Chekhov 573.
57. Ibid., 574.
58. Ibid.
59. Ruhl 20.
60. Ibid., 38.
61. Ibid.
62. See, for example, Virginia Llwellyn Smith, "The Lady with the Dog," in *Critical Essays on Anton Chekhov*, ed. Thomas A. Eekman (Boston: G. K. Hall and Company, 1979), 121–22.
63. Ruhl 39.
64. Ibid., 2.
65. Ibid., 39.
66. See Janet Malcom, *Reading Chekhov: A Critical Journey* (New York: Random House, 2001). Malcom reads Chekhov's ending in a manner that seems almost antithetical to the way I read Ruhl's. She notes how often death affects Chekhov's writing, declaring, "Death is the hinge on which the work swings. 'The Lady with the Lap Dog' is an apparent exception—no one in the story dies or has died. And yet death is in

the air. Gurov's spiritual journey—his transformation from a connoisseur of women to a man tenderly devoted to a single ordinary woman—is a journey of withdrawal from life" (203). See also Beverly Hahn, *Chekhov: A Study of the Major Stories and Plays* (Cambridge: Cambridge University Press, 1977), 262–63.

Chapter 2

1. Michael Kamber and Tim Arango, "4,000 U.S. Deaths, and a Handful of Images," *The New York Times*, July 26, 2008, http://www.nytimes.com/2008/07/26/world/middleeast/26censor.html?pagewanted=all.
2. Charles Isherwood, "A Comic Impudence Softens a Tale of Loss," The New York Times, October 3, 2006, http://theater.nytimes.com/2006/10/03/theater/reviews/03eury.html?pagewanted=all.
3. Elissa Marder, "The Sex of Death and the Maternal Crypt," *Parallax* 15, no. 1 (2009): 5–20.
4. Daniel Sterns, *American Cool* (New York: New York University Press, 1994), 164.
5. Judith Butler, *Precarious Life: The Powers of Mourning and Violence* (London: Verso, 2010), 29.
6. Ibid., 30.
7. Sarah Ahmed, *The Cultural Politics of Emotions* (New York: Routledge, 2004).
8. Jodi Kanter, "Hopeful Sentences: Gender and Mourning Language in Two Contemporary Narratives," *Women and Language* 25, no. 1 (2002): 2.
9. Wendy Weckwerth, "More Invisible Terrains," *Theater* 34, no. 2 (2004): 30.
10. Sarah Ruhl, *Eurydice*, in *The Clean House and Other Plays* (New York: Theatre Communications Group, 2006), 336.
11. Ibid., 336.
12. Ibid.
13. Ibid., 345.
14. Ahmed 11.
15. Ibid., 385.
16. Weckwerth 31.
17. Ibid., 360.
18. Ibid., 363.
19. Ibid., 366.
20. Ibid., 388.
21. Ibid., 373.

22. Ibid., 379.
23. I'm indebted to Kathleen Woodward's analysis of fort-da in *Statistical Panic: Cultural Politics and the Poetics of Emotion* (Durham: Duke University Press, 2009).
24. Ruhl 379.
25. Ibid., 394.
26. Ibid., 395.
27. Ibid., 396.
28. Ibid.
29. Ibid., 406–7.
30. Catherine A. Lutz, "Engendered Emotion: Gender, Power, and the Rhetoric of Emotional Control in American Discourse," in *Language and the Politics of Emotion*, ed. Catherine A. Lutz and Lila Abu-Lughod (Cambridge: Cambridge University Press, 1990), 73.
31. Ibid., 73.
32. Ibid., 74.
33. Charles Isherwood, "The Power of Memory to Triumph Over Death," *The New York Times*, June 19, 2007, http://theater.nytimes.com/2007/06/19/theater/reviews/19seco.html?pagewanted=print.
34. John Lahr, "Guys and Dolls," *The New Yorker*, July 2, 2007, http://www.newyorker.com/arts/critics/theatre/2007/07/02/070702crth_theatre_lahr?currentPage=all.
35. Joan Didion, *The Year of Magical Thinking* (New York: Knopf, 2005), 224–25.
36. See Sandra Gilbert's discussion of this point in her review of *The Year of Magical Thinking* in *Literature and Medicine* 25, no. 2 (Fall 2006): 556.
37. Joan Didion, "The Year of Hoping for Stage Magic," *The New York Times*, March 4, 2007.
38. Butler, *Precarious Life*, 22.
39. Ibid.
40. Ibid., 3-4.
41. Ibid., 10.
42. Robyn Fivush and Janine P. Buckner. "Gender, Sadness, and Depression: The development of Emotional Focus through Gendered Discourse," in *Gender and Emotion: Social Psychological Perspectives*, ed. Agneta H. Fischer (New York: Cambridge University Press, 2000), 250.
43. Jeroen Jansz, "Masculine Identity and Restrictive Emotionality," in *Gender and Emotion: Social Psychological Perspectives*, ed. Agneta H. Fischer (New York: Cambridge University Press, 2000), 181.
44. Didion, "The Year of Hoping."
45. Didion, *Year of Magical Thinking*,150.

46. Ibid., 152.
47. Euripides, *Euripides, 3*, ed. David R. Slavitt and Palmer Bovie (Philadelphia: University of Pennsylvania Press, 1998), http://www.nytimes.com/books/first/e/euripides3-penn.html.
48. John Heath, "The Failure of Orpheus," *Transactions of the American Philological Association* 124 (1994): 163–96.
49. Patricia Foster, "Sideswiped," *Antioch Review* 64 (2006): 814.
50. See page 75 in the book version.
51. Didion, *Year of Magical Thinking: The Play*, 20.
52. Gilbert 555.
53. Didion, *Year of Magical Thinking: The Play*, 36.
54. Ibid., 55.
55. Ibid., 60.
56. Didion, "The Year of Hoping."
57. Jenny Schwartz, *God's Ear* (New York: Faber and Faber, 2008), 19.
58. Sarah Stern, "An Interview with Playwright Jenny Schwartz," accessed December 18, 2012, http://www.vineyardtheatre.org/interview-godsear.htm.
59. Jason Zinoman, "New Dramas, New Voices below 14th Street," *The New York Times*, http://www.nytimes.com/2007/06/03/theater/theaterspecial/03zino.html?pagewanted=2&n=Top/Reference/Times Topics/Subjects/T/Theater.
60. Jeffery Jones, "The Program for Jenny Schwartz's *God's Ear*." This is not a conventional play bill for a production. Instead it was a dramaturgical document created for the show by Jeffrey Jones, Helen Shaw, and David Cote that was aimed to give context for the challenging text and to make it more approachable for audience members.
61. Schwartz 29.
62. Ibid., 50
63. Ibid., 61–62.
64. Ibid., 63.
65. Ibid., 68.
66. Jeffery Jones, program for Jenny Schwartz's *God's Ear*.
67. Ibid., 89.
68. Ibid., 140.
69. Ibid., 116.
70. Cathy Caruth, *Unclaimed Experience: Trauma, Narrative, and History* (Baltimore: Johns Hopkins University Press, 1996), 4.
71. Schwartz 146–47.
72. Ibid., 154.
73. Ibid., 155.
74. Ibid., 157–58.

75. Teresa Brennan, *Transmission of Affect* (Ithaca: Cornell University Press, 2004), 5.
76. Butler, *Precarious Life* (xviii–xix).

Chapter 3

1. The first act of the play was commissioned by the McCarter Theater. The full-length version of the play premiered at the Yale Rep in 2004.
2. Drucilla Barker and Susan Feiner, *Liberating Economics: Feminist Perspectives on Family, Work, and Globalization* (Ann Arbor: University of Michigan Press, 2004), 8–9.
3. Nancy Folbre, "'Holding Hands at Midnight': The Paradox of Caring Labor," in *Toward a Feminist Philosophy of Economics*, ed. Drucilla Barker and Edith Kuiper (London: Routledge, 2003), 222.
4. Ibid., 226.
5. Sarah Ruhl, *The Clean House* in *The Clean House and Other Plays* (New York: Theatre Communications Group, 2006), 10.
6. Alexis Greene, "New Voices: An Interview with Sarah Ruhl," in *Women Writing Plays: Three Decades of the Susan Smith Blackburn Prize* (Austin: University of Texas Press, 2006), 230–31.
7. Ruhl 10.
8. Ibid., 18.
9. Ibid., 19.
10. Ibid.
11. Ibid., 40.
12. Ibid., 45.
13. Ibid., 47.
14. Ibid., 11.
15. Ibid., 65.
16. Ibid., 71.
17. Ibid., 8.
18. Ibid., 74.
19. Ibid., 19.
20. Ibid., 24.
21. Ibid., 26.
22. Ibid., 48–49.
23. Ibid., 82.
24. Ibid., 84.
25. Ibid., 98.
26. Ibid., 100.
27. Ibid., 106.

28. Ibid., 106–7.
29. Ibid., 107.
30. Ibid., 26.
31. Alexis Greene, "Joking Aside: A Conversation about Comedy with Christopher Durang, Gina Gionfriddo, Sarah Ruhl, and Wendy Wasserstein," in *Women Writing Plays: Three Decades of the Susan Smith Blackburn Prize* (Austin: University of Texas Press, 2006), 183.
32. Ms. Mendoza will also play the role of Odessa/Haiku Mom in Quiara Alegría Hudes's *Spoonful of Water*, analyzed in Chapter 5.
33. No academic articles exist that are devoted solely or substantially to *Living Out*. On *The Waiting Room* see Mary K Deshazer, "Fractured Borders: Women's Cancer and Feminist Theatre," *Feminist Formations*15, no. 2 (Summer 2003): 1–26; and Pamela Renner, "Science and Sensibility: Lisa Loomer and Margaret Edson Turn a Lens on the Medical Establishment," *American Theatre* 16 (1999), 34. On *Girl, Interrupted* see Diane R. Wiener, "Antipsychiatric Activism and Feminism: The Use of Film and Text to Question Biomedicine," *Journal of Public Mental Health*4, no. 3 (September 2005): 42–47. On *Bocón*, see Lorenzo Garcia, "Living with/through Loss and Grief in Lisa Loomer's *Bocón!*" *Youth Theatre Journal* 25, no. 2 (2011): 159–74.
34. Jan Breslauer, "As Her Many Worlds Turn," *Los Angeles Times*, August 7, 1994, http://articles.latimes.com/1994-08-07/entertainment/ca-24432_1_lisa-loomer/3.
35. Warren Etheredge, "LIVING OUT—Screenwriter, Lisa Loomer," *The Warren Report*, last modified January 18, 2003, http://thewarrenreport.com/2003/01/18/living-out-screeenwriter-lisa-loomer.
36. Ben Brantley, "'The Doctor Will See You Now.' Uh-Oh," *The New York Times*, November 6, 1996, http://www.nytimes.com/1996/11/06/theater/the-doctor-will-see-you-now-uh-oh.html?n=Top%2fReference%2fTimes%20Topics%2fSubjects%2fT%2fTheater.
37. Breslauer, "Her Many Worlds."
38. Carlo Botero, "Telling the Stories: Interview with Lisa Loomer, Revolutionary Worker #1227," *Revolution Newspaper*, February 1, 2004, http://revcom.us/a/1227/lisainterview.htm.
39. Caridad Svich, "US Polyglot Latino Theatre and its Link to the Americas," *Contemporary Theatre* 16, no. 2 (2006): 189–97.
40. David Roman, "Comment: *Theatre Journals*," *Theatre Journal* 54, no. 3 (2002): vii–xix.
41. Lisa Loomer, *Living Out* (New York: Dramatists Play Service, 2005), 11.
42. Ibid.
43. Ibid., 3.

44. Margo Jefferson, "'Upstairs, Downstairs,' With Nanny-Cam Running," review of Living Out by Lisa Loomer, *The New York Times*, October 1, 2003, http://www.nytimes.com/2003/10/01/theater/theater-review-upstairs-downstairs-with-nanny-cam-running.html?n=Top%2fReference%2fTimes%20Topics%2fSubjects%2fT%2fTheater.
45. Loomer 14.
46. Ibid., 26.
47. Arlie Hochschild, "The Nanny Chain," *American Prospect* 19 (December 2001), http://prospect.org/article/nanny-chain.
48. Ibid.
49. Loomer 62.
50. Breslauer, "Her Many Worlds"
51. Loomer 62.
52. Loomer 64.
53. Dan Bacalzo, "*Satellites* Dish Playwright Diana Son Discusses the World Premiere of Her Play at The Public Theater," *The New York Times*, June 5, 2006.
54. Jason Zinoman, "Theater; Season of the Female Playwright," *The New York Times*, December 21, 2003, http://www.nytimes.com/2003/12/21/theater/theater-the-season-of-the-female-playwright.html?pagewanted=all&src=pm.
55. Despite the popularity and widespread production of *Stop Kiss*, the critical literature on Son is slight. There are multiple theses that treat various aspects of the production process for *Stop Kiss*; there are also several dissertations with chapters on Son.
56. Alexis Greene, "Crossing Borders: A Conversation with Bridget Carpenter, Lynn Nottage, Dael Orlandersmith, and Diana Son" in *Women Writing Plays: Three Decades of the Susan Smith Blackburn Prize* (Austin: University of Texas Press, 2006), 117.
57. Ibid., 121.
58. Diana Son, *Satellites* (New York: Dramatists Play Service, 2008), 8.
59. Ibid., 42.
60. Ibid., 20.
61. Karen Shimakawa's analysis of Young Jean Lee's *Songs of Dragons Flying to Heaven* is useful here. Shimakawa identifies what she calls "a recognizable trope in a play about Asian American female identity:" Playwrights often use food "to illustrate the traditions and relationships that connect diasporic Asians to their home countries/cultures, especially as they bind female progenitors to their culinary inheritors, their Asian American daughters and granddaughters." See Shimakawa, "Performing the Asian American Signature in Law and Literature," in *Signatures of the Past:*

Cultural Memory in Contemporary Anglophone North American Drama, ed. Marc Maufort and Caroline De Wagter (Bruxelles: Peter Lang, 2008). Son employs the trope but also complicates it as she juxtaposes the nourishment Mrs. Chae provides with her racist attitudes.
62. Son 45.
63. Ibid., 50.
64. Ibid., 49.
65. Ibid.
66. Margaret Jane Radin, *Contested Commodities* (Cambridge: Harvard University Press, 1996), 105.
67. Gillian J. Hewitson, "Domestic Labor and Gender Identity," in *Toward a Feminist Philosophy of Economics*, ed. Drucilla Barker and Edith Kuiper (London: Routledge, 2003), 273.
68. Son's strategy is, I think more complex than the previously discussed trap Richard tries to spring for Nancy when he discourages her return to work due to breast-feeding.
69. Ibid., 23–24.
70. Ben Brantley, "Settling Down on Shaky Ground in Diana Son's 'Satellites,'" *The New York Times*, June 19, 2006, http://theater.nytimes.com/2006/06/19/theater/reviews/19sate.html.
71. Son 43.
72. Ibid., 50.
73. Ibid., 51.
74. Sarah Schulman, "Supremacy Ideology Masquerading as Reality: The Obstacle Facing Women Playwrights in America," *Theatre Journal* 62 (2010): 567.

Chapter 4

1. Sarah Ruhl, *Passion Play* (New York: Theatre Communications Group, 2010), xi.
2. Others writers and plays include Sherie Rene Scott's *Everyday Rapture*, Paula Vogel's *Long Christmas Ride Home*, Annie Baker's *Body Awareness*, and Heidi Schrek's *Creature*.
3. Emily Feldman, "Days of Yore," last modified 2011, http://www.thedaysofyore.com/sarah-ruhl.
4. In the 2010 playwright's note, Ruhl simply omits "Now it's 2007." See Ruhl, *Passion Play*, xii.
5. Tanya Palmer, "A Passion for Theater: An Interview with Sarah Ruhl," *Goodman Theatre OnStage*, September/December 2007, 4.

6. Rosemary Radford Ruether, "The Emergence of Christian Feminist Theology," in *The Cambridge Companion to Feminist Theology*, ed. Susan Frank Parsons (Cambridge: Cambridge University Press, 2002), 3.
7. Ibid., 4.
8. Ruhl 14.
9. Ibid., 16.
10. Elisabeth Schussler Fiorenza, "Missionaries, Apostles, Co-workers," in *Feminist Theology: A Reader*, ed. Ann Loades (London: Society for Promoting Christian Knowledge, 1990), 71.
11. Ruhl 25.
12. Ibid., 26.
13. Ruhl isn't alone in asserting this connection in the medieval mind. For example, In "The Wife of Bath's Tale" by Geoffrey Chaucer, the lustiness of the wife is immediately perceptible in her gap-toothed smile.
14. Ruhl 55.
15. Ibid., 60.
16. Ibid., 27.
17. Ibid., 66.
18. Ibid., 76.
19. Janet Martin Soskice, "Blood and Defilement," in *Feminism and Theology*, ed. Janet Martin Soskice and Diana Lipton (Oxford: Oxford University Press, 2003).
20. Soskice 336–37.
21. The Crossroads Initiative, "The Blood and Water from His Side," http://www.crossroadsinitiative.com/library_article/379.
22. Ruhl 86.
23. Ruhl 91.
24. Ibid., 96.
25. Ibid., 120.
26. Ibid., 144.
27. Ibid., 146.
28. Ibid., 147.
29. Louis Montrose, *The Purpose of Playing: Shakespeare and the Cultural Politics of the Elizabethan Theatre* (Chicago: University of Chicago Press, 1996). See chapter 1, "The Reformation of Playing."
30. Ruhl 138.
31. Ibid., 159.
32. Ibid., 188.
33. Ibid., 192–93.
34. Ibid., 181.
35. Ibid., 182.

36. Ibid.,185–86.
37. Ibid., 198.
38. Ibid., 199.
39. Ibid., 207.
40. Ibid., 211–12.
41. Though "VA" now stands for Veterans Affairs, it was Veterans Administration until 1988.
42. Ibid., 217.
43. Ibid., 219.
44. Ibid., 220.
45. Ibid.
46. Ibid., 221.
47. Ibid., 232–33.
48. Ibid., 234.
49. Ibid., 235.
50. Ibid., 240.
51. Valerie Karass, "Eschatology," in *The Cambridge Companion to Feminist Theology*, ed. Susan Frank Parsons (Cambridge: Cambridge University Press, 2002), 255.
52. Eliza Bent, "The Church of Young Jean Lee," *Brooklyn Rail*, http://brooklynrail.org/2007/04/theater/the-church-of-young-jean-lee.
53. Erik Piepenburg, "Faith Confronted, and Defended, Downtown," *The New York Times*, May 6, 2007.
54. Alexis Soloski, "Hell Is for Bohos," *Village Voice*, April 17, 2007.
55. Piepenburg, "Faith Confronted."
56. Bent, "Church of Young Jean Lee."
57. Young Jean Lee, *Songs of the Dragons Flying to Heaven and Other Plays* (New York: Theatre Communications Group, 2010), 6.
58. Jeffrey M. Jones, "What's Wrong with These Plays: An Afterword." in *Songs of the Dragons Flying to Heaven and Other Plays*, by Young Jean Lee (New York: Theatre Communications Group, 2010), 191.
59. Ibid., 193–94.
60. Susan A. Ross, "Church and Sacrament—Community and Worship," In *The Cambridge Companion to Feminist Theology*, ed. Susan Frank Parsons (Cambridge: Cambridge University Press, 2002), 232.
61. Mary Daly, "Beyond God the Father," in *Feminism and Theology*, ed. Janet Martin Soskice and Diana Lipton (Oxford: Oxford University Press, 2003), 42.
62. Lee 15
63. Ibid., 15.
64. Ibid., 16.

65. Ibid., 21.
66. Ibid., 22.
67. Ibid., 199.
68. David Day, "Dusted Reviews: On!Air!Library!," *Dusted*, http://www.dustedmagazine.com/reviews/240.
69. Richard Murphy, "Dance in Worship," Maranatha Life, last modified 1998, http://maranathalife.com/teaching/jew-danc.htm.
70. Tim Sanford, "Artist Interview: Kate Fodor Discusses *100 Saints* with Artistic Director Tim Sanford," Playwrights Horizons, http://playwrightshorizons.org.wehostwebsites.com/showfeature.asp?eventid=10&featureid=3.
71. Ibid.
72. Rob Weinert-Kendt, "On 'Saints' and Longings," *The Los Angeles Times*, May 29, 2011, http://articles.latimes.com/2011/may/29/entertainment/la-ca-100-saints-playwright-20110529. Fodor's experience with baptism might be compared to Ruhl's experience with confirmation. Ruhl was raised in a Catholic home, and she attended catechism classes. When it was time for confirmation, however, she had a crisis of faith. She chose not to go through with the confirmation.
73. Adam Syzmkowicz, "I Interview Playwrights: 261: Kate Fodor," last modified 2010, http://aszym.blogspot.com/2010/09/i-interview-playwrights-part-261-kate.html.
74. Sanford, "Artist Interview."
75. Ben Sisario, "A Playwright Wonders What He Said, She Said," *The New York Times*, April 03, 2004, http://www.nytimes.com/2004/04/03/theater/a-playwright-wonders-what-he-said-she-said.html?n=Top/Reference/Times Topics/Subjects/T/Theater.
76. Sanford.
77. Kate Fodor, *100 Saints You Should Know* (New York: Dramatists Play Service, 2008), 24.
78. Ibid., 31.
79. Ibid., 33.
80. Ibid., 34–35.
81. Nicola Slee, "The Holy Spirit and Spirituality," in *The Cambridge Companion to Feminist Theology*, ed. Susan Frank Parsons (Cambridge: Cambridge University Press, 2002),179–80.
82. Fodor 46.
83. Sarah Coakley, "The Trinity, Prayer, and Sexuality," *In Feminism and Theology*, ed. Janet Martin Soskice and Diana Lipton (Oxford: Oxford University Press, 2003), 258.
84. Fodor 45.
85. Coakley 259.

86. Ibid.
87. Ibid., 264–65.
88. Fodor 41.
89. Ibid., 52.
90. Ibid., 55.
91. Ibid.
92. Slee 180.
93. Fodor 51.
94. Ibid.
95. Ibid.
96. Ibid., 56.
97. Sanford.
98. Ruhl xii.

Chapter 5

1. Caren Kaplan, "Transporting the Subject: Technologies of Mobility and Location in an Era of Globalization," special issue, *PMLA* 117, no. 1 (January 2002): 34.
2. Kaplan 35.
3. Sarah Ruhl, *Dead Man's Cell Phone* (New York: Theatre Communications Group, 2008), 14.
4. Ibid., 15.
5. Krishan Kumar and Ekaterina Makarova, "The Portable Home: The Domestication of Public Space," *Sociological Theory* 26, no. 4 (December 2008): 324–43, http://www.jstor.org/stable/20453115.
6. Ruhl 15.
7. Ibid., 16.
8. Ibid., 18.
9. Ibid., 21.
10. Ibid., 22.
11. Ibid., 29.
12. Ibid., 33.
13. Ibid., 39.
14. Ibid., 40.
15. Ibid., 47.
16. Ibid.
17. Kirsty Best, "Interfacing the Environment: Networked Screens and the Ethics of Visual Consumption," in "Ethics of Seeing: Consuming Environments," special issue, *Ethics and the Environment* 9, no. 2 (Fall–Winter, 2004): 65–85.

18. Ruhl 70.
19. Ibid., 48.
20. Ibid., 52–53.
21. Ibid., 58.
22. Ibid., 59.
23. Ibid., 58–59.
24. Ibid., 75.
25. Mark Poster, "Digital Networks and Citizenship," *PMLA* 117, no. 1 (January 2002), 101.
26. N. Katherine Hayles, "The Complexities of Seriation," *PMLA* 117, no. 1 (January 2002): 117–18.
27. Pico Iyer, *The Global Soul: Jet Lag, Shopping Malls, and the Search for Home* (New York: Vintage, 2001), 59.
28. Ruhl 80.
29. Ibid., 81.
30. Ibid., 83.
31. Ibid., 87.
32. Ibid., 102.
33. Ibid., 62.
34. Ibid., 99.
35. Manuel Castells, *Mobile Communication and Society: A Global Perspective* (Boston: MIT Press), 126.
36. Doran's writing has been staged in both her first home and her new one and includes *Odes and Game Shows*, a show self-produced in England; *Parents' Evening*, her first play produced in the Unites States—at Cherry Lane; *The War Play*, a show self-produced at the Abingdon Theatre while she was studying at Columbia; *Nest*, which was commissioned by Signature in Washington, DC; *Time Unstuck*; *2 Soldiers*; adaptations of *Great Expectations*, *Peer Gynt*, and *The Blind*; *Maestro's Garden*; *Last Best Place*; *Living Room in Africa*; and *Ben and the Magic Paintbrush*, commissioned by South Coast Rep.
37. Bathsheba Doran, *Kin* (Hanover, NH: In an Hour Books, 2011), xvi.
38. Ibid., 2.
39. Castells 172.
40. Doran 4.
41. Ibid., 5.
42. Helen Shaw, "Preview: Kin," *Time Out New York*, March 14, 2011.
43. Castells 174.
44. Doran 40.

45. Patti M. Valkenburg and Jochen Peter, "Who Visits Online Dating Sites? Exploring Some Characteristics of Online Daters," *CyberPsychology and Behavior* 10, no. 6 (2007): 849.
46. Steve Woolgar, *Virtual Society? Technology, Cyperbole, Reality* (Oxford: Oxford University Press), 2002.
47. Doran 64.
48. José Van Dijck, "Facebook as Tool for Producing Sociality and Connectivity," *Television and New Media* 13, no. 2: 160–76.
49. Doran 70.
50. Ibid., 105.
51. Ibid., 108.
52. Ibid., iii.
53. Ibid., iv.
54. Ibid.
55. Anne García-Romero, "Fugue, Hip Hop and Soap Opera: Transcultural Connections and Theatrical Experimentation in Twenty-First Century US Latina Playwriting," *Latin American Theatre Review* 43, no. 1 (2009): 87–102, http://muse.jhu.edu.
56. Like Ruhl, Hudes studied with Paula Vogel.
57. The Goodman Theatre will produce the final part of the trilogy, *The Happiest Song Plays Last*, in its 2012–13 season.
58. Nina from *In the Heights* bears some resemblance to Hudes, and Kevin, Nina's father, seems kin to Hudes's stepfather, while Hudes has admitted that the mother-daughter relationship in *26 Miles* echoes her relationship with her mother (See Alexis Greene, "No Place Like Home," *American Theatre*, October 2008, 33), while Liz Jones and Asher Richelli have also observed in their introduction to Elliot ("Tales of a Chronicler") that Barrio Grrl's heroine "was inspired by Quiara's younger sister" and "Yemaya's Belly was sparked by tales Quiara was told by her father" (263).
59. Ibid.
60. Kate Taylor, "Everything Old Is New Again," *The New York Sun*, October 10, 2006, http://www.nysun.com/arts/everything-old-is-new-again-2006-10-10/41209.
61. Liz Jones and Asher Richelli, "Tales of a Chronicler: An Introduction to Quiara Alegria Hudes's Elliot, A Soldier's Fugue," in *New York Theatre Review (2007)*, ed. Brook Stowe (New York: Black Wave Press, 2007), 262.
62. Frank Rizzo, "Review: 'Spoonful' Funny, Warm, Uplifting," *Hartford Courant*, April 16, 2012.
63. Frank Rizzo, "Legit Reviews: Water by the Spoonful," *Variety*, October 30, 2011, http://www.variety.com/review/VE1117946466d.

64. Gerard Goggin provides some history and perspective on the app: "At the first anniversary of apps in July 2008, Apple claimed that 1.5 billion apps had been downloaded and by November 2009 that more than 100,000 apps were available (Apple 2011c). By January 2011, Apple was celebrating the 10 billionth download . . . and the availability of some 350,000 apps on its store." Goggin, "Ubiquitous Apps: The Politics of Openness in Global Mobile Cultures," *Digital Creativity* 22, no. 3 (2011): 151.
65. Goggin, "Ubiquitous Apps," 152.
66. Ibid.
67. Quiara Alegría Hudes, "Water by the Spoonful" (unpublished manuscript), 2.
68. Ibid., 21.
69. Ibid., 22.
70. Ibid., 36.
71. See Ginny's monologue in *Elliot, A Soldier's Fugue*, in *New York Theatre Review (2007)*, ed. Brook Stowe (New York: Black Wave Press, 2007), 282–84.
72. Hudes 38.
73. Ibid., 40.
74. Greene, "No Place" 33.
75. Hudes 41.
76. Ibid., 13.
77. Natilene I. Bowker and James H. Liu, "Are Women Occupying Positions of Power Online? Demographics of Chat Room Operators," *Cyberpsychology & Behavior* 4, no. 5 (2001): 640.
78. Hudes 2.
79. Bowker and Liu 641–42.
80. Hudes 13.
81. Sarah Nettleton et al., "The Reality of Virtual Social Support," in *Virtual Society? Technology, Cyperbole, Reality*, ed. Steven Woolgar (Oxford: Oxford University Press, 2002), 184–85.
82. Hudes 16.
83. Gazi Islam, "Virtual Speakers, Virtual Audiences: Agency, Audience, and Constraint in an Online Chat Community," *Dialectical Anthropology* 30, no. 1–2: 75.
84. Castells 171.
85. Eric Grode, 'Theatre Talk-Back: A Good Play Can Be Read as Well as Seen," *The New York Times*, April 18, 2012, http://artsbeat.blogs.nytimes.com/2012/04/18/theater-talkback-a-good-play-can-be-read-as-well-as-seen.
86. http://www.variety.com/review/VE1117946466.

87. Hudes 28.
88. Islam 77.
89. Hudes 43.
90. Ibid., 54.
91. Ibid., 69.
92. Ibid., 70.
93. Ibid., 76.
94. Ibid., 81.
95. Ibid., 98–99.
96. Ibid., 106.
97. Ibid., 108.
98. Ibid., 121.
99. Ibid., 109.
100. Ibid., 110.
101. "Facebook's IPO Is Decade's Biggest Flop," Bloomberg Businessweek: Technology, recorded May 25, 2012, http://www.businessweek.com/videos/2012-05-25/facebooks-ipo-flop-is-decades-worst.
102. Ross Douthat, "The Facebook Illusion," *The New York Times*, May 26, 2012, http://www.nytimes.com/2012/05/27/opinion/sunday/douthat-the-facebook-illusion.html?src=me&ref=general.

Chapter 6

1. In her *BOMB* Magazine interview with Sarah Ruhl, Paula Vogel said, "[Like the Goodman Theatre production of *Clean House*] the production of *Eurydice* at Yale also had a transformation of space. It seems to me your work actually calls that out of designers and directors. Whereas the theater of the rational mousetrap, when it insists that characters change, it means the furniture remains stable." Ruhl replies, "If you transform space and atmosphere, you don't have to connect the dots psychologically in a linear way." Vogel, "Interview with Sarah Ruhl," *BOMB* Magazine, http://www.bombsite.com/issues/99/articles/2902 (accessed February 28, 2011). Ruhl clearly puts these ideas to work in the magnificent ending of *In the Next Room*.
2. Karen J. Warren, *Ecofeminist Philosophy: A Western Perspective on What It Is and Why It Matters* (Lanham, MD: Rowan and Littlefield, 2000), 1.
3. After its 2008 Goodman Theatre world premiere, most of *Ruined*'s New York run was in the 2008– 9 season, but after several extensions, it closed in early September 2009.

4. Karen J. Warren, "Ecological Feminist Philosophies: An Overview of the Issues," in *Ecological Feminist Philosophies*, ed. Karen J. Warren (Bloomington: Indiana University Press, 1996), xvi.
5. Ibid., 2.
6. Colleen Mack-Canty, "Third-Wave Feminism and the Need to Reweave the Nature/CultureDuality," *Feminist Formations* 16, no. 3 (Fall 2004): 154–79.
7. Val Plumwood, "Nature, Self, and Gender: Feminism, Environmental Philosophy, and the Critique of Rationalism," in "Ecological Feminism," special issue, *Hypatia* 6, no. 1 (Spring 1991): 3–27.
8. Warren, *Ecofeminist Philosophy*, 198.
9. Sarah Ruhl, *In the Next Room, or the Vibrator Play* (New York: Samuel French, 2010), 11–12.
10. Ibid., 13.
11. Ibid., 15–16.
12. Ibid., 9.
13. Ibid., 38.
14. Ibid., 39.
15. Richard T. Twine, "Ma(r)king Essence-Ecofeminism and Embodiment," *Ethics & the Environment* 6, no. 2 (Autumn 2001), 31–58.
16. Ruhl 53.
17. Ibid., 58.
18. Ibid., 59.
19. Ibid., 60.
20. Ibid., 63.
21. Ibid., 84.
22. Ibid., 84.
23. Ibid., 21.
24. *The Lincoln Center Theater Review*—free to audience members at the theater—provided an excellent overview of the history of and issues surrounding wet-nursing. The article, by Erica Eisdorfer, was titled "11 Things You Never Knew About Wet-Nursing" (*The Lincoln Center Theater Review* [Fall 2009]: 17–18).
25. Delores S. Williams, "Sin, Nature, and Black Women's Bodies," in *Ecofeminism and the Sacred*, ed. Carol J. Adams (New York: Continuum, 1993), 25.
26. Ruhl 21.
27. Ibid., 24.
28. Ibid., 29.
29. Ibid., 32.
30. Ibid., 64.
31. Later on Leo reveals that he told Elizabeth of his feelings for her, and then she slapped him. Ibid., 82.

32. Ibid., 80.
33. Ibid., 82.
34. See also Katherine E. Kelly's reading of this moment in "Making the Bones Sing: The Feminist History Play, 1976–2010," *Theatre Journal* 62 (2010): 659.
35. It is well worth noting here that before Whoriskey, Nottage had had a strong relationship with Seret Scott, who created sensitive productions of many of Nottage's early plays.
36. Kate Whoriskey, introduction to *Ruined*, by Lynn Nottage (New York: Theatre Communications Group, 2009), ix–x.
37. Lynn Nottage, "Out of East Africa," *American Theatre*, May–June 2005, http://www.tcg.org/publications/at/mayjune05/africa.cfm (accessed 28 February 2012).
38. Alexis Greene, "Lynn Nottage Interview 2008," League of Professional Theatre Women, http://www.theatrewomen.org/lynn-nottage-interview-2008 (accessed 28 February 2012).
39. Lynn Nottage, *Ruined* (New York: Theatre Communications Group, 2009), 86.
40. Celia McGee, "Approaching Brecht by Way of Africa," *The New York Times*, January 25, 2009, http://www.nytimes.com/2009/01/25/theater/25McGee.html.
41. Randy Gener, "In Defense of *Ruined*: Five Elements That Shape Lynn Nottage's Masterwork," *American Theatre*, October 2010, 118.
42. I will discuss this point in some detail in the final section of my analysis of *Ruined*.
43. Silvija Jestrovic, *Theatre of Estrangement: Theatre, Practice, Ideology* (Toronto: University of Toronto Press, 2006), 98.
44. Deji Olukotun, "Interview with Lynn Nottage, Pulitzer Prize winning playwright of *Ruined*," FictionThatMatters.Org, January 21, 2010, http://dejiridoo.com/blog1/reviews/full-reviews/interviews/interview-lynn-nottage-ruined-2010-human-rights.
45. Whoriskey xi.
46. Nottage 4, 5.
47. Ibid., 13.
48. Blaine Harden, "The Dirt in the Machine," *The New York Times*, August 12, 2001, 35.
49. Iain Marlow and Omar El Akkad, "Bloodstains at our Fingertips," *The Globe and Mail*, December 4, 2010, F1, http://www.theglobeandmail.com/news/technology/smartphones-blood-stains-at-our-fingertips/article1825207.
50. Nottage 40.
51. Olukotun.
52. Nottage 16.

53. Ibid., 38.
54. Jestrovic 109–10.
55. Nottage 32.
56. Though Fortune was not out mining coltan, Salima's monologue nevertheless resonates with this report from Victoria Brittain: "In addition there is the growing absence of men in the villages, which has left women unprotected. Men who are not in one or another army have been increasingly attracted into the chancy work of digging for diamonds or coltan—the key ingredient for mobile phones—which takes them far from home. The increasing insecurity has increasingly driven the women left behind off the land in recent years. No village has been spared rape, theft, abductions. The various militias' attacks on women have been both in the context of raids on the villages for looting, and in attacks related to coltan. Women tell of having been driven out of their area deliberately to clear it for coltan mining, or of being attacked because their husbands and sons had left home to go to the coltan mines." See Victoria Brittain, "Calvary of the Women of Eastern Democratic Republic of Congo (DRC)," in "State Failure in the Congo: Perceptions & Realities (Le Congo entre Crise et Régenération)," special issue, *Review of African Political Economy* 29, no. 93–94 (September–December 2002): 595–601.
57. Nottage 68.
58. Ibid., 69.
59. Olukotun. In both the Chicago and New York productions of *Ruined*, audiences had access to Tanya Palmer's article, "Weapons of War: The Conflict That Inspired *Ruined*" (provided in the program). Such materials educated audiences about facts that underpinned Nottage's theatrical narrative.
60. Nottage 94.
61. Elin Diamond, "Brechtian Theory/ Feminist Theory: Toward a Gestic Feminist Criticism," *TDR (1988–)* 32, no. 1 (Spring 1988): 82–94.
62. Marlow and El Akkad, "Bloodstains," F1.
63. Ann Fox, "Battles on the Body: Disability, Interpreting Dramatic Literature, and the Case of Lynn Nottage's Ruined," *Journal of Literary & Cultural Disability Studies* 5, no. 1 (2011), 1–15.
64. Nottage 100.
65. Jill Dolan, "Ruined, by Lynn Nottage," *Feminist Spectator* (blog) March 16, 2009, http://feministspectator.blogspot.com/2009/03/ruined-by-lynn-nottage.html.
66. Fox 12.
67. Ibid., 13.
68. Nottage 101.
69. Chris McGreal, "The Cost of a Call," *The Guardian*, August 20, 2001, 2, http://www.guardian.co.uk/g2/story/0,3604,539398,00.html.

70. Nottage 97.
71. Ibid., 101.
72. Ibid., 7.
73. Ibid., 102.
74. Ibid., 8.
75. Kim Gjerstad, "Beer for the Masses, If They Can Afford It," *Kim Gjerstad in Congo* (blog), http://kim.uing.net/1537/home.html?b_pi=1116 (accessed 1 July 2011).
76. Brittain, "Calvary of Women," 595–601.
77. Don Shewey, "A Playwright Who's Unafraid to Admit She's Political," *The New York Times*, February 4, 2001, http://www.nytimes.com/2001/02/04/theater/theater-a-playwright-who-s-unafraid-to-admit-she-s-political.html?ref=kiacorthron.
78. Deborah Gleason-Rielly, "Kia Corthron," in *African American Dramatists: An A-to-Z Guide*, ed. Emmanuel S. Nelson (Westport, CN: Greenwood Press, 2004), 119.
79. Charles Isherwood, "The Force of Water, the Power of Words," *The New York Times*, March 29, 2010, http://theater2.nytimes.com/2010/03/29/theater/reviews/29cool.html?ref=kiacorthron.
80. Erik Haagensen, "A Cool Dip in the Barren Saharan Crick," Backstage, http://www.backstage.com/review/ny-theater/off-broadway/a-cool-dip-in-the-barren-saharan-crick/ (accessed 28 February 2012).
81. Corthron's best-known play is *Breath, Boom*, but her other works include *Wake Up, Lou Riser* (1991), *Cage Rhythm* (1993), *Come Down Burning* (1993), *Splash Hatch on the E Going Down* (1996), *Seeking the Genesis* (1997), *The Venus de Milo Is Armed* (2001), and *Force Continuum* (2001).
82. Lisa M. Anderson, *Black Feminism in Contemporary Drama* (Urbana: University of Illinois Press, 2008), 76.
83. Chris J. Cuomo, *Feminism and Ecological Communities: An Ethic of Flourishing* (London: Routledge: 1998), 38–39.
84. Kia Corthron, *A Cool Dip in the Barren Saharan Crick* (New York: Samuel French, 2010), 19.
85. Ibid., 8.
86. Kara Lee Corthron, "In Dialogue: Kia Corthron's *Cool Dip*," *Brooklyn Rail*, March 2010, http://www.brooklynrail.org/2010/03/theater/in-dialogue-kia-corthrons-cool-dip.
87. Ibid.
88. Corthron 23.
89. Ibid., 33–34.
90. Ibid., 50–51.
91. Ibid., 62.
92. Ibid., 67.
93. Ibid., 68.

94. Ibid., 54.
95. Ibid., 82.
96. Ibid., 83.
97. Ibid., 84.
98. Ibid., 86.
99. Kia Corthron, "Playwright Kia Corthron Takes a *Cool Dip* with a Hot New Drama," *Broadway.com*, last modified 2010, http://www.broadway.com/shows/cool-dip-barren-saharan-crick/buzz/148821/playwright-kia-corthron-takes-a-cool-dip-with-a-hot-new-drama.
100. Kentucky Educational Television, "Black Women Playwrights: Interviews," accessed December 18, 2012, http://www.ket.org/americanshorts/poof/corthron.htm.
101. Corthron 49.
102. Ibid., 60.
103. Ibid., 88.
104. Ibid., 56.
105. Tim Sanford, "Artist Interview: Sarah Ruhl Discusses *Dead Man's Cell Phone* with Artistic Director Tim Sanford," Playwrights Horizons, http://playwrightshorizons.org.wehostwebsites.com/showfeature.asp?eventid=15&featureid=3.
106. Ibid.
107. Corthron 59.
108. Ibid., 87.
109. Ibid., 89.
110. Liza Weisstuch, "Kia Corthron on *Breath, Boom*," *The Boston Phoenix*, February 27, 2003, http://www.bostonphoenix.com/boston/events/theater/documents/02720229.asp. Corthron also referenced Boal in her Playwrights Horizons interview on *A Cool Dip*.

Epilogue

1. Charles Isherwood, "Dramatic Rush from the Beat of Delicate Hearts," *The New York Times*, June 07, 2012, http://www.nytimes.com/2012/06/10/theater/amy-herzog-and-others-bring-new-voices-to-stage.html?pagewanted=all.
2. Whitney Hale, "Kia Corthron to Judge Next Prize for Women Playwrights," University of Kentucky News, last modified 2012, http://uknow.uky.edu/content/kia-corthron-judge-next-prize-women-playwrights.
3. *The Year of Magical Thinking* has played at the Westport Playhouse, the Florida Repertory Theatre, the Court Theatre, the Strand Theatre, the Living Room, and the Main Street Theatre, among others.

4. The brooding, understated *Intimate Apparel* and the zany, over-the-top *Fabulation* represent the contradictory impulses and range of Nottage's bighearted imagination. "The two plays are bookends: I wrote them at the exact same time," Nottage reveals. "For *Fabulation*, I tried to imagine Esther 100 years later, after she's enjoyed the benefits of the women's rights and civil rights movements and become a fully empowered African-American woman, like Condoleezza Rice—and that was Undine. Esther's journey is about *becoming* empowered, whereas Undine feels completely empowered, so I imagined the opposite journey for her. She falls on hard times, goes through this spiral downward, goes back to her roots. In the end, they both achieve the same thing, which is finding self." Randy Gener, "Conjurer of Worlds," *American Theatre*, October 2005, http://www.tcg.org/publications/at/oct05/nottage.cfm.
5. Rob Weinert-Kendt, "Preview: By the Way, Meet Vera Stark," *Time Out New York*, April 18, 2011, http://www.timeout.com/newyork/theater/preview-by-the-way-meet-vera-stark-off-broadway.
6. Nottage modeled this relationship on Theresa Harris's performance alongside Barbara Stanwyck in 1933's *Baby Face*.
7. Hilton Als, "Playing to Type," *The New Yorker*, May 23, 2011, http://www.newyorker.com/arts/critics/theatre/2011/05/23/110523crth_theatre_als.
8. See, for example, Bob Bows, "Legit Reviews: Two Things You Don't Talk About at Dinner," *Variety*, January 30, 2011, http://www.variety.com/review/VE1117946972; and Joanne Ostrow, "Stereotypes Render 'Two Things You Don't Talk About at Dinner' Overdone," *The Denver Post*, February 03, 2011, http://www.denverpost.com/theater/ci_19871349.
9. Hector Tobar, "Their Mother's Day Goal: Redemption," *The Los Angeles Times*, May 10, 2012, http://articles.latimes.com/2012/may/10/local/la-me-tobar-20120511.
10. Michael Giltz, "Theater: 'Wonderlands' with a Thud; 'Pinter' with a Purpose and Then You Die," *The Huffington Post*, last modified 2011, http://www.huffingtonpost.com/michael-giltz/theater-wonderlands-with_b_850839.html.
11. Jason Fitzgerald, "We're Gonna Die," *Backstage*, April 09, 2011, http://www.backstage.com/bso/reviews-ny-theatre-off-broadway/we-re-gonna-die-1005124152.story.
12. Charles Isherwood, "Amid Catchy Choruses, Personal Tales of Life's Brutal Verities," *The New York Times*, April 10, 2011, http://theater.nytimes.com/2011/04/11/theater/reviews/were-gonna-die-by-young-jean-lee-at-joes-pub-review.html.

13. Charles Isherwood, "Dr. Feelgood Isn't Feeling Quite Like Himself," *The New York Times*, February 08, 2012, http://theater.nytimes.com/2012/02/08/theater/reviews/marin-hinkle-in-rx-by-kate-fodor-at-59e59-theaters.html.
14. Anthony Bannon, "'Fifty Ways': A Promising Play Full of Hurt, More Hurt and Hope," *The Chautauquan Daily*, July 24, 2012, http://chqdaily.com/2012/07/24/fifty-ways-a-promising-play-full-of-hurt-more-hurt-and-hope.
15. See Chapter 1 for a brief discussion of *Three Sisters*.
16. Tanya Palmer, "Playing the Part: A Conversation with Sarah Ruhl and Jessica Thebus," *Goodman Theatre Onstage* (April–June 2011): 3.
17. 13 P described itself as operating on an "implosion model:" after the 13 members of the collective self-produced a work, the organization would shut down, or implode. In July 2012, as I was writing this conclusion, that story was receiving considerable attention. See, for example, Alexis Soloski's *The New York Times* article "A Curtain Call for a Grand Experiment," http://www.nytimes.com/2012/07/15/theater/13p-theater-collective-set-for-its-last-production.html; or Shoshana Greenburg's "How Playwrights' Collective 13 P has Changed the Theatre Landscape" *Huffington Post*, http://www.huffingtonpost.com/shoshana-greenberg/13-playwrights-13p_b_1697919.html.
18. Steven Padla, "Yale Repertory Theatre Announces 2012–2013 Season," Yale Repertory Theatre, last modified 2012, http://www.yalerep.org/on_stage/2012-13/_images/2012-13seasonannouncement.pdf.
19. John Lahr, "Surreal Life: The Plays of Sarah Ruhl," *The New Yorker*, March 17, 2008, http://www.newyorker.com/arts/critics/atlarge/2008/03/17/080317crat_atlarge_lahr.

Bibliography

Ahmed, Sarah. *The Cultural Politics of Emotions*. New York: Routledge, 2004.
Anderson, Lisa M. *Black Feminism in Contemporary Drama*. Urbana: University of Illinois Press, 2008.
Als, Hilton. "Playing to Type." *The New Yorker*, May 23, 2011. http://www.newyorker.com/arts/critics/theatre/2011/05/23/110523crth_theatre_als.
Al-Shamma, James. *Sarah Ruhl: A Critical Study of the Plays*. Jefferson, NC: Macfarland, 2011.
Austin, Gayle. *Feminist Theories for Dramatic Criticism*. Ann Arbor: University of Michigan Press, 1990.
Bacalzo, Dan. "*Satellites* Dish Playwright Diana Son Discusses the World Premiere of Her Play at The Public Theater." *The New York Times*, June 5, 2006.
Bannon, Anthony. "'Fifty Ways': A Promising Play Full of Hurt, More Hurt and Hope." *The Chautauquan Daily*, July 24, 2012. http://chqdaily.com/2012/07/24/fifty-ways-a-promising-play-full-of-hurt-more-hurt-and-hope.
Barker, Drucilla, and Susan Feiner. *Liberating Economics: Feminist Perspectives on Family, Work, and Globalization*. Ann Arbor: University of Michigan Press, 2004.
Bent, Eliza. "The Church of Young Jean Lee. Brooklyn Rail." April 2007. http://brooklynrail.org/2007/04/theater/the-church-of-young-jean-lee.
Best, Kirsty. "Interfacing the Environment: Networked Screens and the Ethics of Visual Consumption." In "Ethics of Seeing: Consuming Environments," special issue, *Ethics and the Environment* 9, no. 2 (Fall–Winter 2004): 65–85.
Botero, Carlo. "Telling the Stories: Interview with Lisa Loomer, Revolutionary Worker #1227." *Revolution Newspaper*, February 1, 2004. http://revcom.us/a/1227/lisainterview.htm
Bowker, Natilene I., and James H. Liu. "Are Women Occupying Positions of Power Online? Demographics of Chat Room Operators." *Cyberpsychology & Behavior* 4, no. 5 (2001): 631–44. *Academic Search Premier*.
Bows, Bob. "Legit Reviews: Two Things You Don't Talk About at Dinner." *Variety*, January 30, 2011. http://www.variety.com/review/VE1117946972.

Brantley, Ben. "'The Doctor Will See You Now.' Uh-Oh." *The New York Times*, November 6, 1996. Accessed November 18, 2012. http://www.nytimes.com/1996/11/06/theater/the-doctor-will-see-you-now-uh-oh.html?n=Top%2fReference%2fTimes%20Topics%2fSubjects%2fT%2fTheater.

———. "Settling Down on Shaky Ground in Diana Son's *Satellites*." *The New York Times*, June 19, 2006. Accessed December 1, 2012. http://theater.nytimes.com/2006/06/19/theater/reviews/19sate.html.

Brennan, Teresa. *Transmission of Affect*. Ithaca: Cornell University Press, 2004.

Breslauer, Jan. "As Her Many Worlds Turn." *Los Angeles Times*, August 7, 1994. http://articles.latimes.com/1994-08-07/entertainment/ca-24432_1_lisa-loomer/3.

Brittain, Victoria. "Calvary of the Women of Eastern Democratic Republic of Congo (DRC)." In "State Failure in the Congo: Perceptions & Realities (Le Congo entre Crise et Régenération)," special issue, *Review of African Political Economy* 29, no. 93–94 (September–December 2002): 595–601.

Burns, Christy L. "Re-Dressing Feminist Identities: Tensions between Essential and Constructed Selves in Virginia Woolf's *Orlando*." *Twentieth Century Literature* 40, no. 3 (Autumn 1994): 342–64.

Butler, Judith. *Precarious Life: The Powers of Mourning and Violence*. London: Verso, 2010.

Caruth, Cathy. *Unclaimed Experience: Trauma, Narrative, and History*. Baltimore: Johns Hopkins University Press, 1996.

Castells, Manuel. *Mobile Communication and Society: A Global Perspective*. Boston: MIT Press, 2007.

Chansky, Dorothy. "Usable Performance Feminism for Our Time: Reconsidering Betty Friedan." *Theatre Journal* 60, no. 3 (October 2008): 341–64.

Chekhov, Anton. "The Lady with the Dog." In *Later Short Stories: 1888–1893*, ed. Shelby Foote, 568–85. New York: The Modern Library, 1999.

Coakley, Sarah. "The Trinity, Prayer, and Sexuality." In *Feminism and Theology*, ed. Janet Martin Soskice and Diana Lipton, 258–67. Oxford: Oxford University Press, 2003.

Cohen, Patricia. "Rethinking Gender Bias in Theater." *The New York Times*, June 23, 2009.

Corthron, Kara Lee. "In Dialogue: Kia Corthron's *Cool Dip*." *Brooklyn Rail*, March 2010. http://www.brooklynrail.org/2010/03/theater/in-dialogue-kia-corthrons-cool-dip.

Corthron, Kia. *A Cool Dip in the Barren Saharan Crick*. New York: Samuel French, 2010.

Corthron, Kia. "Playwright Kia Corthron Takes a *Cool Dip* with a Hot New Drama." Broadway.com. Last modified 2010. http://www.broadway.com/shows/cool-dip-barren-saharan-crick/buzz/148821/playwright-kia-corthron-takes-a-cool-dip-with-a-hot-new-drama.

Crossroads Initiative, The. "The Blood and Water from His Side." http://www.crossroadsinitiative.com/library_article/379.
Cuomo, Chris J. *Feminism and Ecological Communities: An Ethic of Flourishing* (London: Routledge: 1998).
Daly, Mary. "Beyond God the Father." In *Feminism and Theology*, ed. Janet Martin Soskice and Diana Lipton, 41–46. Oxford: Oxford UP, 2003.
Day, David. "Dusted Reviews: On!Air!Library!." *Dusted.* http://www.dustedmagazine.com/reviews/240.
Deshazer, Mary K. "Fractured Borders: Women's Cancer And Feminist Theatre." *Feminist Formations* 15, no. 2 (Summer 2003): 1–26.
Diamond, Elin. "Brechtian Theory/ Feminist Theory: Toward a Gestic Feminist Criticism." *TDR (1988–)* 32, no. 1 (Spring 1988): 82–94.
Didion, Joan. "The Year of Hoping for Stage Magic." *The New York Times.* March 4, 2007.
———. *The Year of Magical Thinking.* New York: Knopf, 2005.
———. *The Year of Magical Thinking: The Play.* New York: Vintage, 2007.
Dolan, Jill. "Feminist Performance Criticism and the Popular: Reviewing Wendy Wasserstein." *Theatre Journal* 60, no. 3 (October 2008): 433–57.
———. "*Ruined*, by Lynn Nottage." *Feminist Spectator.* March 16, 2009. Accessed February 28, 2012. http://feministspectator.blogspot.com/2009/03/ruined-by-lynn-nottage.html.
Doran, Bathsheba. *Kin.* Hanover, NH: In an Hour Books, 2011.
Douthat, Ross. "The Facebook Illusion." *The New York Times*, May 26, 2012. http://www.nytimes.com/2012/05/27/opinion/sunday/douthat-the-facebook-illusion.html?src=me&ref=general.
Eisdorfer, Erica. "11 Things You Never Knew About Wet-Nursing." *The Lincoln Center Theater Review*, Fall 2009, 17–18.
Etheredge, Warren. "LIVING OUT—Screenwriter, Lisa Loomer." *The Warren Report.* Last modified January 18, 2003. http://thewarrenreport.com/2003/01/18/living-out-screenwriter-lisa-loomer.
Euripides. *Euripides, 3*, ed. David R. Slavitt and Palmer Bovie (Philadelphia: University of Pennsylvania Press, 1998). http://www.nytimes.com/books/first/e/euripides3-penn.html.
"Facebook's IPO Is Decade's Biggest Flop." Bloomberg Businessweek: Technology. Recorded May 25, 2012. http://www.businessweek.com/videos/2012-05-25/facebooks-ipo-flop-is-decades-worst.
Fiorenza, Elisabeth Schussler. "Missionaries, Apostles, Co-workers." In *Feminist Theology: A Reader*, ed. Ann Loades, 57–71. London: Society for Promoting Christian Knowledge, 1990.
Feldman, Emily. "Days of Yore." Last modified 2011. http://www.thedaysofyore.com/sarah-ruhl.
Fivush, Robyn, and Janine P. Buckner. "Gender, Sadness, and Depression: The Development of Emotional Focus through Gendered Discourse." In *Gender*

and Emotion: Social Psychological Perspectives, ed. Agneta H. Fischer, 232–53. New York: Cambridge University Press, 2000.

Fitzgerald, Jason. "We're Gonna Die." *Backstage*, April 09, 2011. http://www.backstage.com/bso/reviews-ny-theatre-off-broadway/we-re-gonna-die-1005124152.story.

Fodor, Kate. *100 Saints You Should Know*. New York: Dramatists Play Service, 2008.

Folbre, Nancy. "'Holding Hands at Midnight:' The Paradox of Caring Labor." In *Toward a Feminist Philosophy of Economics*, ed. Drucilla Barker and Edith Kuiper, 213–30. London: Routledge, 2003.

Foster, Patricia. "Sideswiped." *Antioch Review* 64 (2006): 810–16.

Fox, Ann. "Battles on the Body: Disability, Interpreting Dramatic Literature, and the Case of Lynn Nottage's *Ruined*." *Journal of Literary & Cultural Disability Studies* 5, no. 1 (2011): 1–15.

Garcia, Lorenzo. "Living with/through Loss and Grief in Lisa Loomer's *Bocón*!" *Youth Theatre Journal* 25, no. 2 (2011): 159–74.

García-Romero, Anne. "Fugue, Hip Hop and Soap Opera: Transcultural Connections and Theatrical Experimentation in Twenty-First Century US Latina Playwriting." *Latin American Theatre Review* 43, no. 1 (2009): 87–102. http://muse.jhu.edu.

Gener, Randy. "Conjurer of Worlds." *American Theatre*, October 2005. http://www.tcg.org/publications/at/oct05/nottage.cfm

———. "In Defense of *Ruined*: Five Elements That Shape Lynn Nottage's Masterwork." *American Theatre*, October 2010, 18.

Gianopulos, Peter. "The Passion of Sarah Ruhl." *Northshore Magazine*, September 2007. http://www.northshoremag.com.

Gilbert, Sandra. "Book Reviews: *The Year of Magical Thinking*." *Literature and Medicine* 25, no. 2 (Fall 2006): 553–67.

Giltz, Michael. "Theater: 'Wonderlands' with a Thud; 'Pinter' with a Purpose And Then You Die." *The Huffington Post*. Last modified 2011. http://www.huffingtonpost.com/michael-giltz/theater-wonderlands-with_b_850839.html.

Gjerstad, Kim. *Kim Gjerstad in Congo* (blog). Accessed July 1, 2011. http://kim.uing.net/1537/home.html?b_pi=1116.

Gleason-Rielly, Deborah. "Kia Corthron." In *African American Dramatists: An A-to-Z Guide*, ed. Emmanuel S. Nelson, 115–24. Westport, CT: Greenwood Press, 2004.

Goggin, Gerard. "Ubiquitous Apps: The Politics of Openness in Global Mobile Cultures." *Digital Creativity* 22, no. 3 (2011): 148–59.

Greene, Alexis. "Crossing Borders: A Conversation with Bridget Carpenter, Lynn Nottage, Dael Orlandersmith, and Diana Son." In *Women Writing*

Plays: Three Decades of the Susan Smith Blackburn Prize, 117. Austin: University of Texas Press, 2006.

———. "Joking Aside: A Conversation about Comedy with Christopher Durang, Gina Gionfriddo, Ruhl, Sarah, and Wendy Wasserstein." In *Women Writing Plays: Three Decades of the Susan Smith Blackburn Prize*, 181–90. Austin: University of Texas Press, 2006.

———. "Lynn Nottage Interview 2008." http://theatrewomen.org/lynn-nottage-interview-2008.

———. "New Voices: An Interview with Sarah Ruhl." In *Women Writing Plays: Three Decades of the Susan Smith Blackburn Prize*, ed. Greene, 230–31. Austin: University of Texas Press, 2006.

———. "What Women Want." *American Theatre* February 2008, 26–29, 62–64.

Greenfield, Adam. "Artist Interview: Adam Greenfield Discusses the Origins of *Cool Dip* . . . with Playwright Kia Corthron." Playwrights Horizons. Last modified 2010. http://playwrightshorizons.org.wehostwebsites.com/showfeature.asp?eventid=30&featureid=3.

Grode, Eric. "Theatre Talk-Back: A Good Play Can Be Read as Well as Seen." *The New York Times*, April 18, 2012. http://artsbeat.blogs.nytimes.com/2012/04/18/theater-talkback-a-good-play-can-be-read-as-well-as-seen.

Haagensen, Erik. "A Cool Dip in the Barren Saharan Crick." Backstage. Accessed February 28, 2012. http://www.backstage.com/review/ny-theater/off-broadway/a-cool-dip-in-the-barren-saharan-crick/.

Hahn, Beverly. *Chekhov: A Study of the Major Stories and Plays*. Cambridge: Cambridge University Press, 1977.

Hale, Whitney. "Kia Corthron to Judge Next Prize for Women Playwrights." University of Kentucky News. Last modified 2012. http://uknow.uky.edu/content/kia-corthron-judge-next-prize-women-playwrights.

Harden, Blaine. "The Dirt in the Machine." *The New York Times*, August 12, 2001.

Hayles, N. Katherine. "The Complexities of Seriation." *PMLA* 117, no. 1 (January 2002): 117–21.

Heath, John. "The Failure of Orpheus." *Transactions of the American Philological Association* 124 (1994): 163–96.

Henry, Astrid. *Not My Mother's Sister: Generational Conflict and Third Wave Feminism*. Bloomington, Indiana University Press, 2004.

Hewitson, Gillian J. "Domestic Labor and Gender Identity." In *Toward a Feminist Philosophy of Economics*, ed. Drucilla Barker and Edith Kuiper, 266–84. London: Routledge, 2003.

Heywood, Leslie, and Jennifer Drake. *Third Wave Agenda: Being Feminist, Doing Feminism*. Minneapolis: University of Minnesota Press, 1997.

Hochschild, Arlie. "The Nanny Chain." *American Prospect*, December 19, 2001. Accessed November 18, 2012. http://prospect.org/article/nanny-chain.

Hudes, Quiara Alegria. "Water by the Spoonful." Unpublished manuscript. October 26, 2011.

Isherwood, Charles. "Amid Catchy Choruses, Personal Tales of Life's Brutal Verities." *The New York Times*, April 10, 2011. http://theater.nytimes.com/2011/04/11/theater/reviews/were-gonna-die-by-young-jean-lee-at-joes-pub-review.html.

Isherwood, Charles. "A Comic Impudence Softens a Tale of Loss." *The New York Times*, October 03, 2006. http://theater.nytimes.com/2006/10/03/theater/reviews/03eury.html?pagewanted=all.

Isherwood, Charles. "Dramatic Rush from the Beat of Delicate Hearts." *The New York Times*, June 07, 2012. http://www.nytimes.com/2012/06/10/theater/amy-herzog-and-others-bring-new-voices-to-stage.html?pagewanted=all.

Isherwood, Charles. "Dr. Feelgood Isn't Feeling Quite Like Himself." *The New York Times*, February 08, 2012. http://theater.nytimes.com/2012/02/08/theater/reviews/marin-hinkle-in-rx-by-kate-fodor-at-59e59-theaters.html.

———. "The Force of Water, the Power of Words." The New York Times, March 29, 2010. Accessed February 28, 2012. http://theater2.nytimes.com/2010/03/29/theater/reviews/29cool.html?ref=kiacorthron.

———. "The Power of Memory to Triumph Over Death." *The New York Times*. June 19, 2007. http://theater.nytimes.com/2007/06/19/theater/reviews/19seco.html?pagewanted=print.

———. "Who's Afraid of Fluid Gender and Time?" review of "Orlando." *The New York Times*, September 23, 2010. Accessed February 28, 2012. http://theater.nytimes.com/2010/09/24/theater/reviews/24orlando.html?pagewanted=all.

Islam, Gazi. "Virtual Speakers, Virtual Audiences: Agency, Audience, and Constraint in an Online Chat Community." *Dialectical Anthropology* 30, no. 1 (2006): 71–89.

Iyer, Pico. *The Global Soul: Jet Lag, Shopping Malls, and the Search for Home*. New York: Vintage, 2001.

Jansz, Jeroen. "Masculine Identity and Restrictive Emotionality." In *Gender and Emotion: Social Psychological Perspectives*, ed. Agneta H. Fischer, 166–88. New York: Cambridge University Press, 2000.

Jefferson, Margo. "'Upstairs, Downstairs,' With Nanny-Cam Running." *The New York Times*, October 1, 2003. Accessed November 18, 2012. http://www.nytimes.com/2003/10/01/theater/theater-review-upstairs-downstairs-with-nanny-cam-running.html?n=Top%2fReference%2fTimes%20Topics%2fSubjects%2fT%2fTheater.

Jestrovic, Silvija. *Theatre of Estrangement: Theatre, Practice, Ideology.* Toronto: University of Toronto Press, 2006.

Jones, Chris. "Snubbed for Years, Playwright Ruhl Finds Hometown Success." *Chicago Tribune*, May 7, 2006. Accessed February 28, 2012. http://articles.chicagotribune.com/2006-05-07/news/0605060225_1_sarah-ruhl-piven-theatre-workshop-prize-winning-playwright-paula-vogel.

Jones, Jeffrey M. "What's Wrong with These Plays: An Afterword." In *Songs of the Dragons Flying to Heaven and Other Plays*, by Young Jean Lee, 183–201. New York: Theatre Communications Group, 2010.

Jones, Liz, and Asher Richelli. "Tales of a Chronicler: An Introduction to Quiara Alegria Hudes's *Elliot, A Soldier's Fugue*." In *New York Theatre Review (2007)*, ed. Brook Stowe, 262–66. New York: Black Wave Press, 2007.

Kamber, Michael, and Tim Arango. "4,000 U.S. Deaths, and a Handful of Images." *The New York Times*, July 26, 2008. http://www.nytimes.com/2008/07/26/world/middleeast/26censor.html?pagewanted=all.

Kanter, Jodi. "Hopeful Sentences: Gender and Mourning Language in Two Contemporary Narratives." *Women and Language* 25, no. 1 (2002): 1–8.

Kaplan, Caren. "Transporting the Subject: Technologies of Mobility and Location in an Era of Globalization." Special issue, *PMLA* 117, no. 1 (January 2002): 32–42.

Karass, Valerie. "Eschatology." In *The Cambridge Companion to Feminist Theology*, ed. Susan Frank Parsons, 243–60. Cambridge: Cambridge University Press, 2002.

Kelly, Katherine E. "Making the Bones Sing: The Feminist History Play, 1976–2010." *Theatre Journal* 62 (2010): 645–60.

Kentucky Educational Television, "Black Women Playwrights: Interviews." Accessed December 18, 2012. http://www.ket.org/americanshorts/poof/corthron.htm.

Kumar, Krishan, and Ekaterina Makarova. "The Portable Home: The Domestication of Public Space." *Sociological Theory* 26, no. 4 (December 2008): 324–43. http://www.jstor.org/stable/20453115.

Lahr, John. "Guys and Dolls." *The New Yorker*, July 2, 2007. http://www.newyorker.com/arts/critics/theatre/2007/07/02/070702crth_theatre_lahr?currentPage=all.

———. "Surreal Life: The Plays of Sarah Ruhl." *The New Yorker*, March 17, 2008. http://www.newyorker.com/arts/critics/atlarge/2008/03/17/080317crat_atlarge_lahr.

Lee, Young Jean. *Songs of the Dragons Flying to Heaven and Other Plays.* New York: Theatre Communications Group, 2010.

Loomer, Lisa. *Living Out.* New York: Dramatists Play Service, 2005.

Lutz, Catherine A. "Engendered Emotion: Gender, Power, and the Rhetoric of Emotional Control in American Discourse." In *Language and the Politics of Emotion*, ed. Catherine A. Lutz and Lila Abu-Lughod, 69–90. Cambridge: Cambridge University Press, 1990.

Mack-Canty, Colleen. "Third-Wave Feminism and the Need to Reweave the Nature/Culture Duality." *Feminist Formations* 16, no. 3 (Fall 2004): 154–79.

Malcom, Janet. *Reading Chekhov: A Critical Journey*. New York: Random House, 2001.

Marcus, Laura. "Woolf's Feminism and Feminism's Woolf." In *The Cambridge Companion to Virginia Woolf*, ed. Sue Roe and Susan Sellers, 209–44. Cambridge: Cambridge University Press, 2000.

Marder, Elissa. "The Sex of Death and the Maternal Crypt." *Parallax* 15, no. 1 (2009): 5–20. *Academic Search Premier*.

Marlow, Iain, and Omar El Akkad. "Bloodstains at Our Fingertips." *The Globe and Mail*, December 4, 2010. Accessed February 28, 2012. http://www.theglobeandmail.com/news/technology/smartphones-blood-stains-at-our-fingertips/article1825207.

McGee, Celia. "Approaching Brecht by Way of Africa." *The New York Times*, January 25, 2009. Accessed February 28, 2012. http://www.nytimes.com/2009/01/25/theater/25McGee.html.

McGreal, Chris. "The Cost of a Call." *The Guardian*. August 20, 2001. Accessed February 28, 2012. http://www.guardian.co.uk/g2/story/0,3604,539398,00.html.

McRobbie, Angela. *The Aftermath of Feminism: Gender, Culture, and Social Change*. London: Sage Publications, 2009.

Montrose, Louis. *The Purpose of Playing: Shakespeare and the Cultural Politics of the Elizabethan Theatre*. Chicago: University of Chicago Press, 1996.

Murphy, Richard. "Dance in Worship." Maranatha Life. Last modified 1998. http://maranathalife.com/teaching/jew-danc.htm.

Nettleton, Sarah, Nicholas Pleace, Roger Burrows, and Steven Muncer. "The Reality of Virtual Social Support." In *Virtual Society? Technology, Cyperbole, Reality*, ed. Steven Woolgar, 176–88. Oxford: Oxford University Press, 2002.

Norman, Marsha. "Not There Yet." *American Theatre*, November 2009, 28–30; 79.

Nottage, Lynn. "Out of East Africa." *American Theatre*, May–June 2005. Accessed February 28, 2012. http://www.tcg.org/publications/at/mayjune05/africa.cfm.

———. *Ruined*. New York: Theatre Communications Group, 2009.

Olukotun, Deji. "Interview with Lynn Nottage, Pulitzer Prize Winning Playwright of *Ruined*." FictionThatMatters.Org. January 21, 2010. Accessed

February 28, 2012. http://dejiridoo.com/blog1/reviews/full-reviews/inter views/interview-lynn-nottage-ruined-2010-human-rights.
Ostrow, Joanne. "Stereotypes Render 'Two Things You Don't Talk About at Dinner' Overdone." *Denver Post*, February 03, 2011. http://www.denver post.com/theater/ci_19871349.
Padla, Steven. Yale Repertory Theatre, "Yale Repertory Theatre Announces 2012–2013 Season." Last modified 2012. http://www.yalerep.org/on _stage/2012-13/_images/2012-13seasonannouncement.pdf.
Palmer, Tanya. "A Passion for Theater: An Interview with Sarah Ruhl." *Goodman Theatre OnStage*, September/December 2007.
———. "Playing the Part: A Conversation with Sarah Ruhl and Jessica Thebus." *Goodman Theatre Onstage*, April–June 2011.
———. "Weapons of War: The Conflict That Inspired *Ruined*." *Goodman Theatre Onstage*. Accessed February 29, 2012. http://www.goodmantheatre .org/_downloads/OnStage_0708_1.pdf.
Parts, Lyudmila. "Down the Intertextual Lane: Petrushevskaia, Chekhov, Tolstoy." *Russian Review* 64, no. 1 (January 2005): 77–89.
Peter, Thomas. "Playbill.com's Brief Encounter with Sarah Ruhl." October 9, 2010. Accessed February 28, 2012. http://www.playbill.com/news/ article/143787-PLAYBILLCOMS-BRIEF-ENCOUNTER-With-Sarah -Ruhl.
Piepenburg, Erik. "Faith Confronted, and Defended, Downtown." *The New York Times*, May 6, 2007.
Plumwood, Val. "Nature, Self, and Gender: Feminism, Environmental Philosophy, and the Critique of Rationalism." In "Ecological Feminism," special issue, *Hypatia* 6, no. 1 (Spring 1991): 3–27
Poster, Mark. "Digital Networks and Citizenship." *PMLA* 117, no. 1 (January 2002): 98–103.
Radin, Margaret Jane. *Contested Commodities*. Cambridge: Harvard University Press, 1996.
Renner, Pamela. "Science and Sensibility: Lisa Loomer and Margaret Edson Turn a Lens on the Medical Establishment." *American Theatre* 16 (1999): 34.
Rizzo, Frank. "Legit Reviews: Water by the Spoonful." *Variety*, October 30, 2011. http://www.variety.com/review/VE1117946466d.
Roman, David. "Comment—*Theatre Journals*." *Theatre Journal* 54, no. 3 (2002): vii–xix.
Ross, Susan A. "Church and Sacrament—Community and Worship." In *The Cambridge Companion to Feminist Theology*, ed. Susan Frank Parsons, 224– 42. Cambridge: Cambridge University Press, 2002.

Roth, Maya. "Revealing and Renewing Feminist Theatrical Engagement: The Jane Chambers Contest for Women Playwrights." *Theatre Topics* 20, no. 2 (2010): 157–69.

Ruether, Rosemary Radford. "The Emergence of Christian Feminist Theology." In *The Cambridge Companion to Feminist Theology*, ed. Susan Frank Parsons, 3–23. Cambridge: Cambridge University Press, 2002,

Ruhl, Sarah. *The American Theatre Wing Presents America's Foremost Playwrights on the Plays That Influenced Them.* Ed. Ben Hodges. New York: Applause Books, 2009.

———. *The Clean House and Other Plays.* New York: Theatre Communication Group, 2006.

———. *Dead Man's Cell Phone.* New York: Theatre Communications Group, 2008.

———. *In the Next Room, or the Vibrator Play.* New York: Samuel French, 2010.

———. "Lady with the Lap Dog." New Dramatists. Unpublished manuscript. March 2000. Word document.

———. *Passion Play.* New York: Theatre Communications Group, 2010.

———. "Re-runs and Repetitions." *Contemporary Theatre Review* 16, no. 3 (2006): 283–90.

———. *Three Sisters.* Unpublished manuscript. July 2009. Word document

———. "No Place Like Home." *American Theatre*, October 2008.

Sands, Emily Glasberg. "Opening the Curtain on Playwright Gender: An Integrated Economic Analysis of Discrimination in American Theater." *The New York Times*, June 23, 2009. http://graphics8.nytimes.com/packages/pdf/theater/speech_slides2x.pdf.

Sanford, Tim. "Artist Interview: Kate Fodor Discusses *100 Saints* with Artistic Director Tim Sanford." Playwrights Horizons. http://playwrightshorizons.org.wehostwebsites.com/showfeature.asp?eventid=10&featureid=3.

———. "Artist Interview: Sarah Ruhl Discusses *Dead Man's Cell Phone* with Artistic Director Tim Sanford." Playwrights Horizons. http://playwrightshorizons.org.wehostwebsites.com/showfeature.asp?eventid=15&featureid=3.

Schuler, Catherine A. "Editorial Comment." *Theatre Journal* 60, no. 3 (2008): vii–viii.

Schulman, Sarah. "Supremacy Ideology Masquerading as Reality: The Obstacle Facing Women Playwrights in America." *Theatre Journal* 62 (2010): 567–70.

Schwartz, Beth C. "Thinking Back Through our Mothers: Virginia Woolf Reads Shakespeare." *ELH* 58, no. 3 (Autumn 1991): 721–46.

Schwartz, Jenny. *God's Ear.* New York: Faber and Faber, 2008.

Sedgwick, Eve Kosofsky. *Touching Feeling: Affect, Pedagogy, Performativity.* Durham: Duke University Press, 2003.

Shaw, Helen. "Preview: Kin." *Time Out New York*, March 14, 2011.
Shewey, Don. "A Playwright Who's Unafraid to Admit She's Political." *The New York Times*, February 4, 2001. http://www.nytimes.com/2001/02/04/theater/theater-a-playwright-who-s-unafraid-to-admit-she-s-political.html?ref=kiacorthron.
Shimakawa, Karen. "Performing the Asian American Signature in Law and Literature." In *Signatures of the Past: Cultural Memory in Contemporary Anglophone North American Drama*, ed. Marc Maufort and Caroline de Wagter, 291–308. Bruxelles: Peter Lang, 2008.
Shklovsky, Viktor. "Art as Technique." In *Russian Formalist Criticism: Four Essays*, ed. Lee T. Lemon and Marion J. Reiss, 3–24. Lincoln: University of Nebraska Press, 1965.
Sisario, Ben. "A Playwright Wonders What He Said, She Said." *The New York Times*, April 03, 2004. http://www.nytimes.com/2004/04/03/theater/a-playwright-wonders-what-he-said-she-said.html?n=Top/Reference/Times Topics/Subjects/T/Theater.
Slee, Nicola. "The Holy Spirit and Spirituality." In *The Cambridge Companion to Feminist Theology*, ed. Susan Frank Parsons, 171–89. Cambridge: Cambridge University Press, 2002.
Smith, Victoria L. "'Ransacking the Language': Finding the Missing Goods in Virginia Woolf's 'Orlando'" *Journal of Modern Literature* 29, no. 4 (Summer 2006): 57–75.
Smith, Virginia Llwellyn. "The Lady with the Dog." In *Critical Essays on Anton Chekhov*, ed. Thomas A. Eekman, 118–25. Boston: G. K. Hall and Company, 1979.
Soloski, Alexis. "Hell Is for Bohos." *Village Voice*, April 17, 2007.
Son, Diana. *Satellites*. New York: Dramatists Play Service, 2008.
Soskice, Janet Martin. "Blood and Defilement." *Feminism and Theology*, ed. Janet Martin Soskice and Diana Lipton, 333–42. Oxford: Oxford University Press, 2003.
Stern, Sarah. "An Interview with Playwright Jenny Schwartz." Vineyard Theatre. Accessed December 18, 2012. http://www.vineyardtheatre.org/interview-godsear.htm.
Sterns, Daniel. *American Cool*. New York: New York University Press, 1994.
Svich, Caridad. "US Polyglot Latino Theatre and its Link to the Americas." *Contemporary Theatre* 16, no. 2 (2006): 189–97.
Szymkowicz, Adam. "I Interview Playwrights: 261: Kate Fodor." Last modified 2010. http://aszym.blogspot.com/2010/09/i-interview-playwrights-part-261-kate.html.

Taylor, Kate. "Everything Old Is New Again." *The New York Sun*, October 10, 2006. http://www.nysun.com/arts/everything-old-is-new-again-2006-10-10/41209.

Theatre Communications Group, "Top Ten Most Produced Plays." Accessed December 18, 2012. http://www.tcg.org/publications/at/attopten.cfm.

Tobar, Hector. "Their Mother's Day Goal: Redemption." *The Los Angeles Times*, May 10, 2012. http://articles.latimes.com/2012/may/10/local/la-me-tobar-20120511.

Tong, Rosemarie. *Feminist Thought: A More Comprehensive Introduction*. 3rd ed. Boulder: Westview Press, 2009.

Twine, Richard T. "Ma(r)king Essence-Ecofeminism and Embodiment." *Ethics & the Environment* 6, no. 2 (Autumn 2001): 31–58.

Valkenburg, Patti M., and Jochen Peter. "Who Visits Online Dating Sites? Exploring Some Characteristics of Online Daters." *CyberPsychology and Behavior* 10, no. 6 (2007): 849–52.

Van Dijck, José. "Facebook as Tool for Producing Sociality and Connectivity." *Television and New Media* 13, no. 2 (2012): 160–76.

Vogel, Paula. "Interview with Sarah Ruhl." *BOMB* Magazine. Accessed February 28, 2011. http://www.bombsite.com/issues/99/articles/2902.

Warren, Karen. *Ecofeminist Philosophy*. Lanham: Rowman and Littlefield, 2000.

———. "Ecological Feminist Philosophies: An Overview of the Issues." In *Ecological Feminist Philosophies*, ed. Karen J. Warren, xvi. Bloomington: Indiana University Press, 1996.

Weckwerth, Wendy. "More Invisible Terrains." *Theater* 34, no. 2 (2004): 28–35.

Weinert-Kendt, Rob. "On 'Saints' and Longings." *The Los Angeles Times*, May 29, 2011. http://articles.latimes.com/2011/may/29/entertainment/la-ca-100-saints-playwright-20110529.

———. "Preview: By the Way, Meet Vera Stark." *Time Out New York*, April 18, 2011. http://www.timeout.com/newyork/theater/preview-by-the-way-meet-vera-stark-off-broadway.

Weisstuch, Liza. "Kia Corthron on *Breath, Boom*." *Boston Phoenix*, February 27, 2003. http://www.bostonphoenix.com/boston/events/theater/documents/02720229.asp.

Wiener, Diane R. "Antipsychiatric Activism and Feminism: The Use of Film and Text to Question Biomedicine." *Journal of Public Mental Health* 4, no. 3 (September 2005): 42–47.

Whoriskey, Kate. Introduction to *Ruined*, by Lynn Nottage, ix–x. New York: Theatre Communications Group, 2009.

Williams, Delores S. "Sin, Nature, and Black Women's Bodies." In *Ecofeminism and the Sacred*, ed. Carol J. Adams, 24–29. New York: Continuum, 1993.

Woodward, Kathleen. *Statistical Panic: Cultural Politics and the Poetics of Emotion*. Durham: Duke University Press, 2009.
Woolf, Virginia. *Orlando*. New York: Harcourt Brace, 1928.
Woolgar, Steve. *Virtual Society? Technology, Cyperbole, Reality*. Oxford: Oxford University Press, 2002.
Wussow, Helen. "Virginia Woolf and the Problematic Nature of the Photographic Image." *Twentieth Century Literature* 40, no. 1 (Spring 1994): 13.
Zinoman, Jason. "New Dramas, New Voices below 14th Street." *The New York Times*, June 3, 2007. http://www.nytimes.com/2007/06/03/theater/theaterspecial/03zino.html?pagewanted=2&n=Top/Reference/Times Topics/Subjects/T/Theater.
———. "Theater; Season of the Female Playwright." *The New York Times*, December 21, 2003.

Index

Ahmed, Sara, 6–7, 8, 33, 35
Alcestis (Euripides)
    Didion and, 42–44
    God's Ear and, 48–49
Als, Hilton, 160
Al-Shamma, James, 4, 166n15
American Cool: Constructing a Twentieth-Century Emotional Style (Stearns), 32
Anderson, Lisa M., 150
Angels in America (Kushner), 61
anger, creativity and, 7
"Anna Around the Neck" (Chekhov), 14
Anna Around the Neck (Ruhl), 25
Anna Karenina (Tolstoy), 25
apps, 117, 183n63
Arena Theatre
    Expecting Isabel as production of, 62
    Passion Play as production of, 76, 85
    Ruhl productions of, 23
Arendt, Hannah, 93
Art as Technique (Shklovsky), 21
Austin, Gayle, 8

Baker, Annie, 159, 166n22
Baltimore Waltz (Vogel), 19
Bannon, Anthony, 162
Barker, Drucilla, 53–54
Beard of Avon (Freed), 2
beauty, social standards of, 61–62
Bengal Tiger at the Baghdad Zoo (Joseph), 3
Bennett, Suzanne, 1, 2
Berkeley Rep
    Dear Elizabeth as production of, 162
    Eurydice as production of, 13
    Three Sisters as production of, 25, 162
Best, Kirsty, 103–4
Beyond God the Father (Daly), 88–89
Bishop, Elizabeth, 162
Black Orpheus, 34
Blue Nights (Didion), 160
Boal, Augusto, 157
Bobbi Boland (Hasty), 2
Bock, Adam, 46
body modification, social standards of beauty and, 61–62
Bogart, Anne, 49
Brantley, Ben, 61, 71–72
Brecht, Bertolt, 21, 140–44, 146, 147, 150
Brennan, Teresa, 51
Breuer, Joseph, 33
Brittain, Victoria, 149, 187n56
Brooks, James L., 62
Buckner, Janine P., 41–42
Burns, Christy L., 17
Bush, George W., 32, 86
Butler, Judith, 32, 40, 51–52
By the Way, Meet Vera Stark (Nottage), 160

Café Vida (Loomer), 161
Callaghan, Sheila, 166n22
caring labor, 53–73
    examples of, 54
    through feminist economists' lens, 53–54
    globalization of, 65–68
    in *Satellites*, 68–73
Caruth, Cathy, 50
Castells, Manuel, 109, 110, 111
Castle Cross the Magnet Carter, The (Corthron), 159

Catching a Wave (Dicker and Piepmeier), 10
Cause for Alarm (Schwartz), 46
cell phone
   as cognitive organ, 106
   See also mobile technologies
Charuvastra, Tony, 23
chat rooms, identity in, 122–23
Chekhov, Anton, 10, 13–14, 33, 34, 170n65
   Ruhl's adaptations of, 25–29
Chipko movement, 132
Cho, Julia, 166n22
Christian fundamentalism, Lee's work and, 87
Christian imagery
   in *A Cool Dip*, 154–55
   feminist theologians' revision of, 76
   in *In the Next Room*, 138–39
   See also religious imagery
Church (Lee), 11, 75, 76
   racism and, 87–88
   themes and interpretation, 86–91
church and state separation, 75
Churchill, Caryl, 1–2, 7
Clark, Andy, 106
class issues
   in *The Clean House*, 54–60
   in *A Cool Dip*, 151–54
   in *Living Out*, 67
   in *Satellites*, 73
   in *Water by the Spoonful*, 116–29
Clean House, The (Ruhl), 4, 11, 18, 20, 53, 62–63
   themes and interpretation, 55–60
Coakley, Sarah, 95–96, 98
Cocteau, Jean, 34
coltan mining, Congolese war and, 142–43, 146–47, 149
comedy
   feminine, 56–60
   Ruhl's vs. Loomer's approach to, 67–68
communication technologies
   identity and, 109–12
   See also mobile technologies

Congolese war, *Ruined* and, 140–50
Cool Dip in the Barren Saharan Crick, A (Corthron), 11, 132
   themes and interpretation, 150–58
Corthron, Kia, 5, 7, 132, 150–58, 159
Cote, David, 173n60
Crumbs from the Table of Joy (Nottage), 140
Cruz, Nilo, 16
Cultural Politics of Emotion, The (Ahmed), 6, 33
Cuomo, Chris, 133, 151

D'Amour, Lisa, 3
Da Vinci, Jane. *See* Loomer, Lisa
Dead Man's Cell Phone (Ruhl), 4, 7, 11, 14, 18, 20, 114, 128–29
   themes and interpretation, 100–109
Dear Elizabeth (Ruhl), 162
d'Eaubonne, Francoise, 132
DeBessonet, Lear, 87
Desdemona (Vogel), 19
Detroit (D'Amour), 3
Diamond, Elin, 146
Diamond, Lydia R., 4
Diaz, Kristoffer, 3
Dicker, Rory, 10
Didion, Joan, 5, 7, 9, 11, 31
   Alcestis and, 42–44
   grief and mourning and, 41–42
   Orpheus and Eurydice myth and, 41, 43–45
   and *Year of Magical Thinking*, 39–46, 51, 160
digital cameras, time-memory relationship and, 104
disability studies, *Ruined* and, 146–47
Dolan, Jill, 5, 9, 10, 147
domestic labor. *See* caring labor
Donne, John, 108
Doran, Bathsheba, 5, 7, 116
   background of, 109–10
   Kin and, 109–16
   plays of, 182n36
   recent work of, 159
Douthat, Ross, 128

Dranke, Jennifer, 10
dualistic thinking, vs. ecofeminist perspective, 132–33
Dunne, John, death of, 41, 43, 44
Dunne, Quintana Roo, 40–41, 45

ecofeminism, 131–33
 A Cool Dip and, 151–52, 156
 Corthron and, 11
 overview of, 132–33
 Ruined and, 141–42, 144–46
ecofeminist spirituality
 A Cool Dip and, 157–58
 essence of, 133
Edson, Margaret, 4, 93
Elaborate Entrance of Chad Diety, The (Diaz), 3
Elliot, A Soldier's Fugue (Hudes), 116, 160
emotion, feminist interpretation and analysis of, 11
emotional expression
 cultural attitudes toward, 32–33
 Didion and, 41–42
 in *Eurydice*, 34–39
emotional journeys, 31–52
 See also *Eurydice* (Ruhl); grief and mourning; *Year of Magical Thinking, The* (Didion)
emotional realism in *God's Ear*, 49
emotional responses, faulty assumptions about, 6–7
Eno, Will, 159
Euripides, Didion and, 41–43
Eurydice (Ruhl), 4, 7, 13, 20, 22, 27, 51, 162
 theme and interpretation, 31, 33–39
Expecting Isabel (Loomer), 62

Fabulation (Nottage), 140, 160, 190n4
Facebook, 113–14
 See also mobile technologies
Feiner, Susan, 53–54
Feingold, Michael, 151
female playwrights
 achieving parity and, 8–9
 values issues and, 5
 working conditions for, 1
feminine comic aesthetic, 56–60
feminism
 emotional connections with, 6–8
 See also liberal feminism; third-wave feminism
feminist economic philosophy, 53–54
 The Clean House and, 55–60
 Living Out and, 60–68
 Satellites and, 68–73
feminist spirituality/theology, 76
 100 Saints and, 94–95, 97
 in *Passion Play*, 77–78
feminist theater, in twenty-first century, 5–6
Feminist Theories for Dramatic Criticism (Austin), 8
Ferber, Edna, 3
Fifty Ways (Fodor), 162
Fiorenza, Elisabeth Schussler, 77–78
Fivush, Robyn, 41–42
Fodor, Kate, 5, 7, 11, 75, 77
 background of, 92–93
 100 Saints You Should Know and, 91–98
 recent work of, 161–62
 on religion, 92, 180n72
Folbre, Nancy, 54
Fornes, Maria Irene, 14, 61
Foster, Jodie, 85
Fox, Ann, 146–47
Fox, Matthew, 94–95
Freed, Amy, 2
Freud, Sigmund, 33, 95–96
Friedman, Melissa, 93
fundamentalism, Christian, Lee's work and, 87

Gaard, Greta, 133
Garcia-Romero, Anne, 116
gender, grief and, 48
gender equity, 1–2
gender identities, 17–18
gender politics, in *Ruined*, 147
Gener, Randy, 141

geographical space
  in *Kin*, 110–12
  in *Satellites*, 71–72
Gerber, Tony, 140
Gersten-Vassilaros, Alexandra, 2
gestic, 146
Gianopulos, Peter, 15, 25
Gibson, Melissa James, 166n22
Gilbert, Sandra, 44
Gilman, Rebecca, 166n22
Gionfriddo, Gina, 166n22
Girl, Interrupted (Kaysen), 62
Gjerstad, Kim, 149
Gleason-Rielly, Deborah, 150
globalization of caring labor, 65–68
Global Soul: Jet Lab, Shopping Malls, and the Search for Home (Iyer), 106–7
God
  longing for, sexual desire and, 95–96
  See also feminist spirituality/theology
God of Carnage (Reza), 165n11
God's Ear (Schwartz), 11, 31, 46–52, 161, 173n60
Goggin, Gerard, 117
Goodman Theatre
  Clean House as production of, 185n1
  Happiest Song Plays Last as production of, 160
  Passion Play as production of, 76, 85
  Ruhl productions of, 23
  Stage Kiss as production of, 162
  Vera Stark as production of, 160
Greene, Alexis, 2
Greene, Nick, 16
grief and mourning
  in *A Cool Dip*, 155
  cultural regulation of, 31–32
  Didion and, 41–42
  in *Eurydice*, 34–39
  Freudian perspective on, 33
  in *God's Ear*, 46–52
  staging of, 51
Grode, Eric, 123
Groff, Rinne, 62, 166n22
Guerilla Girls, 1

Haagensen, Erik, 150
Hall, Katori, 4
Hannah and Martin (Fodor), 92, 93
Happiest Song Plays Last, The (Hudes), 160
Hartford Stage
  Water by the Spoonful as production of, 116–17
Hasty, Nancy, 2
Hayles, N. Katherine, 106
Healy, Ann-Marie, 166n22
Hearts Afire (Loomer), 62
Heath, John, 43–44
Hefel, Katie, 115
Henry, Astrid, 9–10
Herzog, Amy, 159
Hewitson, Gillian, 71
Heywood, Leslie, 10
Hinckley, John, Jr., 85
Hochschild, Arlie, 65–66
home, virtual world understanding of, 122
Homefree (Loomer), 161
Hopper, Edward, 100
Hudes, Quiara Alegría, 3, 5, 7, 9
  mobile technologies and, 99–100
  recent work of, 160
  Water by the Spoonful and, 116–29

identity
  chat room, 122–23
  in *Water by the Spoonful*, 118–19
Inky (Groff), 62
Internet chat rooms. See mobile technologies
Internet dating, 112–13
In the Heights (Hudes), 116, 183n57
In the Next Room, or the Vibrator Play (Ruhl), 3, 4, 11, 27, 131–32
  themes and interpretation, 134–39
Intimate Apparel (Nottage), 140, 160, 190n4
Isherwood, Charles, 16, 31, 39, 150, 159, 161–62
Islam, Gazi, 122
Iyer, Pico, 107

Jackson, Mahalia, 90
Jane Chambers Playwriting Award, for
  The Waiting Room, 61
Jansz, Jeroen, 42
Jefferson, Margo, 64
Jestrovic, Silvija, 21, 142, 144
jokes/humor in *The Clean House*, 56–60
Jolie, Angelina, 62
Jonas, Susan, 1, 2
Jones, Jeffrey M., 47, 49, 87–88, 90, 173n60
Jones, Liz, 117
Jordan, Julia, 2
Joseph, Rajiv, 3

Kanter, Jodi, 33
Kaplan, Caren, 99
Karam, Stephen, 159
Karass, Valerie, 86
Kaufman, George S., 3
Kaysen, Susanna, 62
Kin (Doran), 11, 159
  themes and interpretation, 109–16
Kron, Lisa, 166n22
Kumar, Krishan, 101

LaBute, Neil, 68
"Lady with the Lap Dog, The" (Chekhov), 14
Lady with the Lap Dog, The (Ruhl), 13, 25, 29, 170n65
Lahr, John, 39, 60, 163
Lear (Lee), 161
Lee, Young Jean, 5, 7, 11, 75, 77, 92, 176n59
  background of, 86–87
  Church and, 86–91
  recent work of, 161
Lenya, Lotte, 144
liberal feminism, 8, 9
Living Out (Loomer), 2, 11, 53–54, 60–68
  themes and interpretation, 62–68
Long Christmas Ride Home (Vogel), 2
Loomer, Lisa, 2, 5, 7, 9, 11, 53–54, 73
  background of, 61–62

Living Out and, 60–68
  recent work of, 161
Loraux, Nicole, 32
Lowell, Robert, 162
Lutz, Catherine, 38–39

Mack-Canty, Colleen, 132
mainstream values, play selection and, 8–9
Makarova, Ekaterina, 101
Malcom, Janet, 170n65
Mamet, David, 14
Marcus, Laura, 17
Marder, Elissa, 31
masculinity, contemporary aspects of, 42
May, Elaine, 2
McGee, Celia, 141
McGreal, Chris, 147–48
McRobbie, Angela, 8
Melancholy Play (Ruhl), 162
Mendoza, Zilah, 60–61
Mercier, G. W., 100
metatheatricality, 19
mining, Congolese war and, 142–43, 146–47, 149
mobile technologies, 99–129
  in *Dead Man's Cell Phone*, 100–109
  intimacy and, 99–100
  in *Kin*, 109–16
  in *Water by the Spoonful*, 116–29
monologue, Hudes's reinvention of, 123
Montrose, Louis, 81
Mother Courage (Brecht), 140–41
motherhood
  in *Living Out*, 62–64
  in *Satellites*, 71
mourning. *See* grief and mourning
Mrs. Dalloway (Woolf), 19
Mud, River, Stone (Nottage), 140
musical theater, female writers for, 3

natural world
  women's liberation and, 131–33
  See also ecofeminism
netizen, 106
  See also mobile technologies

212 • Index

Nettleton, Sarah, 121
New Dramatists, 2
Next to Normal, 3
Noonan, Polly, 15
Norman, Marsha, 3, 7
Not My Mother's Sister: Generational Conflict and Third-Wave Feminism (Henry), 9
Nottage, Lynn, 2, 5, 7, 132, 158
  recent work of, 160–61
  Ruined and, 139–50

Oberammergau Passion play, 75–76, 80–81
Odede, Kennedy, 152
Oh, Sandra, 68
Omnium Gatherum (Rebeck and Gersten-Vassilaros), 2
100 Saints You Should Know (Fodor), 11, 75, 76
  themes and interpretation, 91–98
online culture, Hudes's feminist intervention into, 121
online dating, 112–13
online world vs. real world in *Water by the Spoonful*, 117–38
Orlandersmith, Dael, 2
Orlando (Ruhl), 13–14, 16, 29, 162
Orlando—A Biography (Woolf), 14, 16–19
  Ruhl's adaptation of, 16–24, 168n12
Orpheus and Eurydice myth
  Didion and, 41, 43–45
  variations on, 33–39
  See also *Eurydice* (Ruhl)
ostranenie, 21, 24
Othello, 18–19

Palmer, Tanya, 162, 188n59
Parks, Suzan-Lori, 166n22
Parts, Lyudmila, 25, 26
"Passion of Sarah Ruhl, The" (Gianopulos), 25
Passion Play (Ruhl), 5, 17–18, 20, 22, 162
  themes and interpretation, 77–86

Passion play, Oberammergau, 75–76, 80–81
Peter, Jochen, 112
Piepmeier, Alison, 10
Piven, Byrne, 15, 25
Piven, Joyce, 14–16, 15, 24, 25, 29
Piven Theatre Workshop, 14–16, 25
place
  in *Water by the Spoonful*, 119–20
  See also geographical space
plays, percentage by female playwrights, 1–3
Play That Changed My Life, The (Ruhl), 19–20
Playwrights Horizons
  A Cool Dip as production of, 155–56
  Dead Man's Cell Phone as production of, 108
  Hannah and Martin as production of, 92, 95–96
  Kin as production of, 109, 115
  100 Saints You Should Know as production of, 75
Playwrights Theatre Club, 15
Plumwood, Val, 133
Post, Emily, 32
Poster, Mark, 106
praise dance, 91
prayer in *100 Saints*, 95–96, 97–98
Prebble, Lucy, 3
Privilege (Weitz), 62
public sphere, domestication of, 101
Pulitzer Prize
  Clean House nomination for, 53
  Elliot's nomination for, 116, 160
  Ruhl's nominations for, 3, 166n14
  for *Ruined* (2009), 2, 132, 139
  for *Water by the Spoonful*, 3, 116
  women recipients of, 3–4

race and ethnicity issues
  in *The Clean House*, 55–58
  in *A Cool Dip*, 150–51
  in Lee's plays, 87–88
  in *Satellites*, 68–69, 176n59
  in *Vera Stark*, 160

Radin, Margaret Jane, 70
Reading Chekhov: A Critical Journey (Malcom), 170n65
Reagan, Ronald, 84
Rebeck, Theresa, 2, 4, 166n22
Redgrave, Vanessa, 42, 160
religious devotion
  in *100 Saints You Ought to Know*, 93–98
  in theater, 75–77 (see also *Church* [Lee]; *100 Saints You Should Know* [Fodor]; *Passion Play* [Ruhl])
religious imagery
  in *In the Next Room*, 138–39
  transformation of, 26–27
"Re-Runs and Repetition" (Ruhl), 13
Reza, Yasmina, 165n11
Richelli, Asher, 117
Rilke, Rainier Maria, 34
Rizzo, Frank, 117, 123
Roach, Catherine, 133
Roman, David, 62–63
Room of One's Own, A (Woolf), 19
Ross, Susan A., 88
Rostova, Mira, 15
Royal Family (Ferber), 3
Rudin, Scott, 40, 45
Ruether, Rosemary Radford, 76
Ruhl, Kate, 14
Ruhl, Kathy, 14
Ruhl, Sarah, 2
  awards of, 165n14
  The Clean House and, 55–60
  context for, 1–11
  Dead Man's Cell Phone and, 100–109
  and death of father, 15–16, 167n8
  educating, 13–29
  Eurydice and, 33–39, 51, 62, 73, 92, 116, 158
  family of, 23
  literacy predecessors of, 10
  mobile technologies and, 99–100
  Passion Play and, 75–98
  popular commentary on, 4
  Pulitzer nominations and award of, 3, 53, 166n14
  recent work of, 162–63
  religious background of, 180n72
  social and ethical concerns of, 4–5
  success of, 4–6
  Tony nomination of, 3
  on transformation of space, 185n1
  writers "beside," 9–10
Ruined (Nottage), 2, 11, 132, 160
  themes and interpretation, 139–50
Russell, Ron, 93
Rx (Fodor), 161–62

Sackville-West, Vita, 17, 21
Sands, Emily Glassberg, 2–3
Sanford, Tim, 14–15
Sarah Ruhl: A Critical Study of the Plays (Al-Shamma), 4, 166n15
Satellites (Son), 11, 53–54, 159
  themes and interpretation, 68–73
Schuler, Catherine A., 7
Schulman, Sarah, 2, 8–9, 73
Schwartz, Beth, 19
Schwartz, Jenny, 5, 7, 11, 31, 46–52
  God's Ear and, 46–62
  recent work of, 161
Scott, Seret, 186n35
Scott, Sherie Rene, 3
scripts, male- vs. female-authored, 2–3
Second City, 15
Second Stage
  Eurydice as production of, 13, 31, 39
  Living Out as production of, 60, 64
  Vera Stark as production of, 160
  Water by the Spoonful as production of, 160
second-wave feminism, critiques of, 9–10
Sedgwick, Eve, 10
September 11, 2011, attacks of, 31–33
sexual desire, desire for God and, 95–96
Shakespeare, William, influences of, 18–20
Shaw, Helen, 111, 115, 173n60
Shewey, Don, 150
Shimakawa, Karen, 176n59

Shklovsky, Viktor, 21, 24
Sills, Paul, 15
Sister Act (Steinkellner), 4
Slee, Nicola, 94–95, 97, 98
Smith, Molly, 76
social networking. *See* mobile technologies
Somewhere Fun (Schwartz), 161
Son, Diana, 5, 7, 11, 53–54
    recent work of, 159
    Satellites and, 68–73
Songs of Dragons Flying to Heaven (Lee), 176n59
Soskice, Janet Martin, 79, 80
Spanglish (Brooks), 62
Spolin, Viola, 15
Stage Kiss (Ruhl), 19, 162
Stearns, Daniel, 32
Steinkellner, Cheri, 4
Stern, Sarah, 46
St. John of Chrysostom, 79–80
Stop Kiss (Son), 159
straight plays by women, 4
Sullivan, Daniel, 140
Susan Smith Blackburn Prize
    for *The Clean House*, 53
    Living Out nomination for, 60
    for Ruhl's plays, 165n14
    Waiting Room nomination for, 61
Svich, Caridad, 62–63
symbols, transformation of, 20–21
Szymkowicz, Adam, 93

Theatre of the Oppressed (Boal), 157
theological symbology, feminist theologians' revision of, 76
theology, feminist, 76
third-wave feminism, 5, 9–10, 166n18
Three Sisters, The (Ruhl), 15, 162
Thurber, Lucy, 166n22
Tolstoy, Leo, 25
Tony Awards
    female playwrights and, 3–4
    Ruhl's nomination for, 166n14

Top Girls (Churchill), 61
To the Lighthouse (Woolf), 19
Touching Feeling (Sedgwick), 10
Trinity, "earthed" sense of, 95
Twine, Richard T., 136
Two Things You Don't Talk About at Dinner (Loomer), 161

Unclaimed Experience: Trauma, Narrative, History, 50
Untitled Feminist Show (Lee), 161

Valkenburg, Patti M., 112
Vanderbilt, Amy, 32
van Dijck, Jose, 113
Verfremdung, 21, 141, 142
virtual esteem support, 121
Vogel, Paula, 2, 15, 16, 19, 75, 185n1

Waiting Room, The (Loomer), 61–62
war, women's experience of, 139–50
    See also *Ruined* (Nottage)
Warren, Karen, 131, 133
Washburn, Anne, 46, 166n22
Wasserstein, Wendy, 7
Water by the Spoonful (Hudes), 3, 11, 160
    themes and interpretation, 116–29
water imagery/issues
    in *A Cool Dip*, 151–57
    in *Water by the Spoonful*, 122–23, 125–27
    in *The Year of Magical Thinking*, 44–45
Waves, The (Woolf), 19
Weckwerth, Wendy, 33, 36
Weill, Kurt, 144
Weitz, Paul, 62
Wellman, Mac, 16, 36
Wendlund, Mark, 71
We're Gonna Die (Lee), 161
Whoriskey, Kate, 140, 142, 186n35
Williams, Delores S., 137–38
Wing-Davey, Mark, 76

wireless communication. *See* mobile technologies
Wit (Edson), 4
Women's International War Crimes Tribunal for the Trial of Japan's Military Sexual Slavery, 149
women's liberation, natural world and, 131–33
Woolf, Virginia, 10, 13, 14, 16, 33, 34
   Ruhl's adaptation of, 16–24, 168n12
Woolgar, Steve, 113, 124
"Work, The," 15
Wussow, Helen, 21

Yale Repertory Theatre
   Clean House production by, 60
   Dear Elizabeth production by, 162
   Eurydice production by, 31
   Ruhl productions by, 4, 23
Year of Magical Thinking, The (Didion), 11, 31, 160
   themes and interpretation, 39–46, 51
Yew, Chay, 156

Zinoman, Jason, 1–2, 46
Zuckerberg, Mark, 128

GPSR Compliance

The European Union's (EU) General Product Safety Regulation (GPSR) is a set of rules that requires consumer products to be safe and our obligations to ensure this.

If you have any concerns about our products, you can contact us on

ProductSafety@springernature.com

In case Publisher is established outside the EU, the EU authorized representative is:

Springer Nature Customer Service Center GmbH
Europaplatz 3
69115 Heidelberg, Germany

www.ingramcontent.com/pod-product-compliance
Lightning Source LLC
LaVergne TN
LVHW041630060526
838200LV00040B/1516